Alice Faye

Hollywood Legends Series
Ronald L. Davis, General Editor

Alice Faye

A Life Beyond the Silver Screen

Jane Lenz Elder

UNIVERSITY PRESS OF MISSISSIPPI • JACKSON

www.upress.state.ms.us

Copyright © 2002 by University Press of Mississippi
All rights reserved
Manufactured in the United States of America

10 09 08 07 06 05 04 03 02   4 3 2 1

∞

Library of Congress Cataloging-in-Publication Data

Elder, Jane Lenz.
Alice Faye : a life beyond the silver screen / Jane Lenz Elder.
p.   cm. — (Hollywood legends series)
Filmography:
Includes bibliographical references (p.   ) and index.
ISBN 1-57806-210-1 (cloth : alk. paper)
1. Faye, Alice, 1915–   2. Entertainers—United States—Biography.
I. Title. II. Series.

PN2287.F36 E42   2002
791.43'028'092—dc21
[B]
2002020116

British Library Cataloging-in-Publication Data available

For
the Mouse and the Duke

CONTENTS

Acknowledgments   ix

Introduction   3

Chapter 1. Broadway Baby   11

Chapter 2. Vallée's Satin Doll   30

Chapter 3. Scandals   48

Chapter 4. New Studio, New Star   68

Chapter 5. Breakthrough   83

Chapter 6. Treadmill   99

Chapter 7. Queen of the Lot   118

Chapter 8. So This Is Harris   138

Chapter 9. Movies and Motherhood   157

Chapter 10. Goodbye Fox   175

Chapter 11. Return to Radio   193

Chapter 12. Celebrity Fulfilled   213

Epilogue 235

Filmography 249

Bibliographical Essay 263

Bibliography 295

Index 301

ACKNOWLEDGMENTS

When I was a teenager my mother chided me for spending my free time watching old movies. "You'll never get anywhere doing that," she said repeatedly. Perhaps not. Nevertheless, as adolescence recedes and forty looms ever larger on the horizon, I still relish the hours I have spent in the world of celluloid. Writing a film biography merely provides focus, a sense of legitimacy, and an excuse to become better acquainted with some of the people and places related to Hollywood's Golden Age.

Heading my list of acknowledgments is, of course, Ronald L. Davis, professor emeritus of History at Southern Methodist University, who drew on his own experiences as a documenter of film history to advise me on many aspects of this book. Further thanks go to the wealth of people who willingly shared their time and memories of Alice Faye, either in person, on the phone, or by e-mail. These include her friends Jewel Baxter, Gabé Farrell, Kay Gregory, Judy McHarg, Betty Scharf, Nancy Whitaker, and Virginia Zamboni. Alice's fans, many of whom she also counted as friends, proved equally generous. Tim Hollis, of the Lum & Abner Society, helped me track down radio information. Robert Kendall forwarded letters and articles with useful information and insights. Mickey Smith, radio aficionado in the Pharmacy School at the University of Mississippi, shared Phil Harris and Rexall material with me. George Ulrich remained in constant contact, helping me with copies of her movies, CDs and records, and a final shooting script of *Fallen Angel*, and, most important, reading the manuscript with great care at its final stage. Above all was Roy Bishop, whose knowledge and appreciation for Alice Faye and her work was equaled only by his fabulous collection of memorabilia and his willingness to take as much time as necessary to help me do the best possible job. To him I extend particular thanks.

Many of the people with whom Alice worked are long since gone, but those who remain shed important light on not only her sense of professionalism but also her character and personality. These include the inimitable Jane Withers, former radio performer Jeanine Roose, Alice's book collaborator Dick Kleiner, and most of all Paul Ritz of Pfizer Pharmaceuticals. Paul provided me with splendid resources from Alice's years as a Pfizer representative, including films and videos, photographs, and scrapbooks—all of which contained information it would otherwise have been impossible to track down. He shared his personal insights and provided encouragement from the beginning of my work through its final stages.

The assistance of a number of people in California helped me make the best use of my time there. They include Brad Bauer at the Thousand Oaks Public Library, Ned Comstock at the Doheny Library at the University of Southern California, and Barbara Hall at the Margaret Herrick Library of the Academy of Motion Picture Arts and Sciences. Also in California, but in a category all her own, is the fabulous Carol Bruce, whose experience as a band singer and memories of working with Nils T. Granlund and Irving Berlin richly informed the early chapters of this book. For their help with extending my research budget to its farthest possible limits, I thank California friends Robert and Polly Duntley, Virginia and Duane Halpape, Marie Talbot Jordan, and Jan and Bob Winning. At the other end of the country, Robert Nott graciously gave of his time to comb the Billy Rose Theatre Collection at the New York Public Library in search of material related to Miss Faye. In Linton, Indiana, home of the Phil Harris-Alice Faye Collection, I benefited from the knowledge and company of the collection's curator, Regina Kramer, as well as Don Steward, and Jack Shelton, and from the photographic assistance of the late Frank Miller.

Closer to home, I thank Paul Bowser for computer support, Melissa Barden Dowling for intellectual support, James E. Snead for helping me get the first chapter off the ground, and Mildred Pinkston, who allowed me to invade her office to sit and babble. A. N. Kronstadt and Carlotta Sinclair assisted with database searching and interpretation, and Billie Stovall in Central University Libraries at SMU worked miracles with Interlibrary Loan. At the University Press of Mississippi, Seetha Srinivasan, Anne Stascavage, Tammy Oberhausen Rastoder, and the rest of the staff provided friendly and professional guidance through the editorial process, making it practically painless in every way.

Finally, this book could never have happened without the generous assistance of Alice Faye's daughters Alice Regan and Phyllis Middleton. They opened the doors of the collection in Linton, gave me names and phone numbers of people to interview, and provided candid insights into their parents' lives. Biographers only dream of that kind of accessibility, and I thank them for making my first experience in the genre such a pleasant one. Equally important are the contributions of my husband (and fellow cinéphile), who kept the home fires burning in my absences and helped me carve out the time to write from an active family life. A man of many talents, he also proofread, unpacked from our move, maintained the computer, housebroke a puppy, watched *The Gang's All Here*—again, cooked, declared the printer dead and installed a new one, refrained from his natural penchant for suggesting biographical embellishments, and minded our two uncommonly perspicacious offspring, to whom this book is dedicated. The martinis are on me.

Jane Lenz Elder
Dallas, Texas

Alice Faye

Introduction

Alice Faye may be remembered by film historians as much for her abrupt exit from the movies in 1945 as for her preceding eleven years of Hollywood stardom. Tired of dancing, literally, to the tunes that mogul Darryl F. Zanuck put on the silver screen in the lavish musicals produced by Twentieth Century-Fox, she sought meatier roles, the first of which was in Otto Preminger's *Fallen Angel*. When Zanuck butchered the film to make a Roman holiday for another Fox actress, Linda Darnell, Alice walked out of the screening room, paused to write an unrepeatable note to Zanuck, then left the studio for good. Few movie stars of Alice Faye's caliber had ever done such a thing. Only Greta Garbo's retirement from M-G-M after completing *Two-Faced Woman* in 1941 compared, and only Garbo took her retirement from the screen as seriously as did Alice Faye. Many Hollywood observers, including Zanuck, thought that Alice would eventually return to movies. Alice proved them wrong, staying away from movies entirely until she made *State Fair* in 1962, and then again until the late 1970s, when she made cameo appearances in a couple of minor films.

Fortunately for her fans, Alice Faye's life as an entertainer did not begin and end with her film career. To be sure, between 1934 and 1945 she occupied a prime position in the golden age of the big studio system. As the top female star at Twentieth Century-Fox for most of that time, Alice participated fully in the overblown spectacle of Hollywood ritual: the pre-

3

mieres, the nightclubs, and the day-to-day grind of fittings and photo shoots, filming and interviews. On screen and at the box office, she held her own against top musical stars from rival studios, such as Jeanette MacDonald, Eleanor Powell, and Ginger Rogers. Yet Alice was involved in another golden age as well—the golden age of radio. She first sang for Rudy Vallée's *Fleischmann Hour,* one of the most popular programs on the air at the dawn of commercial radio in the early 1930s. While pursuing her film career, she did guest spots on *Lux Radio Theatre* and spent a season as a regular on Hal Kemp's *Music from Hollywood* program. She witnessed the shift in popularity from radio to television with the program she and her husband, bandleader and comedian Phil Harris, produced. It began in 1946 as the *Fitch Bandwagon,* developed into the *Phil Harris-Alice Faye Show,* and was finally cancelled in 1954, when many radio stations began adopting an all-music format in prime time. She also made repeated appearances on the single most popular radio program of all time, the *Jack Benny Show,* on which Phil Harris was a regular. In many ways Alice Faye's radio career proved as significant as her film work. She certainly spent as many years performing in the medium. Radio introduced Alice Faye to the nation, and made her a household name well before her celluloid image flashed across the screens of local movie houses. Radio kept Alice's name and, more important, her voice alive once her fans could no longer count on a steady stream of Alice Faye movies.

What made Alice Faye such a popular performer in both radio and film was, of course, her voice and natural demeanor. These were the common threads of Alice's life, contributing to her success and binding together the episodic activities and tumultuous events of her life. Entertainer and popular music historian Michael Feinstein called Alice's voice "infinitely compelling." From the age of sixteen, when famous New York restauranteur Nils T. Granlund, known in the press of the day simply as N.T.G., pulled her out of the chorus, Alice demonstrated an uncanny ability to put over a song. That talent gave her the means to support herself and her family, to move in circles far removed from those into which she had been born, and change entirely the direction her life might have taken otherwise. Alice once stated that, "The cold facts are that I started with virtually nothing and made it to the point where, in 1940, I was the number-one box office female star in America," but a gift such as her voice could hardly be considered "virtually nothing." Cesar Romero stated it best when he said, "Alice never had a music lesson in her life, but she was blessed with a lovely natural singing voice and had a most persuasive way with a lyric. Her deep, sultry voice was inimitable."

Through her movies and radio work, Alice Faye gave voice to a generation, reflecting its desires, preoccupations, and concerns. Audiences responded by taking her to their hearts, remaining loyal for years after her retirement from movies and radio. So many people named their daughters after her that anyone searching the electronic *Who's Who* database can come up with the names of over a dozen distinguished women born between 1935 and 1955 whose given names are Alice Faye. She was so closely identified with her time that it remains difficult to conjure up images of either the Great Depression or World War II without picturing Alice Faye in the mix somewhere. Her debut in *George White's Scandals* singing the vampy, campy "Oh, You Nasty Man" exploited the nation's fascination with platinum blonde sex kittens. Later she kept depression-era anxieties at bay as she sang to perennial waif Shirley Temple in both *Poor Little Rich Girl* and *Stowaway*. American GIs scattered over the globe in World War II could listen to her sing "You'll Never Know" and feel just a bit closer to the homes and sweethearts they had left behind. Newspaperman Kelly Leiter, penning a very personal obituary for Alice in the *LaFollette Press*, wrote of the youth he spent worshiping Alice Faye. "In my late teens, when I was still the purest sailor ever squeezed into a pair of tight bell-bottoms, my love affair with Alice never waned. I carried an autographed picture of her as my PBY squadron hop-scotched across the Pacific. I saw *Hello, Frisco, Hello* for the first time on a coral atoll. The second time a few months later on the fantail of a seaplane tender. And wondered if Alice would ever know how I felt about her."

Kelly Leiter's devotion to Alice would in no way surprise Alice's friend and fan Roy Bishop, who discovered her for the first time shortly after the death of his mother when he was nine years old. "I missed my mother a lot. She was really beautiful," he said, "and I went to *Tin Pan Alley*. I thought I was going to see a movie where they were banging on tin pans. I walked in the theater as the two blondes were singing 'Hawaii,' and I thought, wow, they're so beautiful. But I gravitated toward Alice, and her warmth just enveloped me. I was sunk. From then on 'til now. It mesmerized me. I just loved her." That warmth, which Alice radiated from the screen in such abundance, was as essential a component of her success as her fabulous voice and is the characteristic people seemed to find most attractive in her. In combination with her singing talent it was unbeatable. Bishop noted that of all the songs performed in films during Hollywood's heyday, Alice introduced the largest number to hit the charts: twenty-three. That number far surpassed the thirteen introduced by better-remembered Judy Garland, or the twelve each introduced by Betty Grable and Doris Day. Throughout her movie career, such leading composers as George Gershwin, Irving Berlin, and Cole Porter named Alice their number one choice as a songplugger.

Alice's popularity, charted by *Box Office Review*, which named her the number one box office draw in America in 1940, is undeniable. The precise nature of her appeal is a bit harder to pin down. *Playboy* mogul and Faye fan Hugh Hefner has claimed that it was the combination of sexiness and vulnerability, which is, in different proportions, what made Marilyn Monroe so popular. Writer Douglas Dean assured his readers that Alice's appeal did not rest in her dancing, her acting, her beauty, or even, surprisingly, her singing. Instead he suggested that it sprang from a sense of her personal dignity and depth: "In her performances there were glimpses of something more than a brassy chorus girl or a street-corner tramp. In this respect she was set apart from Grable and Monroe. (I never heard a smutty story about Alice Faye, did you?) Alice Faye was a lady, and instinctively everybody realized it."

In addition to her success at "expressing the human appetite without making it look smutty," as one film historian described it, Alice also managed to convey a sense of the American work ethic to which her Depression-era audience responded. "Her spirit was very late thirties," wrote Ethan Mordden in *Hollywood Musicals,* "seeing an end to the Depression, but having to work to get there." Alice expressed this through the tilt of her chin, the set of her shoulders, and her walk. "I moved forward with a no-nonsense air," she said when asked about "the Faye walk." "It was nothing I worked on or thought about...I guess my walk reflected my inner determination." Neither Alice nor the characters she played expected good things to come easily. While economic hardship, divisive social issues, and just plain fear did not exist in Alice Faye movies—that was hardly their point—they did contain plenty of heartache and the occasional tightened belt. Audiences knew that Alice would triumph in the end but could also rest assured that she would pay a few dues beforehand.

In that sense Alice's movies paralleled her real life. She triumphed in the final reel but paid for her success as she went. Hard work and strokes of luck removed her from a rough Hell's Kitchen youth and set her on the road to fame and fortune. Perhaps Alice's most significant success was her ability to overcome her chronic lack of self-confidence and sheer stage fright to persevere as a star for so many years. In the advice book she wrote for senior citizens called *Growing Older, Staying Young,* Alice attributed her achievement in keeping her head in the Hollywood spotlight for so many years to her ongoing self-doubt. Her inherent distrust of her own fame made it difficult for her truly to accept the adulation, the financial offers, the proposals of marriage from internationally famous and wealthy men. Roy Bishop remembered witnessing an example of this when he went to dinner with Alice in Beverly Hills. "There were a couple of guys just staring and staring," he said. "Well, I noticed right away they had recognized Alice, but she hadn't. Finally after she became aware of it, she said 'Those guys keep looking over here. Are they friends of yours?' That was Alice."

Celebrities today, who habitually wallow in deep pools of public introspection, might be baffled by the brevity of Alice's allusions to her own insecurity. It represented the only aspect of her interior landscape she cared to reveal and was the only instance in which Alice indulged in anything even remotely approaching the tabloid style self-examination with which our media is saturated. "Everything I wrote I had to really drag out of her," said her book collaborator, Dick Kleiner. "I had to really pad the book. Everything she told me I put in it." Alice had a series of stock stories and quotes that she used throughout the years, varying them slightly to suit specific situations. In interviews she was always gracious and appeared genuinely forthcoming. A close examination of stories and columns released over the course of decades, however, reveals gaping holes in her history she apparently would not discuss. She simply filed away in some remote mental compartment much of her childhood, her relationship with Rudy Vallée, her first marriage, and her dealings with Zanuck, and refused to resurrect them. What joys, tragedies, triumphs, or sorrows these episodes might have reflected neither her book collaborator, her daughters, nor the public will know.

Alice's reticence may have stemmed from self-doubt, an urge to protect herself, a traumatic experience, or just an intense reserve. Alice simply did not open up to people, but as her actions demonstrated, she possessed wit, drive, a sharp temper, and a spontaneity that sometimes led her to leap before she looked. Such things tended to startle acquaintances, who had her pegged as a quiet, tractable woman. Darryl F. Zanuck headed the list of those whom Alice managed to blindside with swift, decisive action when she felt betrayed. Her first husband, Tony Martin, was another. As their respective bafflement over her indicates, Alice was remarkable for exercising as much reticence in private as in public. "Alice kept a lot inside," said her longtime friend and spokeswoman Jewel Baxter. "She wasn't demonstrative. She was very low-key. She never really liked to talk too much about herself, other than little things like this is where I went to school or this is where my mother used to take me to dancing school. There's just so darn many things we never talked about." Her best friend from childhood, Betty Scharf, felt that Alice's silence stemmed from a desire to avoid inflicting her troubles on others. Betty, for example, had very little sense of the details of Alice's troubled marriage to Tony Martin, despite the fact that she considered herself Alice's closest friend at the time. "She never discussed those things with me," Betty said. "She loved me, and I guess she didn't want to burden me with any of her problems. She always wanted me to feel good."

Alice's daughters admit that their mother was not an easy person to know but remain unable to pinpoint the reason. "Mother wasn't real chummy," said Phyllis. "She had a lot of acquaintances but very few friends. Very reserved. And if her dogs could have talked that's who you would need to talk to. Because she talked to her dogs and they knew what she was thinking. I don't think she ever had a confidante." Alice's daughters also noted that she never talked much about her own family and early experiences. "I remember when we went to fill out Mom's death certificate," said Alice Jr., "They asked what was your mother's mother's [maiden] name. Duh! Phyllis and I were looking at each other with no idea." Phyllis said, "I probably know less about her childhood than I know about her friends. She talked about her brothers, but then I knew her brothers, so that wasn't unusual. But she never talked about her father. She never talked about him, period." Neither Alice, Jr., nor Phyllis are clear on the genealogical details of their mother's family, nor do they know the whereabouts of many photographs. "My mother was crazy about her grandmother, who meant a great deal to her," said Alice, Jr. "And yet there are very few pictures of these people available. Mother didn't want to talk about family trees or any of that. But now I'm kind of funny, too. I've taken down a lot of the pictures I had and I don't watch the videos of Mom or Dad and I don't listen to their music. And I'm thinking maybe you do that because it's too painful. So maybe that's the way she was. Her family was dear to her and when she lost them it was too painful. Maybe that was her way of grieving."

From the perspective of the biographer, Alice Faye's lack of commu- nication about her family or her thoughts and feelings at various points in her life makes her a tough subject. Additionally, discrepancies exist in the written record that were perpetuated by Alice during her lifetime. For example, she had as many as three different answers to such fundamental questions as how she got her break in show business or where she first met Phil Harris. Dick Kleiner believed that Alice's ability to recollect anec- dotal material just was not very good. "It's not that she was reticent," he said. "I think her memory was not that great." Roy Bishop remembered sitting next to her at a restaurant table after a performance of *Good News* in San Francisco. As Alice's fans would stop by the table to speak with her, he found himself helping her answer their questions. She could not remember many of the details of her own films and would quietly lean over to him and ask, "Which movie did I sing that song in? What dress was that?" Fortunately material from a wide variety of sources exists to help clarify facts and suggest logical interpretations of motive. In cases where I have relied on pure conjecture, I have attempted to present as many possible interpretations as seem plausible, and have labeled them as such.

Alice Faye was the product of a unique set of economic, familial, and cultural forces. I have tried to present, as fairly as possible, the out- ward and visible signs of her life with as much insight into inward and spiritual motives as can be reasonably assumed in the absence of her own words. I hope that by shedding light on one player in the history of popu- lar culture in the twentieth century, I will illuminate a bit further the ar- eas through which she passed. From the Hell's Kitchen slums, through the nightclubs and speakeasies of New York, to success in radio and movies, and a worthy, working retirement, Alice Faye led a rags-to-riches life. Her greatest riches were her friends, fans, and daughters. I like to think that their thoughtfulness and generosity in helping me pull together this book reflect something of the personality of its subject, an elegant and deter- mined lady who gave her audiences much joy.

CHAPTER 1

Broadway Baby

The showers that had fallen off and on throughout the day were the only reliable harbinger of spring in the sea of tenements on the Manhattan West Side neighborhood known as Hell's Kitchen. Here the unmistakable odors of the neighborhood's slaughterhouses and factories obliterated the fresh scent of the rain, mingling instead with smoke from the trains that delivered the livestock and the sweat of too many bodies living and working together. Noise in this district began early in the day and continued long into the night: the creaking of pushcarts, the stumbling hoofbeats of half-dead horses, the muted voices of domestic peace, and the shriller outbursts of household violence. Even close to midnight, the newborn girl's first cries barely disturbed what passed for peace in that quarter of the city.

Alice Jeane Leppert was born on Wednesday, May 5, 1915, the third child and only daughter of a New York City cop, Charley Leppert, and his wife, Alice. The future queen of movie musicals entered the world in the Hell's Kitchen area of New York City, in a cold-water flat near Tenth Avenue and West Fifty-fourth Street (although in later years neither she nor her mother could recall precisely where). In 1915 Hell's Kitchen was no longer the kind of place its name implied: a wide-open invitation to vice and ruthless human behavior, where crime lords and abject poverty had flourished since the Civil War. Five years earlier, in 1910, a special police force had broken the notorious gangs who gave the neighborhood its un-savory reputation, leaving behind what novelist Theodore Dreiser termed "a very ordinary slum neighborhood, poor and commonplace, and sharply edged by poverty." This grim environment provided the unlikely back-ground for the sweet-faced singer who rose to stardom in the carefree, frothy extravaganzas of Hollywood's golden age.

Alice Faye's roots were purely working-class, like many of the char-acters she portrayed on the screen. Her father walked a beat. Her mother took factory jobs to make ends meet. Studio attempts to camouflage her background suggested a privileged childhood of tennis lessons and horse-back riding, but Alice Faye was a proud daughter of the proletariat who never spoke ill of her section of the city despite its shortcomings. She took the sting out of her Tenth Avenue background by referring to it as "Double Fifth" and said of Hell's Kitchen that it "always sounds as though it must have been an awful place to live. But in reality it wasn't bad at all. Actually, it was reasonably pleasant." She recalled trips to Central Park, where her brother Sonny would pull her on a sled, and playing in the fire hydrants on hot days in the summer. The plump little girl, whose black playmates called her "snowball," seemed to take life as it came, enjoying what was available in her neighborhood and not troubling too much about the rest.

Alice's parents, like most other parents in the district, had few ad-vantages to offer their daughter and two older sons, Bill and Charles, whom they called Sonny. Alice said that the Lepperts "had to scratch to survive." But so did everyone else in a place where poverty was the rule rather than the exception. Like many children, Alice took her surroundings in stride and found them unremarkable. "It wasn't until years later that I ever heard the phrase 'deprived child,' and realized they were talking about kids like me," she said in 1990. "I guess I was deprived, if you meas-ure deprivation in terms of worldly goods, because we had very little."

Faye claimed for her childhood a reasonably stable standard of living in which she never went hungry, although meals at times were meager. "I was always very comfortable, full of good food, and happy. I never wanted for anything," Faye asserted. Nevertheless, one of her most remarkable childhood pleasures was warm feet. "I remember equating warm feet with well-being. If my feet were warm all was right in the world," she said. "If my mom really liked me that day, she'd give me a hot water bottle when I went to bed and I would curl my feet around its delicious warmth. Bliss!"

The Lepperts may have been strapped for cash, but they seem to have wrapped young Alice in a blanket of emotional security. This was especially true of her maternal grandmother. "My grandmother Moffitt lived with us when I was a girl. She was Irish, born in Dublin, and a feisty lady," Alice said. Throughout her life, in interviews and profiles, Alice often invoked the memory of the only grandparent she ever knew. Grandmother Moffit's active presence in her granddaughter's life was perhaps the strongest advantage Alice could claim in her less-than-privileged childhood. Neighborhood kids roamed the streets and often fell prey to the innumerable hazards of city life, but Alice never came home to an empty flat. With her mother away at work, it was Alice's grandmother who nursed her when she was sick and encouraged her to follow her dreams. She anchored the Lepperts' home life, nurturing her young granddaughter and relieving Alice's mother of many of the anxieties common to working mothers.

Otherwise, nothing in her background distinguished Alice Leppert from a thousand other Hell's Kitchen children, or marked her for future success. With her mixed German and Irish ancestry, in fact, Alice could hardly have been more typical. In the years prior to the Civil War, Hell's Kitchen became home to large numbers of immigrants driven out of Germany and Ireland by political instability and famine. They settled on Manhattan's periphery, where conditions deteriorated from bad to worse in the years following the Civil War.

In old New Amsterdam, Manhattan's western shoreline had been well watered and attractive, inspiring the Dutch to name it Bloomindal. In the late nineteenth century, however, it evolved into an industrial center with factories and processing plants supported by a growing pool of cheap labor. The large number of immigrants, the burgeoning manufactures, the Hudson River docks, the adjacent theaters and restaurants of Times Square, and the New York Central Railroad assured Hell's Kitchen's development as a marginal, mixed-use neighborhood.

Social reformer Jacob Riis credited the tenements as providing the rich soil in which depraved humanity flourished, but the fountain that sustained the hoodlums was the New York Central Railroad, which dominated life in Hell's Kitchen. Its yard was the conduit through which flowed a constant and varied source of material goods arriving from Europe via Cunard and White Star. The presence of expensive cargoes in such impoverished surroundings fed the juvenile gangs of the 1860s until they matured into adult criminals and diversified their activities to include armed robbery, daylight burglaries, and protection rackets.

This then was the world in which Alice Faye grew up. In an environment where law enforcement often proved inadequate or corrupt, one can only wonder what led Alice's dad, Charley Leppert, to choose it as his profession. Not much information remains with which to draw a clear picture of Leppert; he had brown hair, brown eyes, and had been born around 1885, give or take a few years. Alice herself seldom referred to him, a notable silence that only raises question about what he was really like. Perhaps he had fought in the Spanish-American War like his brother, Philip, and followed him into the police force after peace was declared. Or perhaps the New York Central Railroad recruited him for the extralegal police force they organized in 1910 to stamp out the gangs preying so relentlessly on the freight yards. This group fought the gangs with a force almost as ruthless as that employed by the gangsters themselves. By "clubbing, shooting, and arresting indiscriminately," said one historian, they captured much of the criminal leadership of the area and put the rest to flight. In the 1920s, Prohibition resurrected a fair amount of gang presence in Hell's Kitchen, but the hoodlums never again regained the stranglehold they held on the area prior to 1910.

The gangs' departure removed the persistent element of danger from the lives of the laboring poor who remained behind in Hell's Kitchen, but otherwise it had little effect on the area's working-class culture. It probably improved the daily life of a beat cop like Charley Leppert only marginally. His duties would still have included a host of unpleasant activities. Leppert most likely worked out of the Eighteenth Precinct Police Station, an ugly yellow brick building on West Forty-seventh Street that remained one of the busiest police stations in the city until 1939 when a WPA-built station on West Fifty-fourth Street replaced it.

On any given day, a policeman in the Hell's Kitchen district dealt with keeping the peace in a climate of poverty, overcrowding, and cultural conflict. At the time of Alice's birth, an influx of Italians into the predominantly Irish-German neighborhood deepened existing cultural divisions and increased the incidence of street fights. The small black community near West Fifty-third Street and Ninth Avenue, which probably included Alice's childhood playmates, exacerbated tensions, although it had been there since the Croton Aqueduct was built in 1840. None of these groups was particularly fond of the police, who had earned a reputation for crookedness and brutality that left them with few friends on the street.

Vice, as well as violence, flourished on Leppert's beat. Toward the east the theatrical rooming houses, boardinghouses, and residential hotels comprised much of the district's housing and attracted a transient population of single adults. Illicit affairs and prostitution involving both sexes thrived, particularly in the 1920s when a group of gay streetwalkers co-opted a section of Forty-second Street falling roughly between Fifth and Eighth Avenues. Toward the west were the docks, with the crews of the great cargo ships and passenger liners mixing it up with the locals on the waterfront. The territory that fell in between held the normal catastrophes of urban life with which cops have to deal: fires, traffic accidents, medical emergencies, and missing persons.

Charley Leppert must have had a pretty strong character, both physically and mentally, to cope with his job description. And he must have derived a certain satisfaction from his work because he continued with it for many years. What effect it had on his personality and home life can only be imagined, however. Such a hard, violent life would have provided him with much reason for bitterness. Economic forces following World War I alone guaranteed that his lot as a policeman contained increasing degrees of misery. Postwar inflation had driven the cost of living up beyond the average patrolman's ability to pay for it. In 1920 the Department of Labor determined the average cost of living for workingmen in various areas of the nation. They based their calculations on the barest amount necessary to maintain a man and his wife and three children: sufficient food, low-rent housing with heat and toilet facilities, and clothing, with only a minimum outlay for medical expenses, modest insurance, a daily newspaper, contributions to church and labor organizations, and Christmas gifts for the children. As the report stated, "This is in no way an ideal budget. It is intended to establish merely the bottom level of health and decency." It did not provide for new furniture, savings accounts, books, or serious medical care.

The report found that the average salary necessary to maintain this dubious standard of living in and around Manhattan in 1920 was $2,342, in contrast to the 1914 "health and decency" level of $1,300. Based on the Department of Labor's statistics, the New York Labor Bureau concluded in a report they prepared for the Patrolman's Benevolent Association in 1922 that police salaries had been inadequate for the past six years and that certain grades of patrolmen were actually worse off in 1921 than they had been before the war. The report also itemized expenses specific to policemen that their salaries did not cover: upkeep of uniforms, station house bills, and charitable collections within their profession. By 1924 an increase of sorts did come through for policemen and firemen: New York City raised their annual salaries the $220 requested, from $2,280 to $2,500—a figure just slightly above the $2,342 determined as the 1920 "health and decency" minimum. Such a small raise, coming several years too late, could not have constituted much of an improvement.

Charley Leppert's low salary impacted the daily lives of his family profoundly, for as Alice once said, her father worked hard but made very little because he was not on the take. "With my grandmother living with us and me and my two brothers to feed and clothe, it was just too much." Alice's mother got a job, which she apparently held throughout Alice's childhood. With Grandmother Moffitt home to look after Sonny, Bill, and Alice, Mrs. Leppert entering the workforce did not represent the domestic catastrophe that it did for other families. Nevertheless, it must have been a blow to Charley Leppert.

Most West Side women worked as unskilled labor in the factories or slaughterhouses because industrial jobs paid better than domestic service in a hotel or private household. Alice's mother was no exception. During this period she worked for the Mirror Chocolate Company and for Coty Perfume. Her daughter recalled that her job in the candy factory "was great for us kids," but that attitude reflects a childish naïveté. Many women at the time assumed that candy dipping would be easier, more pleasant work than what awaited them elsewhere. But working ten to twelve hours a day in a room refrigerated to as low as sixty degrees left women depleted and weakened their resistance to disease. Mrs. Leppert probably considered her job with Coty more pleasant. She most likely worked at the new plant Coty had built in 1915 to capture the market for packaging perfumes and cosmetics. Although still factory work, conditions there were better than at the candy factories or slaughterhouses.

One of the things Mrs. Leppert worked to provide her daughter with was piano lessons. The Lepperts may never have called a doctor—"doctors and hospitals were for the rich or the dying," Alice said—but music was one refinement for which Alice's mother was willing to sacrifice. A door-to-door salesman sold them a piano for a dollar down and a dollar a month. To get the piano into the cramped tenement building, a crew had to remove the front window of the Leppert apartment, attach a block and tackle to the roof, and hoist the instrument up the outside of the building until they could shove it through the window. When times got tough and Mrs. Leppert could not make the monthly payment the crew came back and went through the same procedure in reverse. In later life, Alice used to joke that the comings and goings of the Leppert piano provided one of the great neighborhood attractions.

Alice Faye never did learn to play the piano. She recalled she had just a few lessons and did not learn the things she wanted to. In later life she regretted not learning, but she remembered that often she was simply too busy playing outside to practice. The streets of New York provided a fascinating kaleidoscope of human activity for a child to absorb. Her friend and neighbor in Palm Springs, Gabé Farrell, who also grew up in Hell's Kitchen, said that their neighborhood "was such an experience . . . there was so much learning done." Life on the West Side was lived largely outdoors, to escape the close quarters of the stuffy apartments. After supper, the women would all go downstairs to visit on the stoop, the men would wander down to the corner. Elderly women could prop a pillow on the sill of the front window to watch the world go by, but the children got out into the world themselves to see what was going on. New York presented a never-ending pageant of runaway horses, gang fights, funeral processions, sidewalk crap games, pushcart vendors, and fire alarms.

Alice probably helped her mother or grandmother shop at Paddy's Market, a sea of pushcarts and haggling housewives that held sway under the Ninth Avenue el between Thirty-ninth and Forty-second Streets. Here one could obtain items rejected as unfit in other parts of the city: chipped dishware, day-old bread, overripe fruit, and fish whose time had come. And, of course, there were the lights of Times Square, which stood in marked contrast to the dimly lit streets nearer her home. Alice and her grandmother would walk down Broadway or Seventh Avenue reading the famous names that glittered there and dreaming that someday Alice's might be among them.

Alice Leppert was a shy child but very pretty according to one neighbor who "used to see Alice around." She carried a bit of baby fat, and her hair was a darker shade of blonde than the "amber blonde" of her later career. But with incandescent blue eyes, a turned-up nose, and a timid smile, Alice had every reason to expect at least a modest career in show business.

No one who knew her ever credited Alice Faye with the consuming ambition common to many stars, but certainly her childhood in and around "Double Fifth" created in her a strong desire for a better standard of living. She had seen the long, shiny sedans and elegant clothes of the Broadway celebrities and yearned for a bit of that glamour in her own life.

One of Alice's favorite haunts was Woolworth's, the five-and-dime, which held a fascinating array of cosmetics. Her friend Gabé Farrell said that Alice would spend hours looking at the powders, rouges, and lipsticks. Farrell remembers Alice telling the story of her first brush with crime. She came home after an afternoon at Woolworth's, and her worried mother asked where she had been. On hearing she'd been at the five-and-dime, her mother asked, "Well, what did you get?" "Oh," Alice said, "I was just looking." Her mother put her hand in Alice's pocket and took out a little lipstick. She said, "You were just looking? You go right back to Woolworth's and take back that lipstick." "So," Farrell concluded, "off she went trotting back on over and got rid of that lipstick."

Considering Alice's environment, one incidence of shoplifting seems the model of propriety. She also admitted to sneaking her first cigarette when she was twelve or thirteen because like most in her generation she thought that smoking was sophisticated. Alice's mild behavior stands in marked contrast to much of what went on around her, but her environment probably gave her a sense of the grim realities of life that far exceeded her tender years. Theodore Dreiser observed the reasons for Hell's Kitchen girls going wrong, citing the example of one fifteen-year-old who lived in his building. "Here was too much toil, too much gloom, too much solemnity for her, the non-appreciation which the youthful heart so much abhors. Elsewhere, perhaps, was light, warmth, merriment, beauty, or so she thought." Dreiser's young neighbor seized the first available opportunity to fly from her environment. When she later returned to her family, "with singed wings," her parents threw her "out of the house with shouts and tears of recrimination." This common scenario was not lost on Alice. She was fully aware of the turn many attractive Hell's Kitchen girls chose to take. "If you were pretty, and you grew up on Double Fifth Avenue," she told musical historian Miles Kreuger, "you either hit the stage or hit the streets."

Alice apparently gave her family little cause for concern. She was too preoccupied with show business and too familiar with the consequences of sex to jeopardize her dream of a different life. Her favorite daydream was typical of any city child: living in the country, in a snug, pretty house with a big lawn near a lake. "The trees were all fruit trees, and I would usually have an apple in my hand," she recalled. Other times Alice's dreams reflected her longing for a more distinguished life. She decided she wanted her future husband "to be a person of elegance" and so pictured him in a tuxedo. When she described this fantasy to her mother, however, Mrs. Leppert reminded her daughter that "waiters wear tuxedos."

When she was twelve Alice took a small step toward realizing her dream of a life on the stage. She got her first job working in the dressing room of a dancing school. At one time or another, publicity releases from Twentieth Century-Fox state that she was enrolled in the school, the lessons paid for by her mother, by her brother Bill from whom she borrowed the money, or by her father who had gotten them free from a buddy who had "spotted her talent." But Alice maintained she had worked there. The most plausible story is that her father had arranged the job for her, rather than the lessons. The Lepperts moved a lot but remained in the same neighborhood, had by this time moved to 359 West Fifty-third Street over Sullivan's Café. There Charley Leppert encountered a man named Newsome, who was an instructor for a dancing school. Apparently Leppert, who was proud of his daughter's looks and willing to support her in her ambitions, arranged the job for her.

West Side children went to work early, and Alice and her father knew she was approaching the age when she'd have to go to work in earnest. By her own admission she didn't care for school and was anxious to try out for the chorus. So as she hung up the coats and took care of the tap shoes at the dancing school, she watched the lessons. After work, she went home and practiced the steps in front of her family, her Grandmother Moffitt apparently leading the rest in encouraging all her efforts. Later newspaper stories concocted for Alice the desire to become a schoolteacher should show business not work out, but Alice considered neither teaching nor the possibility that dancing would not work out, at least in a small way. "On payday I would meet mother at the candy factory and have lunch in Chinatown," she said. "We'd stop in at the nearby vaudeville theatre and then afterwards she'd watch as I ran to the stage door and pretended to be one of the stars making her exit."

Alice's dreams took on greater meaning when her Grandmother Moffitt passed away in 1927, at the age of eighty. Alice was twelve, and it was the first great loss she had experienced. One writer asserted that Alice attributed her grandmother's death to the poverty surrounding them; the circumstances resulting in her death are not clear enough now to judge one way or another. Nevertheless, Alice became even more determined to gain a foothold in the theatrical world, just as her grandmother had encouraged her to do. To Alice, the future star of Twentieth Century-Fox, the true luminaries of the entertainment industry came from the haunts of her childhood, the theaters clustered around Times Square and glittering along Broadway. Film production in the middle 1920s had only just begun climbing up from the lowest rungs of the entertainment ladder. To a native New Yorker, even one used to observing its theatrical splendors from the cheap seats, no comparison existed. When Alice said show business, she meant the world created and sustained by the likes of Flo Ziegfeld and his star Marilyn Miller. "I worshipped her for years, because she was so much of everything I wanted to be. I wanted to star in a musical success in the theater. I had that dream ever since I saw her in *Sally.*" Alice would have been between five and eight years old when Miller played in *Sally,* but the stark contrast between Miller's world and her own made an indelible impression.

Show business was a reasonable career choice for a vivacious young New Yorker with no real skills. The money was no worse than factory work, and many West Side girls looked east to Times Square for employment. Alice finished her education when she graduated from the eighth grade at P.S. 84, probably about the time she turned thirteen in 1928. Since her mother worked and her brothers could support themselves by this time, Alice's need to earn an income was not as urgent as many of her classmates' was. By the late 1920s, when Alice finished grammar school, the Lepperts could have gotten by even if Alice had wanted to attend high school. But she was determined to break into the chorus and contribute to the family finances. She saw little reason why she should not try. She had a well-developed figure, a few dance steps in her repertoire, and the support of her family.

Alice passed one of her first auditions at thirteen and landed a spot in the chorus of Earl Carroll's *Vanities* by lying about her age. The *Vanities,* along with Zeigfeld's *Follies* and George White's *Scandals,* took the Broadway review format to the level of high art, with its opulent production values and elegant but scantily clad chorines. Alice had hit the big time on her first try, but in her excitement she let her true age slip, forcing the casting director to release her. From that point on, she routinely added three or four years to her age. "My mother said, 'someday you're going to hate yourself for this. When you're 60, they're going to think you're 64. And you're going to say, 'Damn, why did I do that?' And I said, 'Mom, when I'm 64, I won't even care, I mean, who's gonna live that long?'" Thus the year of Alice's birth became 1912, a misconception she herself perpetrated early in her career and one that gained widespread acceptance.

Not too much later, a wiser (and fictitiously older) Alice Leppert found a place with the Chester Hale dance unit at the Capitol Theater on Broadway at Fifty-first Street. The Capitol was M-G-M's first-run movie house in New York City and, along with the other great picture palaces of that era, the Roxy, the Paramount, and the Strand, it presented live entertainment between feature films. Dancers there kept a grueling schedule, doing five shows on weekdays and seven on weekends, plus rehearsing the following week's routine between shows. Alice admitted, "The hard work knocked the idea of glamour and show business out of my head, but the work was steady and paid $35 a week." Dan Dailey, who co-starred with Betty Grable in many Fox musicals, danced in the house unit at the Roxy around this time. He described how the choreographer and the dance directors would decide on a theme for the upcoming show and then work out the routine. Then the dancers would "just get up there and knock our brains out," he said.

Despite all the hard work, an undeniable magic permeated the air of the Capitol Theater. A *New York Times* reporter described the bustle and excitement backstage at these shows, marveling at the split-second precision of the performances, the dazzling costumes, and the youth of the dancers. He reckoned their ages between sixteen and twenty, although many of them, like Alice, had added a year or two. Alice could have been any one of the young women he described, practicing high kicks in the wings, rushing to change her costume, or chattering excitedly with the other girls.

In true show business fashion, Alice decided to change her name about this time in her life, although her motives remain unclear. Her decision to enter show business had the support of her family, so it is unlikely she did it to protect them. No doubt she thought it was a glamorous thing to do. Perhaps she'd met with confusion about the pronunciation of Leppert and liked the fact that there was only one way to pronounce "Faye." Many publicity releases in later years attribute her choice of surname to the current vaudeville headliner and comedian Frank Fay. Fay was an extraordinarily popular entertainer in the early years of the depression, although today he is more often remembered by show business aficionados as Barbara Stanwyck's first husband. Nevertheless, Alice Faye always claimed, "I liked the name, and it went well with Alice. There was no attempt to copy or adopt anyone else's name. There wasn't much thought or planning behind it."

Alice enjoyed her work in the chorus, especially the camaraderie with the other chorines. During her stint with the Chester Hale troupe, she became especially close with Betty King, another dancer one year her senior. Alice admitted that she hadn't had "many really close, long-lasting friendships" in her life, but Betty King was one person she cherished and maintained contact with throughout her life. "I grew up in the west side of the Bronx," said Betty. "We only met when we were in show business, at the audition for the Capitol Theatre, and we never stopped seeing each other. I loved working for Chester Hale; we worked all the Lowe's theaters in New York. The whole circuit, just around New York."

Betty recalled that they made good money with Chester Hale, "I could pay my family's rent. Her family needed money, too. So we both took care of our families." Around this time, the Lepperts moved downtown, Betty said, and like many young women in the early years of the depression, Alice found herself the primary breadwinner. "She was the mother of the family and the supporter. I don't think she minded that much, because I had to do it, too. I had a step-father and he was in the building line and there was no work for him." Whether Charley Leppert was still working at this point is not certain. Betty said she has no clear recollection of him. "I think I did meet him, but I just don't remember that well. When you get so busy working, your mind is taken up with other things."

Alice stayed busy with the Chester Hale unit for two years and accompanied the troupe on a tour of the major cities of the Atlantic coast, which was the first time she traveled away from New York City on her own. It simply wasn't feasible for her mother to join her. "The truth is," Alice told a journalist in the 1930s, "I couldn't afford to have mother travel with me. I was paid around $40 a week, and had to pay my own living expenses. By eating in cafeterias and living in rooming houses and cheap hotels, I managed to send $20 every week, living on the other $20." Her stint with Chester Hale gave her valuable experience and saw her through two awkward years when other employers might have questioned her age. She grew as a dancer and became more adept at protecting herself in a predatory environment. As one nightclub manager said around this time, "Girls in show business are subjected to more temptation in a day than most other women encounter in a lifetime. It take great mental and moral stamina for a girl to come through, not necessarily to stardom, but merely to retain her decency." Concerned parents could hover beyond stage doors all they wanted to, but in the end a girl's behavior was up to that girl alone. "No amount of care or guarding prepares her for this bewildering business," the manager said. A chorus girl "picks her own way, and what she picks depends on her stamina. The dazzle easily blinds."

The nightclub scene flourishing in New York offered a wealth of opportunities, both honorable and dishonorable, for young dancers. As one historian has pointed out, the number of nightclubs actually increased in Manhattan during the latter half of the Prohibition era, protected by Tammany Hall and Mayor Jimmy Walker, who ceased enforcement of the Volstead Act in 1925. The unregulated criminal element happily provided consumer services related to alcohol, entertainment, and prostitution that legitimate businessmen could not. "If you were in show business and you worked in a night club, the club was owned by a member of the fraternity, for only mobsters had the money to afford places big enough to have entertainment," said one Manhattan impresario.

Alice probably found this setting no more hazardous than the neighborhood she grew up in. In fact, she may not have found it in the least remarkable. When she left the Chester Hale troupe, she immediately found a gig doing a dance specialty at the Hollywood Gardens on Long Island, a brand new venture opened by the radio-personality-turned-restauranteur Nils T. Granlund, known simply as NTG. The Hollywood Gardens was the summertime spin-off of Granlund's highly successful Manhattan night spot, the Hollywood Restaurant. Granlund, who loved the entertainment business as much as he disliked the gangsters, had hit upon a formula for success that saw him, and his imitators, safely through the end Prohibition and the beginning of the Depression. He believed that the gangsters were out to kill the goose that laid golden eggs with their exorbitant cover charges and watered-down booze. To Granlund, like Henry Ford before him, the key to success was volume. "I envisioned a huge cabaret room, large enough to pay off on volume and not so small that it had to peddle liquor to keep afloat. No contemporary trap with its postage-stamp dance floor could offer anything like that...my dream place would duck high prices, fancy foreign headwaiters, and excessive tariffs."

For a minimum charge of $1.50 against the price of their food and drink, with no cover charge and, remarkably, no alcohol, customers at the Hollywood Restaurant enjoyed a six-course dinner and a floor show. The restaurant occupied the second floor of what had once been Rector's, one of New York's most famous turn-of-the-century eating establishments. It could accommodate eight hundred people at a sitting, and was the best bargain on Broadway. The food was good and the floor show spectacular. Granlund, said Durante, "picks out the best-looking damsels on Broadway—queens with complexions like Madam Pompadour's and legs like Barbara Stanwyck's. Nils nearly breaks their hearts with work, but when he's through, he has a live-wire show."

By his own admission, Granlund did not find Alice Faye quite up to his exacting standards for the Hollywood Restaurant downtown but thought she would suit the Hollywood Gardens. It was a huge outdoor venue that held seating for 2,500, separated from a big oval stage by a six-foot moat complete with ducks, swans, and fish. Jimmy Durante said it worked on the same kind of no-cover-charge plan as the Hollywood Restaurant, and even after the stock market crash they filled to capacity every Saturday and Sunday night. "It put on the same kind of capers, with thirty damsels in the semi-nude and a name band," Durante said. "That cost sugar by the ton, but again [Granlund and his] partners got away with it." Granlund himself recalled, "Opening night featured Paul Whiteman's orchestra and twenty-four girls, all good dancers, but not so uniformly beautiful as those we had downtown," he said, adding, "But they didn't have to be with the moat and the waterfowl." Despite being upstaged by the wildlife, Alice soon caught Granlund's eye. He found the "plump little blonde" "adorable and pert," and decided to work her into the act. "NTG was great at discovering these show gals and turning them into performers," recalled Carol Bruce, one of his later protegés who went on to star on Broadway.

Granlund approached Alice shortly after they opened and said, "Look, you're pretty cute and I think you could do something with that tap. Tell you what I'll do, I'll send you to a teacher and you learn an individual number to do in the show." It was a heady offer for a sixteen-year-old but, surprisingly, Alice turned him down flat. Her lack of confidence apparently outweighed her dreams of stardom. She told Granlund that she didn't want to do a solo number, arguing "If you get me out there alone, you'll make fun of me." Granlund acted as his own master of ceremonies, and needling performers and customers alike was part of his performance style. Jimmy Durante recalled that Granlund emceed "in the [Texas] Guinan manner. He rags customers and abuses them, but with the kind of smile you can't forget." The customers loved it, but the prospect of drawing Granlund's fire under the gaze of 2,500 people terrified Alice.

Granlund ran headlong into that combination of stage fright and stubbornness that characterized Alice Faye throughout her life. He concluded, rightly, that "Alice Faye was a girl who knew her own mind," and he saw that arguing with her would get them both nowhere. "I wouldn't have let her quit if she had wanted to, she had too much talent for that," he said. "But she had to be pushed." So he issued an ultimatum: "Either you have that dance ready by Monday, or you don't have a job." She prepared the dance. Granlund said, "I took her by the hand and led her out on to the stage and the more I kidded her, the more the customers loved her. She wasn't much of a dancer, but that didn't seem to matter. She went over big with the audience."

Granlund may have been the first manager to stumble onto that very human quality of warmth and vulnerability that made Alice so popular with men and women alike. He decided to exploit these aspects of Alice's personality further by telling her to prepare a song to add to the dance routine, but not without resistance on Alice's part. This time Granlund got around Alice by offering her a twenty-five-dollar-a-week raise. She may have been shy, but she understood the value of a dollar. Together with what she was earning as a dancer, her salary for the summer season would increase to one thousand dollars. "For $1,000," she said, "I'd sing standing on my head." Instead, she sang backed by Paul Whiteman's orchestra, one of the biggest-name bands in the country, and the audience loved her. Granlund noticed that she became more and more popular as the summer wore on and decided to try her out at his downtown location. "When we closed shop in the autumn, she was the only one from the outdoor show I felt should be given a job in our Broadway establishment," he recalled. Despite her own misgivings, and with considerable pushing from Granlund, Alice was on her way to becoming one of the Manhattan luminaries she wanted to be.

Alice's initial success did not seem to go to her head, however. She worked hard in this period and didn't consider her new working life glamorous at all. "I was too poor. Five or six shows a day, then home to bed. There isn't much chance to do anything else." In a 1935 interview, she discussed her background in the chorus, stating that she was proud of her four years in the chorus and was much less comfortable in front of the line instead of in it. She said, "I was a show girl and loved it. I've never been so happy in my life as I was when I worked in the chorus—it was fun. It was grand training." Doormen and restaurant owners who knew her in this period recalled her as a cheerful, wholesome kid. "There was no monkey business about her," said one. "She was democratic as they come and very hard-working." Another recalled, "Work was dancing and when it was over she got dressed and went home. No waiting around for dates, very quiet and serious."

Some time after her move to the Hollywood Restaurant, Alice tried out for George White's *Scandals,* one of the great trio of annual reviews on Broadway. Between 1926 and 1931 George Gershwin wrote forty-five songs for the *Scandals,* including "I'll Build a Stairway to Paradise" and "Somebody Loves Me." Such opulent productions grew difficult to stage after the stock market crash in 1929, and George White sat out 1930 without staging a review at all. By 1931, however, he was ready to try another edition, which would include Ethel Merman, Ray Bolger, and Ethel Barrymore Colt in her musical comedy debut. To really pack in the audiences, George White had signed a surefire attraction, the singing sensation of the nation, Rudy Vallée. Alice landed a spot in the chorus of the *Scandals* and immediately got her Equity card. Admission into Actor's Equity may have been why Alice considered the chorus of the *Scandals* superior to that of the Hollywood Restaurant—even with Nils Granlund's interest and support. The *Scandals* job paid her sixty dollars a week, which worked out to an annual salary of $3,120. After two years of dancing, sixteen-year-old Alice was now earning more money than her father could after a lifetime on the police force. She could begin to climb out of the ranks of the working poor and, with luck, take her family with her.

At the age of sixteen, Alice Faye's life was about to undergo rapid and unanticipated changes, over which she would have little control. Her background, however, allowed her to meet them with a degree of poise not common in many teenagers. She remained a shy dreamer, longing for the escape that the trappings of celebrity represented, yet reluctant to face the glare of the spotlight alone. The unassuming warmth of her personality and her natural talent as a singer, however, marked her for special attention, whether at the Hollywood Gardens or elsewhere. People noticed Alice. Even better, they liked her.

CHAPTER 2

Vallée's Satin Doll

George White's *Scandals* opened at the Apollo Theatre, on Forty-second Street west of Broadway, on September 14, 1931. It was just as Alice had always imagined it would be: the sense of anticipation, the electric lights, the long, elegant cars gliding to a stop before the theater. George White, resplendent in evening clothes with his dark hair carefully slicked back in the fashion of the day, stood at the curb to greet his patrons, determined to prove that the depression had not licked him. It could count many Broadway producers among its casualties, including the great Florenz Ziegfeld, who would die broke in 1932. George White wanted to demonstrate he was different. After laying out of the game for a year, he had returned to show New York that he could still mount a review worth seeing.

The great Ziegfeld enjoyed staging financially extravagant productions with elaborate costumes. George White, on the other hand, emphasized basic entertainment, enhanced by the prettiest girls available. Ray Bolger, who starred in *Scandals,* remembered, "He did not try to fly with, I mean try to compete with Ziegfeld at all. It was a different type of show; mostly he brought out great stars. Even through Ziegfeld did bring out great stars, Ziegfeld's forte was the elaborate shows like you see in Vegas." At the onset of the Great Depression, that kind of spectacle was simply impossible. As Bolger summed it up, "The difference between Ziegfeld and White, I should think, was about a couple of hundred thousand dollars."

George White's *Scandals* counted as a solid, if not spectacular success, given the times, and Alice's job was secure for the foreseeable future. The show enjoyed a respectable run of 202 performances, because, Bolger remembered, "There was no competition of any importance at that time." The *New York Times* critic Brooks Atkinson dubbed it a "first-rate show," whose "principals and chorus provide the liveliest company the town had seen for some time." He credited Rudy Vallée with winning over the Broadway cynics with the "chuckle of words and tune" in the song "This Is the Missus," and transforming himself in the process from "a lavender myth to a likable reality." Ethel Merman delivered "Life Is Just a Bowl of Cherries" in her "inexhaustible" voice, and Ray Bolger "travestied the old soft-shoe dancing uproariously." Atkinson reserved much of his praise for the sets, costumes, and the musical score, and lavished most of his attention on the comedy sketches performed by Willie Howard—"material that he can stuff full of merriment." He concluded, "There is nothing like low comedy to relieve the imposing dullness of a big musical show." With George White's *Scandals,* he said, "Things look more cheerful in the theatre."

Even in a big Broadway show like the *Scandals,* Alice's work life assumed the same routine she had known in her nightclub and movie palace days. She was one of thirty-two members of the *Scandals* chorus, which White had dubbed "the most beautiful girls on the stage." In 1931 there was a surfeit of attractive young women looking for work. George White could take his pick, and did. Atkinson wrote that not only were the girls pretty, but "they dance, they sing and they look good-natured into the bargain." Alice worked hard and she went home early, only occasionally joining in some of the impromptu company parties backstage. Ethel Merman remembered her as another kid in the chorus. "She used to spend hours talking to me in my dressing room—telling me of her ambition to sing." A later movie magazine profile of Alice claimed that, in addition to her dancing duties, she also understudied Ethel Merman. But all the girls did. George White expected everyone in his shows to know everyone else's part so that in case of an emergency the performance could go on.

Alice was no exception, although the point was moot. Ethel Merman never missed a performance in her life. Only a few weeks' trial run in Atlantic City in August altered Alice's usual routine and provided some variety for the sixteen-year-old. The seaside felt good after the stifling air of the city, even if the show left little time to relax and enjoy herself. By September the show returned to Manhattan for the opening, and Alice returned to her normal life. Then unexpectedly, at some point early in the run of *Scandals*, the show's star, Rudy Vallée, noticed Alice.

By all accounts, the sixteen-year-old Alice was a standout. She had danced off much of her baby fat and was left with an especially curvaceous figure. She had elegant long legs and arresting blue eyes. Ray Bolger, who also starred in *Scandals*, said, "She was the most beautiful thing you've ever seen. She was blond, and her legs seemed to reach from under her armpits all the way down to the ground. Really the most fantastic body." Vallée, a self-proclaimed connoisseur of fantastic bodies, had recently founded his own talent agency, and was therefore in a position to take a more professional interest in Alice than did the other men in the show. He watched her closely and decided he liked what he saw. Vallée's interest ensured that Alice's life would never be "normal" again.

Alice Faye attracting the attention of Rudy Vallée in 1931 was like Lady Diana Spencer capturing the Prince of Wales's attention fifty years later. As one of Vallée's musical directors, Walter Scharf, put it, "Rudy Vallée was the Elvis Presley, the Glen Miller, the Frank Sinatra, and the Michael Jackson of the early 1930s. All rolled into one." Vallée was the first true entertainment icon of popular culture, the first sensation produced and packaged by the new medium of radio. At the time, he was probably second only to Charles Lindbergh in his ability to command the attention of public, press, and presidents alike. He had the same clean-cut, blond good looks as Lindbergh, with a collegiate twist. He boasted a Yale pedigree, a punctilious way of speaking, and a soft "crooning" style of delivering a song that was almost completely untouched by the still-not-wholly-acceptable influences of jazz.

Vallée started out in the mid-1920s when vocalists with dance bands were the exception rather than the rule. He hit upon his crooning style to compensate for his voice, which was not at all powerful. At the same time, nightclubs began to introduce masters of ceremonies into their entertainment formats, and this new role generated some of the decade's greatest stars, Vallée among them. He pulled together a small band named the Connecticut Yankees in 1925. As leader of this group, he combined the roles of vocalist and master of ceremonies in an affable, self-effacing way that proved extremely popular.

Today Rudy Vallée is often dismissed as the "campy crooner" who sang through a megaphone and played the stuffy boss in *How to Succeed in Business without Really Trying*. The postmodern world has little use for the icons of yesteryear, but Vallée's success was truly phenomenal in many ways. One of those ways was Vallée's exceptionally astute management of his own career. As one writer put it, "Little that developed was not the result of his careful planning, strong determination, and the recognition of opportunities when they presented themselves." His soft singing style in particular lent itself to the broadcasting technology of the time. Additionally, Vallée was quick to realize radio's potential, grabbing as much air time as possible. He was one of the first commercial "radio personalities," singing and announcing an hour-long show every Thursday evening at eight o'clock sponsored by Fleischmann's Yeast and produced by the J. Walter Thompson advertising agency. Yet Vallée took radio's "dance-band-with-plugs formula" a step further by pioneering the variety format. Beginning the hour with his trademark "Heigh-ho everybody! We earnestly crave your attention, and we strive earnestly to please you," he opened with a solo number, introduced a guest star, read a monologue, then did another song. The rest of the hour generally included comedy sketches and scenes from Broadway shows performed by original cast members, all glued together with what one writer described as Vallée's "somewhat self-important manner. Always the youthful well-mannered fellow, he presided over the show like a snooty maitre-d'."

By 1930, the *Fleischmann Hour* had replaced the Palace as the prestige booking of show business, with regular guest appearances by the biggest names in vaudeville. At the same time, Vallée diversified his activities to capitalize on the mass hysteria that accompanied his acceptance as one of the century's first bona fide heartthrobs. He toured the country making personal appearances, and he also opened his own nightclub. Vallée published his memoirs, *Vagabond Dreams Come True,* in February 1930, and within two months it was in its ninth printing. He also began his own talent agency, signing and representing performers whom he felt had promise. His relentless efforts paid off handsomely. As the grip of the depression tightened its hold on the United States, Vallée was rumored to earn in the vicinity of seventy-five hundred dollars a week. He was the quintessential celebrity of the era, which one historian has described as "the apotheosis of the consumption idol that had been forming in the 1910s. The star entertainer, making fabulous sums, living in luxury, was a democratic figure, one who offered the tangibility of the new life to an even wider audience" than had the society figures of an earlier generation. Such a figure had an even wider appeal in the early 1930s, when grim economic circumstances left people hungry for proof that the American dream could still come true.

Many discrepancies exist about the circumstances that first drew Alice Faye to Rudy Vallée's attention, with many people claiming credit for having "spotted" her. The most widely accepted version of the story is that at an impromptu backstage party, the company of *Scandals* was fooling around with a record-making machine and Alice was persuaded to record the popular Maurice Chevalier song "Mimi." Vallée's lawyer, Hyman Bushell, heard the record and played it for Vallée, who signed her to a personal contract with his orchestra. Vallée's version of the story, described in *My Vagabond Lover,* was that "a top producer and a real bastard louse of a man, George White, had put out feelers for me to star in the eleventh edition of his *Scandals* show on Broadway. As I was introduced to the cast, which included Ethel Merman and Ray Bolger, one very, very young sweet little face stood out from all the rest. I learned her name was

Alice Faye and she was only fifteen [sic] years old. A few years later I managed to persuade her to sing with my band."

Nils T. Granlund wrote yet another version of the story in his memoirs. He said that Rudy Vallée had known about Alice from her summer work at the Hollywood Gardens. He had become a frequent visitor, after his lawyer Bushell heard her sing and urged him to come listen. As Granlund said, "He and his orchestra were rehearsing with George White's *Scandals* and Rudy was scouting for this show, though I didn't know until later that he had propositioned Alice. She went to work in the Hollywood [Restaurant] and a few days later I was talking to Rudy. 'Man, what kind of hold do you have over these girls? I offered Alice Faye $175 to appear in the *Scandals* and she turned me down.'" Granlund concludes the story by saying that he "had to put up quite a front of big-brother sternness" to convince Alice to try for the *Scandals* job.

Elements of truth mixed with substantial doses of bravado exist in each version. Contemporary evidence suggests Vallée's story may be the closest to the truth. He said he found Alice captivating and memorable, an opinion with which many concurred. She would have to have been for Vallée to remember such a small event as their meeting. He was living the chaotic life of a superstar in 1931. Throughout the summer, while Alice was doing her spot at the Hollywood Gardens, Vallée seldom ventured out of the public eye. He worked on several projects at once, traveling all the time, and meeting hundreds of people every day. Additionally, his personal life was undergoing profound changes. He married a former M-G-M screen actress named Fay Webb, a wedding that he announced with hyperbolic fanfare at the NBC building in Manhattan. On July 10 Vallée staged a reception where, as the *New York Times* reported, the newlyweds entered the party escorted by twelve uniformed attendants with seven radio announcers and two dozen cameramen to relay the news to a waiting world.

Vallée may have decided that Alice had a special appeal, but he didn't act on his instincts right away. Alice may not even have known that she had caught his eye. Throughout the run of *Scandals* on Broadway and during its national tour the following spring, Alice remembered being just another chorus girl used to looking in shop windows when she was new in town, and thanking her lucky stars that she had a job. White closed the New York show in February 1931, after 202 performances. Theater mavens conceded that it was a respectable run given the hard times, but none of White's previous editions of *Scandals* had closed so quickly. White found it a disappointing indicator of the reality that had set in on Broadway since the theater district's peak season of 1927-28, when 264 shows opened. Rising costs of production and competition from the movies had begun eroding business on the Great White Way even before the 1929 Crash. The long-term effects of the depression merely accelerated the process. White bowed to the reality of the times when he opened the *Scandals* in Boston in March 1932 with reduced prices. The show that had cost as much as $5.50 to see in New York would cost far less in Boston: $3.00 for an evening performance and $2.50 for a matinee. "I am motivated by one cardinal fact—the majority of playgoers are no longer in a position to pay $5 to see a musical, much as they may want to," said White.

White kept prices down throughout the rest of the tour. From Boston, the show traveled to the major cities of the East, Philadelphia, Washington, D.C., Pittsburgh, Richmond, Baltimore, then another two weeks in Philadelphia, before heading west to Ohio, Michigan, and Illinois. Some publicity pieces mention the possibility of the show moving on to California to play during the run of the Olympic Games in Los Angeles. Alice, who stayed with the show throughout its national tour, had never been so far away from her home and family. Only the Chester Hale tours in and around New York had exposed her to any kind of life on the road. Now she was venturing farther afield than any member of her family had since they came to America the century before. Whether it left her feeling lonely or exhilarated she never said. During the *Scandals* tour she celebrated a birthday away from her family for the first time in her life. What the company thought was her twentieth birthday, but was really her seventeenth, came during a one-week stand in Cincinnati.

Eventually the *Scandals* tour ended and Alice returned to New York, but precisely when Rudy Vallée offered her a job as his vocalist is not clear. Her good friend Walter Scharf, who was Vallée's principal assistant for two years, said that she worked with Vallée from 1932 to 1934. Another source says Alice didn't debut with Vallée until 1933. No clear record remains to indicate what exactly Alice did in the summer and fall of 1932. The advertisements for Vallée's 1932 summer tour and for the autumn broadcasts of his radio show do not mention Alice's name, although she may have been present in an unadvertised capacity as Vallée tried her out with audiences. Or she may not have worked for Vallée at all. A 1934 *Modern Screen* article refers to her working in the chorus at both the Palais d'Or and the Chin Restaurant at some point in her New York dancing days. Or she may have returned to Nils Granlund at the Hollywood. If she worked with Vallée, he didn't advertise her before 1933. Perhaps he felt that, with her inexperience as a singer, she did not warrant a buildup for a while.

Nevertheless, Alice had joined the orchestra officially by the winter of 1932-33. Her first advertised appearance with Rudy Vallée and his Connecticut Yankees occurred during his 1933 tour at a Junior League dance for four thousand in Jacksonville, Florida. On January 28, she received her first notices: "Miss Alice Fay [sic] was, according to popular verdict, 'a knockout.'" A reporter for the local high school paper, clearly dazzled by Alice's sophistication, referred to her as "young, pretty, and unmarried. She has platinum blonde hair and a low sweet voice. She smokes occasionally, loves to dance, and prefers tossing 'blues' numbers." The high school reporter probably never realized that the platinum blond torch singer was exactly his age and, under different circumstances, could have been his date to the dance.

Life on the road with an orchestra was a world away from high school but an education in itself, often a difficult one. Alice traveled from place to place crowded into cars and buses with the rest of the performers. Some venues, she discovered, had dressing rooms, many did not, leaving her to change into her stage clothes and apply her makeup in the ladies room. Her hair was cut and styled wherever a salon could be found, and curlers went in overnight whether she slept in a hotel or on the bus. Meals were catch-as-catch-can. Alice recalled eating at all different times of the day, wherever they happened to be, "mostly in some greasy spoon diner around the corner from the ballroom where I was singing."

A life of looking adorable regardless of the circumstances provided Alice with good training. While she coped with the irregular hours and impromptu meals, she learned a great deal about handling herself in new situations, unfamiliar surroundings, and with strange people. To be sure, she was not alone. Despite the drawbacks of living in such intimacy with a forty-man orchestra, she felt protected. Used to the presence of two older brothers, Alice now found herself with two score, along with an assortment of orchestra wives. Alice was almost certainly the youngest member of the group. They nicknamed her Cuddles and treated her like a kid sister, a role to which she was accustomed. They became her family. A photograph of the group taken at Vallée's summer lodge in Maine in 1933 shows a dimpled and smiling Alice hugging her knees in the center of the assembled band members, looking for all the world like a team mascot.

After her first printed reviews in Jacksonville, Alice began to attract notice more consistently as the orchestra continued its 1933 tour. The audience called her back for an encore at a February 7 Coronation Ball in Tampa. The Chicago *News* on April 22 hailed her as Vallée's latest discovery, and said she'd been singing with the orchestra and on Vallée's Thursday night broadcasts "for some time now." The band's appearance in Vallée's home state of Maine, at the end of May, drew the most publicity. The Lewiston newspaper wrote that "there is added interest in the fact that Rudy is bringing with him the torch singer in his band, Alice Faye. Miss Faye has been heard with Rudy on radio programs but little about her has appeared in magazines, and local radio fans will be interested to see and hear her." Her reviews from that appearance asserted that the "charming little blonde with a personality" was one of the hits of the evening.

Alice could take pride in the job she was doing. Her accomplishments rested on hard work. Vallée enjoyed a reputation as a taskmaster, who fined his performers, including Alice, a set fee for mistakes. "He wanted his people to be perfect, and I think we all respected this," she said. "I was fined one dollar for every minute I was late to rehearsal and another dollar for every lyric I flubbed." The girl from Hell's Kitchen understood the value of those dollars, concluding, "Needless to say I did my homework, knew my lyrics letter perfect, and was always on time." Meeting Vallée's demands for perfection gave Alice a sense of professionalism it might otherwise have taken her years to acquire. Conquering her stage fright came more slowly. One published version of her *Fleischmann Hour* debut describes her getting up to sing "Honeymoon Hotel," doing it perfectly, then fainting dead away on the last note. It is a melodramatic story meant to illustrate Alice's self-effacing temperament. Yet it also underscores how high stakes in the new medium of live radio were, especially on a nationally popular show. There was simply no room for mistakes.

The advent of broadcast radio represented the first step in twentieth-century America's love affair with "home entertainment," and Rudy Vallée let Alice Faye in on the ground floor. His assistant Walter Scharf said that "the radio was bigger than anything had ever been before," bigger even than television, because it unobtrusively provided the sounds that became part of the fabric of peoples' days. "It was there all the time, turned on without upsetting the family routine," he said. Programming had undergone a substantial transformation in its first decade of life. Local broadcasts by small-time vaudevillians, social reformers, quacks, boosters, and charlatans quickly gave way to long-distance networks providing professional programs packaged by advertising agencies. By 1927, the National Broadcasting Corporation had two national networks, the "red" originating from station WEAF and the "blue" from station WJZ, both in New

York. Advertising agencies began to see the marketing potential of these national networks. Within five years such agencies as the J. Walter Thompson agency established radio departments that wrote and produced not only radio advertising for their clients but the programs as well.

The ad agencies developed audience surveying to better serve their clients engaged in program sponsorship. They discovered in America an increased interest in the urban experience, such as the music of popular dance bands broadcast live from New York and Chicago hotels, and an overall preference for more slickly packaged entertainment than had been available in radio's earliest days. Corporations could feed this demand by sponsoring radio programs whose stars would be inextricably linked to their products in the minds of the public. Early radio entertainers, who had not been widely known before they went on the air, often got "branded" with the name of their sponsor's product and had trouble shifting to other programs with different corporate sponsorship. In 1929, Fleischmann's Yeast, which had advertised nationally for years but was new to radio, reversed that trend by taking a different approach. They decided to hire the biggest star they could find to host their show, calculating to benefit from the prestige of having their name linked with the star's rather than the reverse strategy of building up an unknown performer until his name was identified with the company's. The biggest star of the day was, of course, Rudy Vallée. They signed him to host the *Fleischmann Hour,* which premiered two days after the stock market crashed in 1929. It became the most popular variety show on radio and ran for ten years.

Radio's development as a commercial medium meant that big companies spent big money for big names. Vallée consolidated his place as host of the number-one variety show by inviting the best entertainers in show business to appear as guests on his program. Edgar Bergen, Milton Berle, Burns and Allen, and Eddie Cantor all made their radio debuts on the *Fleischmann Hour.* Theatrical notables like Noel Coward and Bea Lillie also appeared with Vallée. He even hired a little-known Danish comedian/pianist named Victor Borge to warm up the studio audience before air time. By 1932, stars approached Vallée for guest spots rather than the other way around. Other notables he attracted included Fanny Brice, Bob Hope, Red Skelton, and Orson Welles. Listeners recognized and responded to the quality of the talent and the lush way in which Vallée showcased it.

Vallée worked very hard to live up to his white-tie-and-tails image and consistently delivered a class act. Each detail of the show received his personal attention. As a result, Vallée took his role as Alice Faye's Svengali seriously to the point of re-creating her image. Many orchestra leaders left decisions about their singers' appearances to the singers themselves. Rudy, however, had other ideas. His third wife, Eleanor, said he preferred women who were the opposite of the Alice Faye type: slinky, in high heels, with long fingernails and red lipstick. That is exactly the "look" he encouraged Alice to adopt when she began with the orchestra. Rudy, she said, "liked girls in satin, so I wore satin and lightened my hair in the fashion." Photographs from this time show Alice as a pert femme fatale, with platinum blonde hair, a devastating figure, deep red cupid-bow lips, and pencil-thin eyebrows arching upwards.

Alice looked every inch the vamp as she stood in the spotlight in skin-tight satin to do her torch numbers. No one would guess that she was still a seventeen-year-old kid working to overcome a bad case of stage fright. Her biggest problem, one common to most novice singers, was what to do with her hands. When she was nervous, people several feet away could see the way that they trembled. One of Faye's habitual singing postures, hands held together often with a handkerchief or scarf between them, probably developed during this time as a defense against the shakes. She had something to hold onto, yet gave the appearance of remarkable poise. As her confidence grew, so too did her ability to use her hands in a freer, more expressive way.

As Alice gained more experience, she appeared more frequently on the *Fleischmann Hour,* singing swing numbers to offset Vallée's romantic ballads. The formula proved successful, yet Vallée could not convince his sponsors that Alice was an asset to the show, and they refused to pay her out of the program's budget. Fortunately Vallée, who had a healthy ego and a profound faith in his own ability to spot talent, willingly backed his opinion with his checkbook. Vallée paid Alice's salary out of his own pocket, willing to wait for public opinion to prove that his sponsor was wrong. Her $120-a-week salary was double what she earned as a dancer in *Scandals,* and a princely sum for anyone living through the early years of the depression. Alice flourished professionally in the circumstances Vallée created for her, and the nation slowly began to notice her and look forward to her Thursday night radio appearances.

Naturally, Alice's biggest asset was her voice, and she was more fortunate than either she or Vallée knew in how well it suited the primitive broadcasting technology of the time. Popular music in the late twenties and early thirties favored female vocalists with a near-operatic soprano, like the M-G-M star Jeannette MacDonald. Alice Faye's husky, resonant alto had a vastly different quality, which one radio historian described as the sound of "a girl of the proletariat, city-tough, yet just folks." Columnist Louella Parsons credited Alice Faye as "the first to create interest in the throaty, husky type of feminine crooning." Alice set a new trend in singing. Her low, soft, "crooning" style worked well from a technical standpoint, too. Radio's sensitive carbon microphones contained filaments that tended to shatter at the sound of harsh, high notes. Strong stage voices, like those of Al Jolson or Ethel Merman, simply did not work as well on radio as the intimate vocalizations of Vallée and Faye. Still the sponsors held out, and Vallée continued to pay Alice's salary himself.

This stalemate may have continued indefinitely had fate not intervened in a dramatic way. In a rainstorm at four in the morning on August 21, Vallée lost control of his sixteen-cylinder Cadillac touring car in the middle of Delaware. His dozing passengers, Alice, Seabury Waring, and Lester and Faye Laden, startled awake as the car flipped on the shoulder of a deserted road. Everyone emerged from the overturned vehicle unharmed except Alice, who had been thrown from the car. As Vallée and the others searched for her in the rainy darkness, the cars carrying the rest of the orchestra managed to pull to a stop before hitting the overturned Cadillac. They found Alice lying in the mud several yards away. Alice remembered, "Rudy apparently fell asleep at the wheel and the car went off the shoulder and flipped completely over. My lower back took the brunt of the fall."

Vallée and his band had just finished an engagement in Atlantic City and were traveling to another one in Norfolk, Virginia, when the accident occurred. They took Alice from Bridgeville to Greenwood, Delaware, where she was treated by Dr. Gottred Metzler. She had sustained a severe cut over her left eye, an injured shoulder, and multiple bruises. They left Vallée's wrecked Cadillac in Greenwood and continued to Virginia Beach, checking into the Cavalier Hotel by mid-morning. An orderly carried Alice inside, where she rested until she could board the afternoon train to New York. The deep cut over her eye concerned everyone, and Vallée wanted her to get to New York as soon as possible to see what could be done for it. She returned to Manhattan that afternoon. The next day, she consulted a plastic surgeon, who, as the *New York Journal* put it, "will operate in an effort to prevent her beauty from being marred by a long and jagged gash in her forehead." Alice underwent surgery, which was successful. By the following week Alice left the hospital to recuperate in what the papers called her "Long Island home"—a flat in the Bronx she shared with her mother and brothers.

The accident and its consequences were painful for Alice and presented her with the inconvenience of a few weeks' lost wages. She filed a petition with the state compensation board and waited for her scars to heal so she could perform again. Otherwise, she thought nothing about the car accident warranted a great deal of attention. The press thought otherwise, however, and gave the story national attention. From their perspective America's foremost (married) pop idol in a midnight car accident with his blonde protégée was a sensational story, and they played it to the hilt. Later Alice would say that the wreck and its attendant publicity "left scars on my body and my psyche." By reason of her association with Vallée, photographs of a bandaged Alice being carried into the Cavalier Hotel appeared in newspapers from New Bedford, Massachusetts, to Louisville, Kentucky, and beyond. Some of the accompanying stories were benign, with headlines such as "Rudy Vallée's Car in Crash, Girl Pal Hurt." Others were hugely exaggerated: "Rudy Vallée Near Death as Car Overturns." The remainder cast the story in a predictable light, emphasizing Alice's presence in the passenger seat of Vallée's car in the middle of the night and neglecting to mention that the car carried three other passengers as well. Vallée and Fay Webb, his wife of one year, had already separated and reconciled on several occasions. Their marriage was troubled, and the press knew it.

The press wanted to know just how proximate Alice and Rudy were, and appearances worked to the media's advantage. A wealthy, world-famous bandleader with a rocky marriage spending months on the road in the company of a lovely young singer who owed her career to him played straight into the hands of the gossip columnists. What lay beneath surface appearances was irrelevant. The two could issue any number of denials, which they did over the years, but they went largely ignored. Until her death, Alice maintained that she and Vallée had never had an affair. In later years, Vallée declared that they did but that the affair did not occur until after Alice's marriage to Tony Martin had foundered. Throughout the early 1930s they had a variety of opportunities, and both were young and attractive. If they did succumb to temptation, however, it would have been a fleeting incident. Too many people surrounded them for a full-blown passionate affair between Vallée and his singer to go unnoticed, and the financial rewards for feeding such a hot piece of information to the press were too great. Nevertheless, the rumors that began with the car accident would continue to grow and plague Alice for some time to come.

One aspect of the publicity surrounding the accident proved positive, however. The newspapers kept Alice's name before the public as she sat on the sidelines while her face healed. Fans of the Rudy Vallée show noticed her absence from the Thursday night broadcasts and responded with cards and letters in numbers so great that the sponsors could no longer avoid acknowledgment of Alice's contributions to the *Fleischmann Hour's* success. They finally relented and gave Alice a contract, which regularized her position and secured her place in radio. Vallée's reputation for spotting talent was sustained. Almost without trying, Alice Faye had become a household name across America. The interest generated by the car accident and the intimacy of Alice's voice won the public and the sponsor over. She had less of an effect on one new acquaintance, however; while she waited for her injuries to mend, Alice came to watch the orchestra perform at the Pennsylvania Roof. One night, Vallée introduced her to another bandleader named Phil Harris. Harris described Alice as a vision with a black eye, fifteen stitches in her forehead, and adhesive tape around one ear. "She couldn't smile because she'd been smacked in the mouth," he said. Clearly, the introduction sparked little interest at the time.

By the end of September, when Alice could perform again she appeared with the orchestra in a series of gigs in and around New York. On October 11 she had a personal triumph when "Rudy Vallée and his Connecticut Yankees with Alice Faye," as the billing read, opened the "Hollywood Revels of 1934" at the Hollywood Restaurant. After the opening, Irving Caesar, a New York music publisher, wrote a personal review in a letter to Vallée: "Incidentally, tell Alice that the comments at our table about her work would have been very cheering to her if she had overheard them. She was better than good, and before another year has rolled around, I think, she will be doing outstanding work." The newspapers concurred and typically continued to link the two performers personally as well as professionally. In an October 13 story about the show, the *New York Mirror* captioned a publicity photo of Vallée and Alice with the first of many wedding rumors: "Rudy Vallée is denying reports that he would soon marry Alice Faye, singer."

Several weeks later, at the beginning of December, Alice had a brief opportunity to solo for a few weeks at the Embassy Club on Fifty-seventh Street. Their singer, the headliner Helen Morgan, was drinking and despondent and had returned home to Cleveland for two weeks to work herself out of a deep trough of depression. Walter Scharf, who worked as Morgan's accompanist at the Embassy at the time, said that the inexperienced Alice got the job by "kidding the proprietors of the Embassy that she could do more" than just "getting up in the middle of a number, singing a couple of choruses and letting the band do the rest." The proprietors of the Embassy Club were not the kind of people to bluff. A man named Al Howard managed it for the mob and kept things well organized. His arrangement with the authorities guaranteed that not even a perfunctory raid would disturb the peace of his establishment. As a result, the Embassy's patrons, recalled Walter Scharf, "were the highest in high society, men in starched shirts and tails and the women in long satin dresses, with the most expensive jewelry seen outside the grilles of Tiffany's." They enjoyed the food, the drinks, and the thrill of the proximity to real gangsters, where the atmosphere of latent violence added spice to an evening's entertainment.

Al Howard called Alice's bluff and hired her as Morgan's replacement. His faith in her threw Alice into a panic over how she would cope in the spotlight without the security of Vallée and the Connecticut Yankees backing her up. She knew that club performers had to be good to rise above the noise of drinks and dinner. Many singers did not enjoy working in nightclubs, where they had to compete with the clinking of knives and forks, the bustling waiters, and rambunctious or drunken customers. The customers' lack of attention, in particular, could devastate a novice performer. Other vocalists relished the challenge of nightclub work, which allowed them to exercise their ability to capture the audience's attention and hold it through a set despite the hubbub. At this point in her career, Alice belonged to the former school of thought.

The minor-key numbers Helen Morgan favored concerned Alice particularly. "I can't do it," she lamented to Walter Scharf. "I don't know how to sing this kind of material." Scharf helped her overcome her anxiety by suggesting songs more suited to her style, "exciting, modern songs that went with her appearance and the range of her vocal chords." For reasons long since forgotten, Alice's lighting posed a problem, too. The electricians had experimented, ultimately finding a special kind of lamp for her, which undoubtedly added to her tension. It took effort on everyone's part to prepare Alice's act and make it really effective, but when Alice opened, the results were spectacular. The songs Scharf selected worked, and his presence onstage as her accompanist eased Alice's fears. The electrician's new lighting gave her a "sparkling sheen" and an "uncanny confidence" that dazzled the gangsters who owned the club. They and their patrons, Scharf asserted, were the first to hear the definitive Alice Faye sound, "with that deep voice sending shivers down their spines."

Alice's solo turn at the Embassy was a huge hit. "She seemed to bring an extra kind of class to a very classy supper club," said Scharf.

The acclaim she earned at the Embassy Club demonstrated that Alice could succeed on her own, and it is possible that she believed she had reached the pinnacle of her ambitions. But in the months ahead as she followed along in Rudy Vallée's wake, she would find herself venturing into a medium where she would prove a far greater success than he.

CHAPTER 3

Scandals

While Alice toured the country, sang on the radio, and coped with her small share of the limelight, her friend Betty King continued to work in the chorus and began dating Alice's brother Sonny. Alice did not approve. She loved Betty and knew how hard Betty had worked to support her mother and stepfather. Alice wanted the best for her friend, and, to her way of thinking, the best didn't include Sonny. She loved her brother but displayed an almost ruthless pragmatism when she declared she did not want Betty to get too serious about him. "My brother isn't making enough money," Alice said. Betty said that Sonny suffered from arthritis from an early age, and his disability prevented him from working consistently. Sonny was not in a business of any kind, "just doing little things around to make a dollar here and there once in a while," Betty said. She remembers Alice really putting her foot down. "Betty," she said, "you are not going to marry my brother. He doesn't deserve you because he can't give you the kind of life you should have. You watch, you're going to meet someone that's going to be just good, keep you going, and give you a good living." Shortly thereafter, Alice took matters into her own hands and introduced Betty to Walter Scharf.

While she performed at the Embassy Club, Alice was so pleased with Walter Scharf that she had suggested he leave Helen Morgan and join Rudy Vallée's company. She mentioned him to Vallée, and insisted Vallée come up to the club, saying, "Rudy, he's the best pianist in the world. You've got to hear him." Vallée liked Alice's suggestion, and he hired Scharf as his principal assistant. Vallée's sense of perfection guaranteed that the work was not easy, but Scharf recognized a good opportunity when he saw one. In addition to the exposure that came with working for someone so famous, Vallée paid his employees double the going rate for musicians at this time, a payroll that included twenty-eight musicians and thirteen entertainers. Scharf earned five hundred dollars a week with Vallée. When Alice introduced Walter to Betty King, the two hit it off immediately. Soon Alice, Betty, Walter, and Rudy were going out and about together. "We were good company," Betty said. "We dined together quite often, especially after Walter went to work for Rudy."

Alice had briefly returned to her usual spot singing with Vallée and his group at the Hollywood Restaurant once she finished at the Embassy Club. Her newfound popularity packed in the customers for the few nights Rudy Vallée and the Connecticut Yankees continued to play there. But Vallée was already looking ahead to his next professional move. He was leaving Granlund's Hollywood to accept a new offer from the real Hollywood. Fox Studios planned to film an adaptation of George White's *Scandals* as a vehicle for perennially popular Vallée. In true workaholic fashion, Vallée intended to work on the film by day, perform with his band by night, and continue the Thursday broadcast of the *Fleischmann Hour* from Los Angeles. He knew his presence in southern California might exacerbate tensions in his nasty and drawn-out divorce action against Fay Webb, which was in the California courts. Webb had established legal residence there when she returned home to her father, the police chief of Santa Monica. Personal complications notwithstanding, Vallée wanted a second chance in films. His only previous foray into movies, a poorly received movie called *Vagabond Lover*, had left him discouraged and anxious for a chance to redeem himself as a screen actor. He accepted Fox's offer and risked the chance of repercussions in his divorce suit with Fay Webb.

In the second week of December 1933, Alice and the rest of Vallée's forty-person company embarked for Los Angeles. Alice recalled in 1987 that she had had no thoughts of breaking into movies. "I went along because I was singing with the band," she said, but her memory in this case proved faulty. Vallée had arranged for her to have a small part in the film. From the time he signed his own contract, Vallée had pestered George White about using Alice in the movie. About the time that Alice returned to work at the Hollywood, White telegraphed from Los Angeles to say that he had secured a featured role for Alice, doing a song with the provocative title "Oh, You Nasty Man." Vallée's lawyer, Hyman Bushell, went to work outlining the contractual provisions that would allow Alice, as an artist signed with Vallée's talent agency, to appear in the picture.

Even with Vallée and his orchestra going with her, Alice found the thought of traveling to Hollywood intimidating. She asked Betty King to come out to California and work as her stand-in. "She said, 'You have to be out there with me. I'm not going to be in California without you,'" Betty said. "You come out there and be my stand-in and you'll make much, much more money," Alice promised. Her offer also meant that Betty could stay close to Walter Scharf and away from Sonny. Typically, in later interviews Alice said nothing about the train trip to California, but she would have the breadth of North America to consider the challenge of performing in a motion picture, which she probably found as frightening as her many previous opportunities. The prospect of California in winter was more pleasant, especially since she could bring her mother along and treat her to a few months of sunshine.

Newcomers to southern California inevitably remarked upon how clean and bright it was compared to the east. Alice's future film costar Don Ameche raved, "It was clean. The curbs were white, and the streets were immaculate, and the homes were immaculate, and the palm trees." Alice's immediate impressions on her arrival on the Golden State Limited on December 9, however, were not recorded by the press, who customarily grilled newcomers on that subject. Instead members of the press were keenly interested in the Vallée divorce. Fay Webb was a hometown girl, the daughter of a local official. Instead of the customary questions about the weather and her hopes of success in the upcoming film, Alice faced a contingent of suspicious pressmen as she stepped off the train. "Alice Faye denies romance, role with Rudy Vallée only basis for friendship," said the *Los Angeles Times*. "Blonde Dancer Just a Pal," said the *Examiner*. In the face of Alice's denials of the alleged affair, the reporters had to content themselves with merely reiterating the rumors, but they were sniffing for blood.

The actual work on *George White's Scandals* began more smoothly. Alice's sequence was shot and considered successful. The production hit a snag, though, when the leading lady, the English dramatic actress Lillian Harvey, abruptly walked out. At the time, the story circulated that Harvey considered the part insufficiently important for her. She had demanded an expanded role and then quit when the studios refused. "But the truth was," Alice later said, "that she was simply not right for the role as it had been written." Alice classified it, correctly, as "a light bit of froth," for which Harvey felt she was badly miscast. "Harvey and the studio both knew it," she said.

The sequence of events that followed Harvey's exit could not have been more predictable had it been written for Busby Berkeley's backstage musical, *Forty-Second Street*; Alice Faye's life was about to become a Hollywood cliché. "I went to a dinner party with Rudy Vallée," who, as her agent, had suggested her for the part, she recalled. "I met Mr. [Sidney] Kent, then the head of Fox. He liked me and said, 'I'd like to see that girl tested.'" Vallée recollected a slightly different version of the story, in which the Fox brass saw the rushes of Alice performing "Oh, You Nasty Man," judged her as "sensational," and immediately demanded, "We want this girl for the lead!" Whichever way it happened, Alice got the part, at a salary of five hundred dollars a week, negotiated for her by Vallée. That amount may not have been staggering by Hollywood standards, but it was by Alice's, and it constituted her first introduction to the extravagant world of the big studio system.

Through Rudy Vallée and his promotion of her talents, Alice had inadvertently stumbled onto the best route to success and stardom in Hollywood. In a 1949 book called *Your Career in Motion Pictures,* a compilation of advice from the biggest names in movies, two of Alice's future costars, Dana Andrews and Betty Grable, argued that the easiest path to stardom was success in another medium. Andrews said, "Had I been an extra at the studio, part of an atmospheric group, I might have gone unnoticed for months or even years." Instead, a Goldwyn scout spotted him in a featured role on stage at the Pasadena Playhouse. Grable *had* gone unnoticed for years as a contract player at both RKO and Paramount. Twentieth Century-Fox offered her a leading role only after she achieved success on Broadway in Cole Porter's *DuBarry Was a Lady.* "If you want to get into motion pictures, *don't* go to Hollywood," she wrote. "My best opportunities in Hollywood came to me when I was not directly looking for work at the studios."

Demonstrated ability on stage or in radio could get a performer into the studios, but it could not guarantee a smooth transition to film work. Don Ameche, who, like Alice, performed on the radio before Twentieth Century-Fox signed him, argued that every medium was different. "You can't say you are an accomplished performer in radio unless you really know radio and what radio was all about. And it didn't make you an accomplished performer in pictures at all." Film work exposed Alice to a set of anxieties far more unnerving than any she had found before. Movies combined all the horrors of occupying the spotlight alone without an orchestra or chorus to provide support. Movie equipment and technicians were far more intimidating than radio's microphones and sound engineers. Ultimately, Alice found she enjoyed acting in films, but she never reconciled herself to viewing her own work. "I could never watch myself on screen. I would lose my lunch," she said. "I'd just die."

Fortunately the character Alice played (originally named Mona Vale but renamed Kitty Donnelly after Lillian Harvey bowed out) did not require much dramatic ability. The film adaptation of *George White's Scandals* retained the review format, with the acts held together by the thinnest of plots: a backstage romance between the show's two principals, Vallée and Faye, is threatened by Vallée's infatuation with a society debutante. Their relationship is saved by George White, playing himself. He contrives a wedding number for the closing act, substituting a real minister who performs a real ceremony unbeknownst to Vallée and Faye. They have just signed a marriage license, assured by White that it is their contract for the upcoming season. Once wed, White's trick is revealed, love triumphs, and the camera fades on the happy couple.

Alice derived a certain amount of assurance from the costumes and the makeup. They allowed her to feel like another, more glamorous person. "I never thought I was really beautiful when I was young," she recalled. "When the people at the studio were through putting me together, by ten o'clock in the morning I thought I was pretty beautiful." Working with the familiar Vallée as her costar eased her professional tensions, as did the support the studio system provided for young talent. Alice likened the studio to "one vast graduate school for performers," where she was coached in movement and speech, and finally received the first formal dance lessons in her life. Still she feared that the bubble might burst. "I was so unsure of myself that I was convinced one morning I would wake up and find that all this about being a movie star had been a dream," she said. "I really wasn't a movie star at all, just a kid from New York struggling to make it in the chorus line. I needed all the help in the confidence department that I could get."

On the morning of January 9, 1934, however, Alice woke up to find that her movie star bubble was in eminent danger of bursting. Fay Webb had filed a special maintenance action in her divorce suit against Vallée, naming Alice Faye as one of three co-respondents. The charges, outlined in the *New York Times,* placed Alice Faye's nascent film career in serious jeopardy. Webb alleged that Vallée had been "intimate on numerous occasions" with "Alice Faye, movie actress," as well as "two Jane Does." At this point in what the *Times* referred to as the "Vallée matrimonial shipwreck," it was less likely that Webb based her accusations on fact than on rumors in the newspapers. Sensational coverage abounded, a typical example of which was a serialized life of Vallée by Adela Rogers St. Johns: "On the road in strange cities, Alice and Rudy fought loneliness together. Naturally they ate together, made the long jumps together, shared work and play, ran in and out of each other's rooms and dressing rooms as people in their profession do, without any thought," St. Johns wrote. Her conclusion that "such things bind two people very close," neglected to mention the other thirty-eight or so men and women traveling with them at the same time and sharing in the same circumstances.

Alice countered the charges that day, telling the *Los Angeles Examiner* that the suit was "ridiculous." "Mr. Vallée is my friend and employer and has been that ever since he engaged me as part of his orchestra organization," she asserted. "As a member of the orchestra I have traveled with them in many different sites and in many different places." As Alice might have put it, her Irish was up, and her usual shy reserve gave way before it. Alice knew that kind of story would distress her friends and family as much as it distressed her. "I just loved Alice so much, I didn't pay any attention to those things," said Betty Scharf. "Her moral standards were good. I didn't want anybody putting her down about any of those things." Alice insisted that the records containing the charge and the specific details of her alleged "misconduct" be opened to the press, knowing she would be exonerated.

The circumstances in which Alice now found herself were further complicated by a temporary restraining order obtained by Fay Webb's attorney preventing Fox from paying Alice her weekly salary of five hundred dollars. A hearing on January 18 freed her previous week's pay, but not until January 25 did a judge rule that Alice could continue to draw her studio salary every week until the case was settled. In the meantime, she continued to defend herself. The papers published Fay Webb's list of twelve cities in which Faye and Vallée purportedly disported themselves, beginning with Alice Faye's debut in Jacksonville, Florida, the previous January, and continuing throughout the orchestra's spring tour. Faye countered by describing a distraught Vallée preoccupied throughout the tour with trying to contact his wife: "Time and again I noticed him sending wires to Mrs. Vallée, writing her letters and making long distance calls," she said. "I know that he begged and pleaded with her to join him." She added that throughout the tour she was in the company of the band members and several of their wives and seldom found herself alone with Vallée. In a later statement, Alice justified her role as Vallée's protégée by declaring, "I owe my radio career, my picture career, everything I am to Rudy Vallée. I'd be pretty much of an ingrate if I didn't feel grateful down to the tips of my shoes. He took me out of the chorus line and boosted me up the ladder. He's responsible for every bit of my success."

Both Alice and Vallée maintained for the rest of their lives that Webb's accusations had no basis in fact. Had firm evidence of an intimate relationship between the two existed, Webb could surely have used it to better effect earlier in her divorce action. Webb was firing a broadside hoping to hit something, and hoping too that the press might dig up something on its own. If Alice and Vallée had indeed been "intimate on numerous occasions," no third party ever came forward to confirm it. As it was, the allegations involving Alice ceased to be an issue as the case wore on. An article in the August 1934 issue of *Modern Screen* summed up Alice's situation best: "Alice Faye was lucky. Her innocence in the Vallée break-up was established before too late." In Hollywood, sometimes even the establishment of innocence could not salvage a damaged career, as the Fatty Arbuckle case in the 1920s demonstrated. Fox could have let Alice finish *George White's Scandals*, then given her the boot; her contract was only good for the duration of that one picture. Once again, however, Alice's timing proved fortuitous. By the time she had finished *George White's Scandals* in February, much of the hubbub surrounding Fay Webb's accusations had diminished, in part because of Alice's own forthright behavior. Alice had become a "forgotten factor in the case," which *Modern Screen* interpreted as the "break in her favor" that led Fox to offer her a long-term contract.

The studio bosses liked her performance in the movie and signed her in February, a month before *George White's Scandals* scheduled release date.

Alice had weathered the worst publicity storm of her career and emerged intact, with a Hollywood contract to boot. Late in her life, she said that *George White's Scandals* "will always be near and dear to my heart" because "one always remembers one's first fondly." Distance must have lent enchantment when she said that. It could not have been an easy period to live through as she adjusted to working in films and to dealing with the ruthless glare of negative publicity. But as usual, little time existed in which to dwell on it.

No sooner had *George White's Scandals* wrapped than she found herself in her second film, a non-musical drama called *Now I'll Tell*. The screenplay had been written by Inez Norton, the widow of Arnold Rothstein, one of the gamblers involved in the scheme to fix the 1919 World Series. It starred Helen Twelvetrees and Spencer Tracy as a couple on the brink of divorce because of his gambling and infidelity. The studio cast Alice in a supporting role as Peggy Warren, the "other woman," a move that seemed calculated to capitalize on Alice's recent notoriety. The one song Alice was allowed to sing, entitled "Foolin' with the Other Woman's Man," simply enhanced that image. Dressed in a slinky evening gown of black satin, accented with jewels and black feathers, with heavy makeup and tousled platinum curls, she looked every inch the homewrecker. The message came across loud and clear. Between Alice's publicity stills depicting this role and those from *George White's Scandals* in which she and Vallée appeared together in formal wedding attire, it is no wonder that her name continued to surface in conjunction with Vallée's whenever the press mentioned either one of them.

As she worked, the eighteen-year-old New Yorker tried to adapt to the relaxed pace of southern California, but she found that life in Hollywood, or at least her life, lacked the excitement and sparkle she had always known in Manhattan. Part of the problem was that Alice knew so few people. Back in New York, Rudy Vallée had to make his own adjustments.

Always a difficult man, he became practically impossible as he cast about for a replacement for Alice. "That was certainly not his favorite pastime," said Walter Scharf. "He hated to audition and the way he behaved showed just how much he hated it." It had been gracious of Vallée to allow Alice to pursue a movie career instead of holding her to her contract with him. He apparently realized that Fox was giving Alice a greater opportunity than he had had in trying to break into movies. Rather than stand in her way, Vallée simply urged her to live up to their expectations as best she could. In fact, he wrote to Winfield Sheehan, longtime studio boss and survivor from the William Fox days, thanking him for the consideration shown Alice, and "to express my hope, which I know is yours, that she justifies our faith in her."

Alice was striving to do just that. On the set of *Now I'll Tell*, she worked well with her costars, the little-remembered Helen Twelvetrees and the legendary Spencer Tracy. She recalled being in awe of Tracy, "I was very young when I worked with Spencer and my mouth was just hanging open," she recalled. Her reaction, however, may not have been due to his acting ability. Tracy drank constantly during the period he was under contract to Fox, feeling underappreciated and anxious about his future with the studio. Tracy's worries about his career and his unhappy marriage manifested themselves in drunken and reprehensible public outbursts.

Alice found herself discreetly fending off Tracy's advances on the set, particularly his tendency to grope her thigh under the table during their nightclub scenes. Nevertheless, Alice liked the role she played in *Now I'll Tell*. It allowed her a chance to sing, even though the picture was a drama. "I guess I'll always sing in pictures," she said, "and I'm glad because I love rhythm and blues singing." The sound crew employed an unusual method to record her number in the film. Instead of recording the song separately and playing it back during filming, as was customary, they filmed and recorded the sound simultaneously in one take. Alice actually sang on film, rather than lip-synching. Two other incidents made the film notable in a minor way. First, it was the only time in her career that Alice played a character who died, as homewreckers inevitably had to do in order to appease the production code. Second, it featured a brief appearance by a new child actor named Shirley Temple, with whom Alice would costar in later films.

While Alice worked in *Now I'll Tell,* the studio released *George White's Scandals.* Finally, the press could discuss Alice in terms of her professional, rather than her personal, life. She fared better than the movie as a whole. *Picture Play* called *George White's Scandals* "frequently empty," and "one of those picture which you can see if you're in an indulgent mood," advising that "Alice Faye will be seen in other films and perhaps they will be better ones." The *Hollywood Reporter* attributed the movie's good-natured air to Jimmy Durante and Alice Faye, while asserting that "high amid its faults are Mr. Vallée's earnest efforts to be humorous." Predictably, the number "Oh, You Nasty Man" commanded much attention, with the *New York Times* remarking that the "flashy blonde newcomer" put over the lyrics "in great style." *Dallas Morning News* critic John Rosenfield said, "Miss Faye, who figured in the recent Vallée headlines, is revealed as an expressive ha-cha singer with a moist Cupid's bow for a mouth and the rest very like Harlow."

Because of the ultra-sophisticated image Vallée had urged Alice to cultivate, comparisons between Alice and M-G-M star Jean Harlow were inevitable. In fact, one Hollywood sob sister wrote a feature about Alice entitled "Look Out Harlow!" in which she contrasted the two actresses. Alice simply endured what one writer termed the "sex-pot apprenticeship" that most starlets went through. Since nothing succeeded like imitation in the film industry, logic dictated that Alice must be made to look like an existing star. She already looked like a femme fatale; the Fox cosmetologists simply enhanced what was already there to achieve the resemblance to Harlow. "The studio makeup department changed my makeup to match my hair coloring and plucked my eyebrows into skinny little lines, and during those few years I did wear a lot of powder, rouge, and mascara, and the whole bit," Alice said. "I always felt at night as though I had to peel my face off before I got down to the real me." At one point Alice even shaved off her eyebrows. "I really wanted to look like Dietrich, with penciled eyebrows and suits," Alice said.

On March 27, Fox announced that Alice's next vehicle would be a production called *She Learned about Sailors,* but before filming began she made a quick trip back to New York. As she traveled, the press recorded her every move, fueled no doubt by the Fox publicity machine. Alice flew east with her mother, leaving Los Angeles on April 5. She refused to comment on the reason for her trip to the *Los Angeles Times,* whose reporter gushed, "Could it be Rudy Vallée, the crooner?" She stopped in Indianapolis, then Pittsburgh, where the *Pittsburgh Sun* headlined its story about her "Girl in Vallée Case Here." The same week the *Milwaukee Journal* noted that Rudy Vallée had given Alice a chow puppy, which must have made an interesting addition to her luggage. By the time she arrived in New York, the *New York Enquirer* reported that she was to be guest of honor at a party at the Hollywood Restaurant. This was a return engagement at the Hollywood Restaurant on April 12 for a one-night-only performance with Vallée and his orchestra. She declared it was a kick seeing her name in the electric lights over the entrance. "And it was so wonderful to be able to go back and be sweet to some of the ones who had treated me terrible," she confessed. The *New York Journal* also noted that the State Compensation Bureau awarded Alice a cash settlement of four hundred dollars plus twenty-five dollars a week for the weeks between August 22 and September 28, 1933, when she had been unable to work because of the car accident with Vallée.

At the same time, the press busily built up another sensational romance for Alice. This time they linked her with Nick Foran, a Princeton football player and son of a multimillionaire, to whom she was supposedly engaged. Distinguishing fact from the fantasy produced by both the papers and the studio publicists became almost impossible. According to published accounts, the twenty-three-year-old Foran ventured out to Hollywood in search of a screen test and there met Alice, whom he dated for three months. Foran's father, president of the bank in Flemington, New Jersey, and a former Collector of the Port of New York, reputedly objected to the relationship on the grounds of Alice Faye's notoriety. In a statement to the press, the elder Foran stated, "Miss Faye may be a very lovely girl, but from the unpleasant publicity she has received I do not think it would be wise for my son to become engaged to her. So if Nick becomes engaged to Miss Faye I shall be compelled to disinherit him." A disinherited scion of a wealthy family was just the kind of news opportunity that the press needed to resurrect Alice's reputation as an adventuress, and, typically, it did.

In the midst of this media barrage, however, a few reporters began to tumble to the fact that Alice Faye was really a quiet young woman who abhorred the glare of publicity. One of the earliest articles to employ this angle described her as a "mysterious lady," who declined to comment about her personal life. In Hollywood Alice lived up to her growing reputation as a retiring personality, making only a few public appearances—usually escorted by one of her brothers, who had joined Alice and their mother in California. Nineteen-year-old Alice had entered a new and demanding profession, and the negative publicity that her new work generated understandably concerned her family.

Betty King, who lived with the Lepperts in California, remembered fondly how careful Alice's mother was. "Oh, I loved her," Betty said. "She took care of me when I came out here like she was my mother." Alice Leppert took her responsibility seriously and looked after both girls like a hawk, setting curfews and refusing to allow them out with certain dates. Clearly, the glamour of Hollywood had not gone to her head, as it did with other celebrity mothers. Alice Leppert knew how to love and protect her daughter and her daughter's friend and could not have been further removed in her outlook from the typical stage mother. "Her mother was fabulous," said Betty. "I hate to say it because my real mother was wonderful, but Alice's mother was more my mother than my own mother." Alice arranged for Betty to continue working as her stand-in and insisted she live with the Lepperts. Betty said, "And not only that, but she wouldn't let me pay any rent, or buy any of the food or anything." Betty remembered Alice saying, "You don't have to pay for anything; you're going to have a hundred dollars a week to help your family." Both girls continued to act as the economic mainstay of their respective families. Alice's transition to film work simply meant that she and Betty could improve their families' standard of living.

Throughout 1934, Alice worked too hard to have a full nightlife. After her quick trip to New York in April, she returned to do two more pictures at Fox: *She Learned About Sailors* and *365 Nights in Hollywood*. Both of these films were low-budget B movies, shot at Fox's lot on Western Avenue, a smaller studio that was "very intimate and quiet and very different" from the newer lot used for A pictures after Fox merged with Twentieth Century, said Fox child star Jane Withers. Alice feared that being cast in less important features meant studio bosses wanted to phase her out of movies entirely. On the contrary, B pictures were where the moguls sent contract players to acquire on-the-job experience. Lynn Bari, another Fox actress at the time, likened B pictures to today's television work, where producers allotted no more than twenty-four to twenty-eight days per film and screenwriters constantly revised the scripts. Alice had to work both fast and well to pull off a good performance under these circumstances.

Twentieth Century-Fox star Dan Dailey recalled that in the days before the Screen Actors Guild, pictures were filmed six days a week. A day's work on A pictures averaged from nine in the morning until six in the evening, but B pictures were "pretty close from" nine in the morning to eleven or twelve o'clock at night. Betty Scharf said that, during the shooting of *She Learned about Sailors* and *365 Nights in Hollywood*, "they didn't want Alice to get too tired. A couple of times they dressed me the same as her and did long shots of me dancing for her." Performers maintaining this kind of schedule often had neither the time nor the inclination to indulge in Hollywood's nightlife.

In addition to providing novice actors like Alice with valuable experience, B movies constituted an important component of the big studio system. The equivalent of any other factory-produced "bulk" product, they kept Fox's national chain of theaters supplied with new movies, and kept expensive equipment and technicians constantly employed. B pictures were a critical component of the industry because they absorbed overhead costs. "There was so much studio space and manpower then, we always kept busy with many pictures," said Fox producer Otto Lang. Sol Wurtzel headed Fox's B picture unit. Wurtzel was a tall, dark-haired man with a mustache and a reputation for being a thoroughly nice man. He enjoyed gambling, sports, and turning a consistent profit.

Wurtzel generated Fox's most consistent profit line with popular programmers such as Will Rogers's folksy, inexpensive comedies, the "Charlie Chan" series, and a string of low-budget dramas introducing Shirley Temple. His productions were, as one film historian put it, "always competent, and sometimes very good." Both *She Learned about Sailors* and *365 Nights in Hollywood* met these criteria. They were well received by the public, garnered solid, respectable reviews for Alice Faye, and made money. Wurtzel's bread-and-butter films proved essential to the life of the company, which had spent several years tottering on the brink of financial disaster, losing talent (like Spencer Tracy) to other studios, and producing unsuccessful A pictures. The chief of A productions was Winfield Sheehan, a holdover from the days when William Fox owned the studio. In the early thirties, Sheehan underwent a creative slump. Despite his success with the award-winning *Cavalcade,* critics found his films increasingly repetitive, featuring dull plots and sluggish performances. Fox's New York office found them unnecessarily expensive. The overall economic climate of the nation, combined with a decline in the quality of Fox's product under Sheehan, posed a serious threat to the studio's continuing existence.

Ongoing legal complications from Fox's previous administration did nothing to help the situation. In 1925 William Fox, the head of the successful Fox Film Corporation, recapitalized his company. He issued stock to the public under the name of Fox Theatre Corporation and utilized the revenue in an attempt to gain primacy in the motion picture industry. During the next four years Fox acquired a number of small and medium-sized theater chains across the country, developed and promoted the "Movietone" system of sound on film, and attempted a takeover of Loew's, Inc., the holding company that controlled both the two-hundred-theater Loew's Circuit and M-G-M Studio. To accomplish his ends, Fox stripped his companies of cash and negotiated millions of dollars of short-term loans. His cash-depleted companies could not generate sufficient revenue, however, to service this debt. This problem was compounded by serious injuries William Fox sustained in a car accident in July 1929, which prevented him from working at full capacity. He had built an empire on an insubstantial foundation, and, three months later when the stock market crashed, it toppled. William Fox lost control of his business, eventually declared bankruptcy, and ultimately went to prison for bribing the judge in his bankruptcy case.

The Fox companies went into receivership and were reorganized by Chase National Bank, which in 1932 appointed Sidney Kent president of Fox Films. Kent turned out to be a gifted manager, who reorganized the theater division and thereby improved Fox's troubled distribution system. As a result Fox actually made a profit in 1933. But an improved distribution system only helped if there was a good product to distribute. By the middle of 1934, it became clear to Kent that Sheehan was a liability the company could no longer afford, and he began to cast about for a new head of production. In the meantime, he began to cut costs aggressively. Alice, who was filming *George White's 1935 Scandals* at the time, remembered money being a constant problem throughout the production. "Not only did they cut corners," she said, "but they often cut the whole enchilada." At one point during filming, the producer approached Alice to request that she not drink so much water. "It costs seventy-five cents a bottle," he reminded her.

George White's 1935 Scandals was another Sheehan production, filmed at the newer lot near Beverly Hills. Alice again received good reviews, as well as top billing, but the movie suffered from the same lack of imagination and verve that troubled the rest of Fox's top-of-the-line films. One reviewer wrote, "Miss Faye lusciously fulfills the double requirements of heroine and singing star," and *New York Times* critic Howard Barnes called Alice "the premiere chanteuse of the musical" who proved "exceedingly resourceful at putting over its most infectious songs." He went on to damn the overall production, however, stating that "neither the tunes nor pageantry are potent enough to charm away its frequent laggard stretches." Symptomatic of Sheehan's lack of vision was the fact that *George White's 1935 Scandals* featured the screen debut of a promising young dancer named Eleanor Powell, whom he failed to sign to a long-term contract. M-G-M snapped her up, and she became one of the most famous film dancers of the thirties.

Sheehan's next move seemed equally inexplicable. No sooner did the *New York Times* make Alice a bankable asset by declaring her the "premiere chanteuse of the musical" than the studio loaned Alice Faye to Walter Wanger for *Every Night at Eight,* where she costarred with singer Frances Langford and her old friend from New York, George Raft. Perhaps Fox's financial woes meant that they were not in a position to utilize Alice effectively right away, or perhaps they were able to generate some income by loaning her out at a higher rate than they were currently paying her. Whatever the reason, Alice starred in *Every Night at Eight,* in which she played part of a female singing trio who combined forces with orchestra leader George Raft to land a spot in radio. As part of the loan-out agreement, Alice received better billing (second after Raft) than Frances Langford, although Langford had the better role. Alice sang the Jimmy McHugh song "I Feel a Song Coming On" with such bombshell aplomb that audiences were struck once again by the resemblance between Alice Faye and Jean Harlow.

For her next project Alice returned to Fox for *Music Is Magic,* the last of her films produced under the Sheehan regime. It showed. With a running time of a scant sixty-six minutes, *Music Is Magic* could barely justify its designation as a feature-length film. *Variety* commended Alice for her "neat work" but classified the film as a "flighty affair." Its musical num-bers were brief and carelessly staged, and its costumes and scenery looked as if they had been recycled from other productions. Still, Alice received top billing, and this was her first movie released under the logo of the newly reorganized company. During late 1934 and early 1935 Fox presi-dent Sidney Kent had conducted negotiations that led to the merger of the ailing Fox studios with a recently founded production company called Twentieth Century, headed by a cinematic dynamo named Darryl F. Zanuck. The new company would be called Twentieth Century-Fox.

The specifics of the two companies' business suggested that a merger was an ideal solution to their respective problems. Twentieth Century had been founded in 1933 by Joe Schenck, Darryl F. Zanuck, and William Goetz, whose father-in-law, Louis B. Mayer, provided him with his share of funding. From its beginning, however, Twentieth Century lacked both a studio and a nationally organized chain of theaters in which to exhibit its product. Instead it distributed its films through United Artists. In con-trast, Fox owned two movie lots and a string of theaters, recently brought up to date by Sidney Kent, but lacked a producer with sufficient energy and vision to stir the studio out of its creative doldrums. Fox's assets of $36 million generated a net profit of $1.8 million in 1935, whereas Twen-tieth Century managed to generate a $1.7 million profit with a company whose assets (little more than its personnel) were valued at $4 million. The deal constituted the biggest film merger since M-G-M was formed a decade before. Under its terms, Spyros Skouras became president in New York and Zanuck assumed the position of vice president in charge of pro-duction in Hollywood.

Darryl F. Zanuck was a small-town Nebraskan with an eighth-grade education and a gift for story development. He arrived in Hollywood in the 1920s after fighting in France during World War I. His start in movies seemed inauspicious—he landed a job as a scriptwriter for *Rin Tin Tin* at Warner Brothers. He proved so successful with the canine serial star, how-ever, that he soon attracted the attention of Jack Warner, who moved him to more important projects. He had a gift for creating plots out of whole cloth from newspaper headlines and thereby introduced the gritty gangster films, like *Public Enemy,* for which Warners became famous. Realizing he would never achieve a top position at the family-run Warners, he left there for a ground-floor position as one of the founders of Twentieth Century.

The people who worked with him either loved or loathed Darryl Zanuck, but almost everyone respected his abilities. "He was smart as hell as far as that went," said Lynn Bari, "and he had some pretty good people around him, too. Awfully good writers, awfully good producers, real gentlemen, not fly-by-nighters." Yet despite the excellence of the people with whom he worked, Zanuck was perhaps the most relentless of all the moguls in sacrificing the desires of his subordinates to the greater benefit of the studio's operations. Screenwriter Philip Dunne summed up Zanuck's approach when he said, "Writers did not write scripts for directors, they wrote them for Darryl. Directors were assigned, as writers and actors were assigned: by his decision." Zanuck played an integral part in crafting all of his productions, spending hours in story conferences, keeping a dozen plot lines in his head, haranguing scriptwriters in person, and bombarding them with memos from a distance. His ability to fix a problematic script was legendary. His comments were usually perceptive, often astute, always incisive.

A hallmark of the Zanuck approach was the emphasis on the story rather than the actors, a logical strategy considering the dearth of bankable performers he inherited from Fox. Over the previous five years the studio had developed few new stars, relying instead on the fading popularity of Warner Baxter and Janet Gaynor. The only surefire stars around whom Zanuck could build a movie were Will Rogers and Shirley Temple. Rogers had occupied a top-ten position in the popularity polls since 1932. Temple was named the number one box office draw in 1935 and remained there for the next four years. Shortly after the merger, however, Twentieth Century Fox sustained a major blow when Will Rogers died in a plane crash in Alaska. Rogers had been an enormous moneymaker for the studio.

Zanuck had counted on Rogers's box office appeal when he agreed to become studio chief, because Rogers had a reputation as a workhorse whose films could be produced inexpensively. Without the lucrative Rogers vehicles he'd planned on, Zanuck needed to develop new stars quickly. In the meantime, it was little wonder that Zanuck chose to de-emphasize actors in favor of the story itself. It would buy him the time he needed to find some more talent.

It was only a matter of time before Zanuck began to take stock of his contract players, just as a new organization man would take inventory in any other kind of factory, looking for materials out of which to create a marketable product. If there was anyone on the Fox lot Zanuck could develop into a bankable performer, he would. Shirley Temple could not last forever.

CHAPTER 4

New Studio, New Star

The upheavals occurring at the top reaches of the studio's administration had little immediate effect on the day-to-day lives of the contract players. During most of 1935 Alice Faye continued to work in the Sheehan productions to which she had been assigned. The studio released these films at regular intervals throughout the year: *George White's 1935 Scandals* in March, *Music Is Magic* in November, with Paramount's *Every Night at Eight* reaching the screens in August. Between releases, the Fox publicity machine, under the direction of Harry Brand, kept her name before the public as much as possible. "I'd read stories about Alice Faye in the papers—stories the studio publicity department had planted—and I would wonder who that girl was," Alice said. "It didn't sound like anybody I knew."

The fictive Alice Faye of the studio's imagining maintained a busy and, at times preposterous, schedule according to the newspapers. In November 1934 they reported that she had a clause inserted in her contract that allowed her to quit work at 4:00 P.M. on Thursdays in order to listen to the *Fleischmann Hour* each week. Another piece claimed she simply had a radio installed on the set. The previous month the *New York Times* ran an item announcing that Alice had been cast in the lead role of a screen version of Dante's *Inferno*. In May 1935 the papers said she had achieved her goal of owning a mink coat and that she planned to become an opera singer after her career in movies came to an end. And always there was

the speculation about her personal life. As the rumors of her involvement with Vallée died down, the press linked her name with Nick Foran,
then actors Lyle Talbot and Nelson Eddy, then finally nobody at all. The
dearth of men in her life purportedly prompted this claim: "Alice Faye declared recently she'd rather have a $1,000 husband than a $1,000,000
contract."

Alice's real life, in contrast, continued to be consumed with the consequences of her rapid rise to fame. She felt overwhelmed by the shift
from New York to Los Angeles, the shift from band singer to movie actress,
and the shift from poverty to affluence. Like so many other film industry
successes, she considered herself undeserving and something of a fraud.
Unfortunately, her hectic schedule provided little time for the reflection
necessary to make the mental adjustment to all the new demands she
faced. "There I would be," she said, "unsure and unsteady, wondering
why I was there and how I could possibly justify the big money I was getting and the luxurious life I was leading." Many "overnight successes" in
countless other industries felt similarly anxious. Alice could not realize
just how common her confusion about her new circumstances were or
how easily self-doubt lured the unwary into self-destructive behavior. In
the studio environment, such psychological distractions as alcohol, drugs,
sex, or gambling were readily available, and she may have been aware of
other performers who chose those means of escaping their problems. Their
solution was not Alice's, however. For whatever reason—her family, an
innate sense of morality, or simply a stubborn sense of self-preservation—
Alice grappled with her sense of inadequacy without resorting to pills,
drink, or financial and sexual recklessness. She thereby avoided one of
the biggest hazards of a movie career, one that ruined the lives of many of
her costars in years to come.

Alice continued to live quietly, enjoying her family and friends, who
had their own adjustments to make. Her brothers had moved to California
sometime in 1934, and she and her mother rented a house, with a swim-
ming pool, to accommodate everyone. Sonny, according to Fox press re-

leases, had been an agent for General Motors in New York, although given his chronic arthritis one wonders what kind of responsibilities this position entailed. His decision to join his mother and sister in California was doubtless influenced by his need to seek relief from his illness. Once he arrived Alice helped him find work as an assistant director at Fox. Later in 1934 Sonny met and married an M-G-M contract actress named Bonnie Bannon and they set up house for themselves. Alice's other brother Bill, who had had a position of some sort with Chase National Bank in New York, became her business manager when he arrived in Los Angeles. In contrast to many celebrity relatives who quietly embezzled thousands, Bill banked Alice's salary and put her on a strict monthly allowance. He eventually earned a reputation as a sound and trustworthy manager, handling the business affairs of Walter and Betty Scharf over the course of many years.

Walter Scharf and Betty King had continued to see each other in California while Betty worked as Alice's stand-in on *George White's Scandals* and Walter worked for Rudy Vallée. When Vallée returned to New York, Walter went with him, but it quickly dawned on him that he missed Betty, and they decided to get married.

Because Betty did not want to return to New York to live, Alice found an opening for Walter at Twentieth Century-Fox. "Rudy got so mad at me because he said I was responsible for Walter leaving his band," said Betty. "He wasn't that bad about Alice staying in California to be in pictures, that I can recall. If he was, she didn't tell me about it. But at the end Rudy didn't like me very well because I said that I wanted to live in California." Betty recalled that Alice said, "Don't pay any attention to Rudy. Walter is going to do much better living in California and being in the picture business." Alice was right. Walter enjoyed a long and successful Hollywood career, working with her on her films as well as with other legends in the business, such as Bing Crosby, Irving Berlin, and later Barbra Streisand.

By the end of 1935, Alice, her family, and her best friends had settled into a comfortable new life. Alice found herself working harder than she ever had before, but she was adjusting to the routine of the film world, meeting the professional challenges of stardom, and enjoying the privileges her new life afforded her and those she loved. One of those privileges, of course, was the ease with which Alice had been able to find work for both her brothers and her friends, the Scharfs. She never expressed resentment at having to contribute to their support while she worked in New York and in her early days in California. That kind of thinking was simply not in her character. "She was a wonderful, good person," said Betty Scharf. "She was so generous, there wasn't another person like her." Alice derived satisfaction from her ability to help support her family and best friend in the economically troubled 1930s. She must have been particularly pleased, though, to see them securely placed in jobs of their own, in the practically depression-proof film industry. With only her mother to support, Alice enjoyed a greater freedom from responsibility than she had known since the age of thirteen.

Stunning news in November, however, shattered Alice's hard-won complacency and opened the door for another round of brutal publicity—the first bad press she received in eighteen months. Late that month her father, from whom her mother had been separated for several years, collapsed and was taken to Bellevue Hospital. The authorities there could not trace any friends or relations of the shabbily dressed man. His wallet identified him as Charles Leppert but contained no other evidence of his connection to anyone beyond a photograph of Alice Faye. In desperation, the hospital contacted Alice in California.

Charley Leppert was seriously ill. Alice, her mother, and her brothers boarded a train for New York, switching to a plane in Chicago, but they failed to arrive in time. Charley Leppert died in Bellevue Hospital, in a charity ward, on Thanksgiving Day. The press leapt on the story immediately. "Alice Faye's Father Dies in Charity Ward," cried the *New York Mirror*, following the next day with "Alice Faye's Father Rests Rich in Death." Conflicting stories abounded. One implied that Charley Leppert had been shut out of the family circle, living in rented rooms because "he had not been able to carry out his desire to live with his daughter and wife and two sons in Hollywood." Another quoted lawyer Hyman Bushell as saying that Leppert, "a kindly, grizzled, rapidly graying man in his early fifties," had spent a month in California with his family just that summer. The Twentieth Century-Fox publicity machine tried to exercise damage control by asserting that Leppert had been living with his family all along and had merely returned to New York to make the necessary preparations for a big family holiday when tragedy struck. Rudy Vallée's agent in California, Richard English, even wrote a magazine article called "The Truth about Alice Faye's Tragedy" in which he attempted to rebut the hostile rumors.

The *New York Journal* gave the most reasonable-sounding account when it stated that Charley and Alice Leppert had been separated for a number of years and Charley simply preferred to live in New York. At some point Charley had retired from the police force and found a position as a shipping clerk in a hospital supply company. His children's relocation to the West Coast did not necessarily mean he lived in isolation. His brother Philip, who was also a policeman, lived in the Bronx, and he also had a sister in New York, Mrs. George Gardner. Alice mentioned in an interview in 1937 that she had sent her father money regularly, and, while she seldom mentioned him, she did not seem to react with hostility when his name came up. But the exact nature of Charley Leppert's relationship with his family in general, and Alice in particular, remains a mystery.

Charley Leppert was laid to rest in Woodlawn Cemetery on December 2, 1935, but, unfortunately for Alice, there was more bad publicity to come. Five days later, on December 7, 1935, Alice went to court with a petition to have her name legally changed from Leppert to Faye, on the grounds that she had been known by that name since the age of thirteen and that it "has now become indispensable." Judge Bernard L. Shientag granted her petition, and the press had another field day with what it interpreted as an unforgivably callous gesture. "Alice Faye buries her father, then petitions to have her name changed," said the *New York Evening Post*, giving the story added emphasis by reiterating the impoverished circumstances in which Charley Leppert had passed away. They did not mention whether Alice's mother and brothers, who also changed their names to Faye, did so at this time. The national press followed the New York paper's lead, with one newspaper remarking that the rough treatment Alice had received from the media regarding her father had at least reunited her with Rudy Vallée, with whom she had not been in touch in months. Alice was clearly not destined to win this round with the press, and one wonders what persuaded her to choose such an inauspicious time to legalize her stage name.

Ironically, late in her life, Alice stated that one of the aspects of the big studio system she admired was the way in which their performers were always shielded. "The studios protected the stars they had under contract," she said. "They carefully monitored publicity." Dan Dailey remember that Fox's publicity department "did everything. You could have your own publicity agent if you wanted, but they had such a tremendous staff." He said, "They'd assign maybe a certain number of actors to one person, who would just handle those few people. So you didn't really *need* anybody." Twentieth Century-Fox made every effort to put a palatable spin on the events surrounding Alice's father's death. Toward the end of her life, Alice recollected that "our names and faces and reputations weren't smeared all over those sleazy tabloids, like those of the poor stars of today," perhaps forgetting the way in which the press smeared her own name in this incident and, to a greater extent, during the Rudy Vallée-Fay Webb divorce. After these two episodes, Alice's relationship with the press proceeded more smoothly, simply because she had learned to treat reporters with extreme wariness, refusing to give them anything that they could use against her. These episodes undoubtedly contributed to Alice's lifelong reticence, as well as her ability to toss off remarkably bland quotes. Twentieth Century-Fox's publicity department probably kept a sharp eye on her as well.

Alice might have derived a sense of security from this system after her own public relations mishaps. She might have felt safer knowing that the publicity department, under Harry Brand, wanted to safeguard her image just as much as she did. Brand was a low-key man who rarely let the substantial pressures of his work bother him. Alice's experiences may have helped reconcile her to the kind of fluff that Brand and his people made up about her: the childhood riding lessons and an ambition to sing opera, for example. Stories like these did not hurt her as badly as the allegations printed during the Vallée divorce. The stuff the studio produced was basically harmless, if a little silly. Those ridiculous stories gave her something to talk about with the reporters and helped protect her real self. Many stars in the big studio system rebelled against precisely this kind of smokescreen, but Alice recognized the safety that could come with playing along with Harry Brand and his publicists.

Alice expressed an appreciation of the way in which the big studio system worked, even after she had retired from film work. "I liked the studio system at the time, and in retrospect, I still believe it was good," she said. "For one thing there was a continuity to one's career; they tried to advance you from small parts to bigger ones to biggest ones." She remembered Twentieth Century-Fox as a big graduate school for actors and actresses. Cesar Romero, who remembered the same thing, said, "Every studio had its drama coach and they trained young players, they all went to school." All of the major studios in this period worked this way. For inexperienced performers in need of training, the big studio system held decided advantages.

Studio coaching, however, did not stop with an actor's performances. Alice said, "The studio told you what lessons to take, how to do your hair and your makeup, what clothes to wear." For the most part, Alice went along with the studio's prescriptions, finding they relieved her of many anxieties. They assigned a wardrobe woman named Olli Hughes to Alice. "She got to know me and my clothing so well that she was a great comfort to me." Studios took even more elaborate precautions with their performers' hair and makeup. "Most Hollywood stars were as close to physically perfect as nature and the law allowed," Alice said, "but in my era they wouldn't permit even the slightest blemish to go uncovered." Just as the Twentieth Century-Fox publicity department worked overtime to insure that no untoward information about a star's life reached the public, so too did the studio's makeup and costume departments perpetuate the illusion of perfection by never allowing the world to see anything less than a star's best face, best hair, best ensembles. Some stars, like Alice early in her film career, found this kind of protection a relief. Others found it inherently restrictive.

Even as she praised it advantages, Alice acknowledged the rigidity of the system. "You had no choice of the parts you would play; they were all assigned to you, and you played them or else you were suspended without pay. They selected the people you would date for important functions. They told you how much money you would make and, unless you fought them, they would bank it for you and only let you have an allowance." Normally docile, Alice put her foot down when it came to her finances, turning her salary over to her brother Bill to handle for her. Ironically, he too put her on an allowance, but he remained conscientious in his management of her affairs and she never regretted her confidence in him. Like many other performers, she sometimes felt the urge to break out of the studio's control in larger ways. "But," she said, "more often I just leaned back and relaxed and enjoyed it all."

Alice's first movie for the new Twentieth Century-Fox organization opened in the theaters in January 1936, a month after the death of her father. With *King of Burlesque,* the studio presented her with the opportunity to play the character who carried the film, Pat Doran, a singer-dancer in love with burlesque impresario Kerry Bolton. Bolton breaks into legitimate musicals using the talented Pat but then marries the once-wealthy society figure Rosalind Cleve. The heartbroken Pat flees to England, where she becomes the toast of the London stage, while Bolton goes broke staging a "classy" spectacular for one of Rosalind's protégées. Bolton and Rosalind divorce, Pat hires a phony "angel" to back Bolton's comeback show, which is, of course, a hit, and Bolton and Pat are reunited. The plot of *King of Burlesque* is identical to Alice's later success, *Hello Frisco Hello*, reflecting Darryl Zanuck's habit of recycling story lines in his musicals.

Alice realized that in giving her the pivotal role in the movie, the studio was placing more responsibility on her shoulders than ever before. She also knew that the new management would be paying close attention. She had been around long enough to know that, as she said, "all it takes is a couple of pictures in a row that fall on their faces and a career can be over. Like that." As it worked out, her performance in *King of Burlesque* was well-received—more so than her frizzy platinum hair, which *Variety* assessed as "too fluffy." This film marked the beginning of the end of Alice's apprenticeship. In her next, *Poor Little Rich Girl*, Alice starred alongside the studio's biggest bankable star, Shirley Temple. "We were all aware that to be in a Shirley Temple film was a pretty thankless job," Alice said. "You had to work to hold your own." Nevertheless, playing opposite Temple indicated that the studio was thinking of Alice Faye in terms of larger things to come. Change was in the air. The bosses had obviously taken a cue from the reviews of *King of Burlesque* and toned Alice's hair down to a sleeker style in a more becoming natural blonde color. *Poor Little Rich Girl* helped tone down her image too. As Shirley Temple's surrogate mother for most of the film, Alice had the opportunity to display some of the human tenderness that was inconsistent with her earlier image as a Jean Harlow-style bombshell.

The plot revolved, naturally, around Shirley Temple's Barbara Barry, the daughter of a soap tycoon whose nurse is struck by a car as Barbara waits for her inside a train station. Barbara grows tired of waiting and wanders off to take a "vacation" from her affluent but overly-regimented life. She is discovered by vaudeville hoofers Jimmy and Jerry Dolan, who incorporate her into their act by having her pose as their daughter. They land a spot on a rival soap magnate's radio show. Barbara's father eventually hears his daughter singing over the airwaves and realizes she is not at boarding school as he thought. He rushes to the radio station, confronts his business rival, and is eventually reunited with Barbara.

One of *Poor Little Rich Girl's* song and dance routines was a showstopper. The final number in the film, it featured Shirley Temple, Jack Haley, and Alice Faye doing a lengthy precision tap routine to the song "I Love a Military Man." It certainly gave Alice the opportunity to put all the studio's lessons to work, since it is unlikely that she ever dealt with such a complicated routine as a New York chorus girl. While filming on the dance routine went smoothly, it did indeed take time and great effort to dub the sound of the taps in a recording studio afterwards. Temple remembered working for hours in the dim recording booth. "Our job as a trio was to match our tap noises in synchrony with the long and athletic filmed segment being projected against a screen," she said. "Dancing together, it took only one false tap from any of us to ruin the take." Haley in particular had trouble synchronizing his steps without the music to guide him, while Temple managed to do it perfectly each time. Tempers ran short, time ran out, and eventually the sound engineers recorded Temple's taps separately so she could go home at the end of her legally permitted workday. Unlike their young costar, Haley and Faye remained at the studio. They broke for dinner and returned to the recording studio afterwards to work for as long as it took to get the sound of their dance right.

Alice stood out in *Poor Little Rich Girl*, in spite of the old stage adage about working with animals and children. Her screen persona was warm and the precision tap dance finale dazzling. Even though she received less screen time than in any of her movies since *Now I'll Tell*, she drew attention to herself. *Variety* noted that "Alice Faye demonstrates that she is worthy of more important assignments." She got one with her next picture, *Sing, Baby, Sing*. In search of stories, Zanuck fell back on newspaper headlines, just as he had done in creating the gangster genre at Warner Brothers. He based *Sing, Baby, Sing* on newspaper coverage of the cross-country romance of actor John Barrymore and Elaine Barry. The script, which had been in the works since December 1935, went through many revisions, on which Zanuck urged his writers to "stay more to real story of Barrymore—hoke ruins it."

Alice directly benefited from this kind of careful attention to the script. *Sing, Baby, Sing* was her best role to date and she shone in it, much to the delight of the talent-hungry Zanuck. After viewing rushes one day, he sent off a memo to director John Crowell and producer Kenneth McGowan, who were trying to cast *This Is My Affair*. "I have just come from the projection room and saw three cut dramatic episodes of [Alice Faye] from *Sing, Baby, Sing*," he wrote. "I have never seen her look so gorgeous, her new hairdress has changed her into a new girl; she is glamorous, exciting, and certainly a young Mae West in physique and attitude ... you can bet your last dollar that Faye will be a star," said the man who was in a position to make her one.

The process began almost immediately after that. The Twentieth Century-Fox publicity machine sprang into life on Alice's behalf and quickly went into overdrive. On June 30 they released a story based on a poll taken among men at the studio regarding Alice's new hair color. Nine to one expressed themselves in favor of the darker "amber blonde." On July 7, they informed the public that Alice called a half-hour break on the set of *Sing, Baby, Sing* to serve a cake to celebrate the thirteenth anniversary of her hairdresser, Gale Roe. On July 28, while still working on *Sing, Baby, Sing*, a wasp stung Alice, and Harry Brand's staff churned out two paragraphs describing the incident. Subsequent stories, produced at regular intervals, continued to keep her name before the public: Alice's plans for a vacation in Bermuda, her special order for a car horn that sounded like the foghorn on the Hudson River Ferry, her practice of placing a drop of perfume on light bulbs, which worked until one light bulb exploded (she escaped uninjured). A complicit American press dutifully digested each of these stories and regurgitated them to an eager public throughout the remainder of 1936.

None of these insipid stories revealed the true Alice; their purpose was pure ballyhoo. The star they promoted could have been almost any woman in Hollywood, again reflecting Zanuck's perception of his performers as types rather than as individual personalities. Some film historians have derided Zanuck for his decision to promote such "bland" performers as Alice Faye and her contemporaries Tyrone Power, Don Ameche, and Sonja Henie. "None of these were exactly movie star material," said one. Others recognize the larger issue that concerned Zanuck, one that concerned every other studio boss in Hollywood: developing enough talent to star in enough product to feed the insatiable demands of the public. One historian stated that Zanuck knew that Faye and her fellow Fox contract players "had something that, with the proper genre, could be packaged and sold to moviegoers." Zanuck recognized that Alice was the key ingredient in *Sing, Baby, Sing,* and he began to lay plans to turn her into one of the staples of his formulaic, but fun, musicals.

In the meantime, Alice had encountered one of the studio's handsome newcomers on the set of *Sing, Baby, Sing.* She first met Tony Martin during a production party for *Poor Little Rich Girl* in 1936. The young baritone had a brief unbilled appearance in the movie as a studio singer at the radio station where much of the movie's action took place, and, due to an ironic set of circumstances, he wound up lip-synching to the previously recorded vocalizations of another singer. His first break had occurred when Darryl F. Zanuck, who had first heard Martin sing at the Trocadero nightclub in Los Angeles, determined to build him into a star, signing him the same day as two other young hopefuls, Don Ameche and Tyrone Power.

Martin's studio apprenticeship was very similar to the one Alice had gone through two years before. He played cameos and bit parts here and there and finally landed a song in *Sing, Baby, Sing.* "It was my first real movie. I was nervous. My usual self-confidence left me for a time," he said. He remembered appreciating the way in which Alice tried to put him at ease on the set, and from then on they were fast friends. His *Sing, Baby, Sing* role was small, but his number, "When Did You Leave Heaven" by Walter Bullock and Richard Whiting, garnered extra attention for Martin when the Motion Picture Academy nominated it as one of the best songs of 1936. It also spent thirteen weeks on *Your Hit Parade*. After that brief moment of glory, however, Tony Martin went back to the B's, appearing in Sol Wurtzel's Jones family serial, *See America First*, followed by *Pigskin Parade*. He had another chance with a small part in *Banjo on My Knee*, starring Barbara Stanwyck and Joel McCrea, but his career in films seemed stuck.

In the meantime, Martin enjoyed as much social life as his limited salary afforded him. He and the other Fox performers with whom he became friends—Tyrone Power, Don Ameche, and the Ritz Brothers—enjoyed a restaurant called Sugie's Tropics, which offered Chinese food and exotic rum-based cocktails. "Most of the time," he recalled, "I'd see Alice Faye there...usually with her brother Bill." Citing her good looks and easygoing demeanor, he said, "I think that's where I fell in love with her." Alice, who remained as reticent throughout her life about Tony Martin as she did about everything else, apparently reciprocated his feelings. Sometime in the late summer or early fall of 1936 they began seeing each other.

With events in her personal life taking a promising turn, Alice began to enjoy a professional sense of accomplishment she'd never felt before. *Sing, Baby, Sing*, she said, "was the first picture in which I got good notices from the critics and it was the first time that I really felt I'd made good in the movies. Up to then I'd been neither fish nor fowl." *Film Weekly* said "Alice Faye, looking much more charming than she has ever done before, carries the burden of the musical numbers, and sings them with a persuasive lilt that is impossible to resist."

Only Alice's wardrobe in the film came in for criticism. "The costumes I was squeezed into," she said, "were dismissed by one reviewer as 'atrocious' and I think he was kind." As Twentieth Century-Fox's rising star, the public expected better of her and did not hesitate to say so. Neither did Darryl Zanuck, who thought her face looked too full and that she bordered on "chubby." "He said I had better do something about it. And fast, if I wanted to stay under contract," Alice remembered. As a result, she said, "I usually had cottage cheese and sliced tomato for lunch." Between the diet and the dancing, Alice achieved a weight of 120 pounds, which suited her five-foot, four-inch frame.

Learning to withstand the intensified scrutiny of stardom proved a tough assignment for Alice, but perhaps because of this criticism, the studio provided her with an assortment of elegantly simple and modest costumes for her next film, *Stowaway,* her last outing with Shirley Temple. She played Susan Parker, who is traveling to China to marry her fiancé, accompanied by her fiancé's busybody mother. She discovers a stowaway on board, Shirley Temple, a ward of missionaries to China who have been killed in a provincial uprising.

As Zanuck stated in a story conference, "This is by far the most serious set-up we have ever had for Temple and therefore the construction must be more sound." To the benefit of Alice, and Robert Young, whom Zanuck had borrowed from M-G-M specifically for this project, Zanuck insisted that "the romance and its complications is [sic] of even more importance than Shirley. The whole idea of this story is based upon a romance which we have to believe in." To that end, Alice enjoyed two solo numbers in *Stowaway:* a reprise, with adult lyrics of "Goodnight My Love," and "One Never Knows."

Another aspect of *Stowaway* with which Zanuck took great care were the scenes set in China. "The Chinese must be played by real Chinese actors," he noted. His attitude was unusual in an industry noted for simply trying to make Anglo actors, from Myrna Loy to John Wayne, look Oriental. Twentieth Century-Fox hired a tutor named Bessie Nye from UCLA to coach Shirley Temple on the phrases she would be speaking in the film so she could interact appropriately with the cast. Unfortunately, Nye taught Temple in the Mandarin dialect. Most the Chinese actors on the film were from a province where a different dialect was spoken. The result undermined Zanuck's best intentions. Temple recalled, "Each of us was spouting a language as mutually unintelligible as if between an Australian aborigine and a reindeer herdsman from Lapland."

The cast and crew of *Stowaway* hit a snag at the end of October when Alice fell ill with the flu. Louella Parsons noted that "Tony Martin is a daily visitor to her hospital room for the brief few minutes the doctors allow." The studio shot around her as much as possible but finally had to shut down until her return. After nine days in Cedars of Lebanon hospital, Alice reported to the set, but then Shirley Temple became sick. Temple recalled that when Alice's illness halted the production, "I seethed in secret; it was the first medical delay in any of my films." It was also the first in any of Alice's. Temple acknowledged that her "vindictive attitude" backfired. "The very day she returned I developed a high fever and was sent home. Again film production was shut down. For the next two weeks I lay in sickbed with plenty of time to reflect on the possibility of divine retribution for my initial uncompassionate attitude."

Twentieth Century-Fox released *Stowaway* on Christmas Day, and it eventually grossed over one million dollars in domestic receipts. It was one of their best productions of the year, and certainly one of the most profitable. Film historians have found the quantity of Zanuck's 1936 output more remarkable than its quality: fifty features, fifty-two two-reelers, thirty one-reelers, and twenty-six cartoons. Zanuck knew he needed more than an aging Shirley Temple to meet the needs of the studio's production schedule. He needed Alice Faye. *Stowaway* demonstrated that, stripped of the bombshell image and costumed in elegant gowns, Alice could hold her own against any musical star in Hollywood. As 1937 rolled around, Darryl Zanuck prepared to put her to work for the studio. Alice would become Twentieth Century-Fox's biggest female musical star, one of its hardest-working performers, and one of its top generators of revenue. Only later would Alice learn the price she would pay for Zanuck's dependence on her.

CHAPTER 5

Breakthrough

On November 25, 1936, Rudy Vallée's ex-wife, Fay Webb, died suddenly following an abdominal operation. Even the press in Los Angeles, where she died, barely mentioned it. The media apparently considered the woman who caused Alice so much misery old news, missing a potentially sensational story. As Rudy Vallée's secretary Evelyn Langfeldt wrote to Hyman Bushell, during the operation Webb's intestinal wall collapsed and peritonitis had set in. Webb's constitution, Langfeldt said, had been weakened by an illness similar to tuberculosis, and she suggested the possibility that it was related to alcohol or drug use. Langfeldt even mentioned hearing an unconfirmed rumor that the unhappy Webb had been taking dope for some time. The whole incident held nothing for Alice, whose name had not even come up in the scant news coverage.

By this point in her career, Alice was too big a star for the tabloids to smear her without repercussions. Tony Martin remembered her during this period as "one of the queens of Hollywood," earning a commensurately large salary well above his own few hundred a week. Given her status as one of Fox's top moneymakers, Alice enjoyed the full protection of Harry Brand's publicity department. By the time of Fay Webb's death, Harry Brand's efforts had already been concentrated on exploiting Alice's relationship with Tony Martin—thereby minimizing the old Vallée connection as well as doubling the studio's exposure on any given story featuring the

two contract players. On December 10, Brand released a brief piece announcing simply that Alice Faye and Tony Martin were "officially an item."
The same day, he generated a lengthier story outlining the trouble the
two busy stars encountered as they tried to find time for one another.

In contrast to the usual Hollywood public relations bilge, this particular piece contained more than a grain of truth. A few years later it would
prove remarkably prescient because it sounded one of the major themes
of Alice Faye and Tony Martin's relationship: their respective careers consumed so much of their time that there was little time left for either themselves as individuals or as a couple. Brand's publicity release profiled a "typical" week in Alice and Tony's recent life: on Monday, while Alice worked
on recording for *Stowaway*, Tony filmed *The Holy Terror* with Jane Withers, it
said. They lunched at different hours, then Tony spent the evening rehearsing for the *Burns and Allen* radio show in which he was now a regular.
Tuesday was the same, with Alice's recording extending into the evening,
and Tony performing at a benefit. On Wednesday Alice began working on
On the Avenue; Tony had a lunch meeting with a columnist. In the evening
he performed on *Burns and Allen*, and Alice rehearsed for the *Kraft Hour*
radio show. Alice continued with *On the Avenue* on Thursday, posing for
"beauty stills" during her lunch break. She performed on the *Kraft Hour*
that evening, while Tony worked on the night scenes for *The Holy Terror*.
At lunch on Friday Alice did a magazine interview and Tony posed for
portraits. In the evening he rehearsed for a recording session, while she
went to bed early for a 5:00 A.M. call the next day. Saturday saw Tony
recording at Decca, while Alice filmed and then made the rounds of various nightclubs with a reporter from a fan magazine. On Sunday Alice
rested while Tony did additional scenes for *The Holy Terror*. Then from
seven to ten that evening Alice had a recording session for Brunswick
records.

Despite the obstacles their schedules presented, Alice Faye and Tony
Martin were crazy about each other. Tony admired Alice's humanity, as
well as her obvious physical assets. "She was a real girl," he said, "not one

of these paint-and powder dolls that were all over Hollywood then. Alice Faye was a person." Alice, in turn, seemed to admire the same qualities in Tony. As he recalled, "I think maybe she was tired of those swinging rich guys she'd been seeing, and felt more at home with me. I was simple to talk to, easy to understand. I had no pretenses—I wasn't rich enough or eccentric enough to have any."

The two performers got along well together. Tony couldn't afford elaborate dates, and Alice apparently didn't really enjoy them. Alice felt particularly uncomfortable in crowds and found personal appearances daunting. In two short years she had ascended to the A-list of Hollywood's social scene, so she and Tony were able to attend parties hosted by the likes of Errol Flynn, Cesar Romero, and Joan Crawford, in addition to premieres, ceremonies, and other Hollywood occasions. But those events counted as business. On her own time, Alice apparently preferred more relaxed, commonplace activities. "She liked a few luxurious things," Martin said, "orchids, good clothes, hats particularly—but in most things she preferred the ordinary to the exotic." Martin remembered most of their dates as simple affairs: drinks and dinner alone or, if he'd been rehearsing the radio show, with George Burns and Gracie Allen. Alice and Gracie got along well and enjoyed each other's company. Occasionally Tony and Alice attended the movies. "She was a sex symbol. She didn't act like one," he said. "I knew her as a laughing girl who insisted on being home in bed by ten if she had an early call the next morning."

Their courtship proceeded slowly, in part because Alice so often had early calls at the studio. In fact, she could not have chosen a worse time in her life to get seriously involved with someone. Darryl Zanuck had been hatching plans since the middle of 1936 to costar Alice in the biggest musical Twentieth Century-Fox had produced to date, Irving Berlin's *On the Avenue*. Alice was, as Zanuck noted in one memo, "climbing to stardom so rapidly that we are unable to keep up with the demands of the exhibitors in connection with her. After seeing her in the one dramatic scene in *[King of] Burlesque*," Zanuck continued, "Berlin begged for her and wrote the part for her." Zanuck was not about to squander Alice's newly minted drawing power. Over the next few years, very little of Alice's time would be her own. In 1937 alone she worked in five major motion pictures.

The first of these was *On the Avenue,* which Zanuck produced as Fox's alternative to RKO's wildly popular musical *Top Hat.* He hired *Top Hat's* composer, Irving Berlin, to do *On the Avenue's* entire score; he brought in Dick Powell, the star of his 1933 smash musical at Warner Brothers, *42nd Street,* casting him opposite dramatic actress Madeleine Carroll in the leading roles. Alice, who headed up a supporting cast of Fox regulars such as the Ritz Brothers and Joan Davis, costarred in a role tailor-made to showcase her talents as a singer and dancer. One Berlin biographer stated that "everything about *On the Avenue* was designed to put the Fred Astaire-Ginger Rogers musicals to shame; it had a larger cast, more lavish sets, more songs by Irving Berlin, a more complicated plot—virtually every element that could be stuffed into one hundred minutes of cinematic entertainment." What it lacked, however, was a leading couple with the chemistry of Astaire and Rogers, distinctively styled sets epitomizing the deco glamour of the 1930s, and a streamlined plot with a handful of familiar characters to move the action along. Nor did the presence of Zanuck's pet comics the Ritz Brothers, a trio with neither the wit of the Marx Brothers, nor the burlesque genius of the Three Stooges, enhance the picture. A pleasant and, on the whole, entertaining movie, *On the Avenue* is best summed up as "an ambitious misfire," in the words of one film historian.

The movie did contain several successful elements, most notably Alice Faye singing Irving Berlin's songs. Alice played Broadway baby Mona Merrick, the female star of Gary Blake's (Dick Powell) hit review. In this incarnation of the traditional backstage musical, Alice lost the man to Madeleine Carroll's Mimi Caraway, but won all the great numbers, from the movie's opening shot of her singing "He Ain't Got Rhythm" to the show's biggest production number "Slumming on Park Avenue" (for which her legs deserved billing on their own). She also enjoyed appearances in Powell's rendition of "I've Got My Love to Keep Me Warm" and "The Girl in the Police Gazette," during which she remembered wearing "these stockings with jewels sewed onto them, which was pretty snazzy." Alice's best number, which remained on radio's *Your Hit Parade* for several months, was the torch standard "This Year's Kisses," sung in the heart-on-your-sleeve style that she perfected. *On the Avenue* opened at Radio City Music Hall, where RKO had premiered its Fred Astaire and Ginger Rogers successes, on February 12, 1937. RKO had nothing to worry about. *On the Avenue* met with a mixed reception; the reviewer for the *New York Herald Tribune* stated that "the tolerant thing to do would be to discuss the Berlin songs at length."

Zanuck fared much better with Alice's next vehicle, *Wake Up and Live,* released barely two months after *On the Avenue's* premiere, on April 23. Drawing on the world of radio for inspiration, Zanuck created a film story out of the then-current Walter Winchell-Ben Bernie airwaves feud. Several other producers had the same idea. Universal dramatized the W. C. Fields-Charlie MacCarthy radio feud in *You Can't Cheat an Honest Man,* while Paramount exploited the Jack Benny-Fred Allen feud in *Love Thy Neighbor.* Radio gossip columnist Winchell and bandleader Bernie played themselves in *Wake Up and Live,* receiving top billing for doing so. Fox billed Alice third, although she appeared in only ten scenes. The real workhorse of the movie was Jack Haley, who got sixth billing behind character actors Patsy Kelly and Ned Sparks, even though he appeared in the majority of the scenes and provided the focal point for the action.

Haley played Eddie Kane, a vaudeville headliner struck by a case of "mike fright" as he auditions for the radio spot that will win him fame and fortune. He winds up as an usher at the Federal Broadcasting Company and seeks help in overcoming his fear from Alice Faye (as Alice Huntley), a motivational broadcaster whose message is to "wake up and live." During a Bernie broadcast, Haley inadvertently sings into an open mike and becomes the airwaves newest sensation—"the Phantom." Bernie and Winchell's rivalry is given new impetus by their scramble to be the first to discover his true identity.

As for Alice, she played a winning, but disappointingly small role, getting the man this time, but not much screen time. She first appears almost twenty minutes into the movie to sing "Wake Up and Live," then sings only one more of the movie's seven Mack Gordon and Harry Revel numbers. This was an arresting, but difficult, tune called "There's a Lull in My Life," which one film historian called "an Un Bel Di" of the swing era in that singers' reputations are made or shredded on it. Her abbreviated appearance nevertheless won raves across the United States, and in England critics for such periodicals as *Film Weekly* and *Picturegoer* noted the improvement in her acting and an increasingly relaxed quality in her demeanor. John Rosenfield of the *Dallas Morning News* stated flatly that she was "the absolute tops in torch songstresses" and "carrolled thrillingly."

Wake Up and Live premiered at the Roxy Theater in New York, and audiences flocked to it, setting a one-day attendance record of 38,825. They found it entertaining fare, as *Variety* noted, "fast-stepping, sparkling, without a foot of waste material or a dull moment." Its engaging plot holds up well even today, assisted to some extent by its charmingly "modern" sets and dialogue. It possesses a naive optimism regarding technology and showcases the lost world of radio broadcasting, from the live audience "singalong" shows to the ranks of uniformed studio ushers saluting and marching in formation. Yet *Wake Up and Live* succeeds by innocently reflecting a bygone era in broadcasting that Zanuck's later portentous attempts at radio nostalgia, like *The Great American Broadcast,* fail to do. It's an engaging slice of Americana, art deco style.

Alice's reviews in *Wake Up and Live* solidified her new status as one of Fox's top stars, and Zanuck left her little time for either resting on her laurels or nurturing relationships outside of the studio before assigning her to her next project. "Back then we used to make movies one after another," Alice recalled in the 1980s. "That was all I did. That was my whole life. I called it Penitentiary Fox, but I was always happy to go back. I didn't know anything else." If Alice wanted emotional support and friendship, she had to find it on the lot because that was where she spent almost every waking moment. The need of overworked performers to create a surrogate family from the cast and crews of their films led many to recall studio life as "one big happy family" in their reminiscences. As absurd as the notion of Darryl F. Zanuck, Louis B. Mayer, or Harry Cohn as benevolent patriarchs of loving extended families seems, the working hours the moguls imposed on their stars—ten to twelve hours of filming often followed by evening appearances at various industry functions—necessitated players forming personal attachments to people with whom they spent their daily lives. Alice remembered that "there was the wardrobe woman and the makeup man and the cameraman and the director and that was my whole life." In the late spring of 1937 she began *You Can't Have Everything* and discovered a new friend with whom she would work in five additional movies, Don Ameche.

Like Alice, Don Ameche came to movies from radio, where he had created a relaxed style of acting that he found translated well to the screen. But in contrast to his own technique, Ameche remembered Alice as an excellent performer with a surprising capacity for anxiety. "She was so nervous," he said. "Oh, such insecurity, you just can't imagine. It's a wonder she stayed in the business as long as she did. It had to take so much out of her." Alice admitted to feeling insecure but simultaneously protected by the insular world she inhabited. "I was kind of shy and I was protected," she remembered. "I had all the protection of all the good people I worked for and for the time being it was just great." Late in her life Alice recalled looking back and wondering why she was so "uptight." "But that was the way I was then," she said. She had a poor body image combined with a lack of self-confidence and "very little sense of pride in my own work."

Alice represented a minority of one in her low opinion of herself. Everywhere else, at the box office and at the studio, she was regarded as a genuinely warm, talented girl with a beautiful voice. Tony Martin knew from the beginning that she was a woman worth competing for. "I think Ty Power fell in love with her about the same time I did," he said. "So we competed for Alice. I finally got lucky—Ty Power left town." Don Ameche conceded that even Darryl Zanuck "maybe chased Alice Faye around. But," he added, "a lot of people chased Alice Faye around." Even the plot of Alice's current movie, *You Can't Have Everything,* turned on the notion of her character, a writer, selling a play on the basis of her looks. The attention and acclaim, however, failed to boost Alice's poor self-image. The one thing she felt confident doing, she said, was singing. "I have faith in my singing because I feel natural when I'm singing," she said, adding that she felt that if her voice went, she'd have nothing left.

While her voice held good, Alice undertook a regular spot as the featured vocalist on a radio show called *Music from Hollywood,* sponsored by Chesterfield Cigarettes and featuring Hal Kemp's Orchestra. A half-hour show on Friday evenings on CBS, it was broadcast live twice, at 4:00 P.M. for the East Coast, and at 7:00 P.M. for the West Coast (other time zones carried the one of their choice). Alice appeared on twenty-four of the programs throughout 1937. Walter Scharf recalled that coming on top of her six-day workweek at Fox, the broadcasts were a chore for Alice, "but she never complained." Scharf orchestrated her numbers while Jule Styne, whom Zanuck had hired to supervise music at Fox, acted as Alice's vocal coach and arranger. Scharf recalled his amazement at the ease with which they worked with Hal Kemp, a gifted musician who died of pneumonia following a car accident in December 1940. Kemp's orchestra, Scharf said, "was geared to a certain style of playing and Alice's orchestrations were like studio recordings. With a bit a coaching from me, they acclimated themselves to the studio style for Alice's numbers, while still retaining some of the Kemp style."

Alice's nerves caused her to flub her debut on the program. *Variety* noted in its review that "swinging into a vocal early in the session, singer Alice Faye hopped in too soon. She was forced to a complete stop, had to ask Kemp to 'take it again,' and wait for the introductory bars all over again." Since the broadcasts were live, they went out over the airwaves mistakes and all. But, as singer Rosemary Clooney remarked, Alice "was a very good singer with true emotion. She left her mark on every song she introduced." Zanuck did not encourage his stars to record, so the *Music from Hollywood* program was the only venue apart from Alice's movies where her fans could hear her exceptional voice. She often performed the songs associated with her from her movies but from time to time would tackle other hits of the day including "Night and Day," "Nice Work If You Can Get It," "Basin Street Blues," and "The Lady Is a Tramp." The broadcast's recordings also captured Alice at her prime in front of a live audience, preserving a voice that deserved to make far more recordings than it did.

In the midst of all this professional activity, Alice's relationship with Tony Martin stalled, although not as a result of her hectic schedule. In fact, Tony enjoyed a supporting role in *You Can't Have Everything,* in which he sang a romantic ballad with Alice called "Afraid to Dream." As a member of the cast, he became almost as much a part of Alice's daily working life as her cameraman and wardrobe lady. In May 1937 *Radio Mirror* declared the couple's attachment the "Romance of the Month," but around this time, Alice turned cool. Martin clearly wanted to marry her but just as clearly hesitated. "Pretty soon," he said, "Alice recognized what was happening— or, rather, what was not happening." Not one to sit pining for a proposal, regardless of her screen image, Alice took action by moving Tony to the periphery of her social life.

Martin attributed his reluctance to propose to three issues. The first was the difference in their backgrounds: Alice was a German-Irish Episcopalian from Manhattan, Tony was really Al Morris, a Jewish boy from Oakland, California. Conversations with George Burns, a Jew who had married Catholic Gracie Allen, helped Martin overcome his doubts on this score. Burns said that if Tony truly loved Alice and couldn't see himself living without her, the only thing to do was "become an Episcopalian and marry her." The second issue concerned the disparity in their incomes. Tony remembered Alice making $5,000 a week at this time, although one columnist, Hubbard Keavy, estimated it as closer to $1,500 a week (another year would pass before she renegotiated her contract with Fox for a weekly income of $2,500 a week). Nevertheless, she earned far more than his salary of $185 a week from the studio and $150 a week from the *Burns and Allen* show. Rather than facing this problem head on, Martin avoided it. "The question of the relative status of our income I just sort of shunted to the back of my mind," he said. That attitude was clearly the wrong one to take, as later events would reveal. Martin's future with Alice might have enjoyed more security had he squarely faced down his own feelings about the difference in their relative prestige as judged by Hollywood.

At this stage of Alice and Tony's relationship, however, Tony's concern about what his mother would say constituted the biggest stumbling block. "I wanted to marry this girl, but I was afraid of what my mother would say," he remembered. "And what's worse, I couldn't think of getting married without her approval and blessing. So I procrastinated." Faced with a lover who could not stand up to his mother, Alice became unavailable. Her mother and her brother Bill thought she could do better for herself anyway. Martin began to find it difficult to reach her by telephone and soon learned that Alice and actor George Brent were seeing each other. But relationships were not at the forefront of Alice's mind. In early June a momentous event transpired that placed a coveted movie role within Alice's grasp, and she did not hesitate to reach out for it. The part was that of Belle Fawcett; the movie was one of Zanuck's biggest productions to date, the disaster drama, *In Old Chicago*.

In the years since Zanuck had assumed control of production at Twentieth Century-Fox, he employed the strategy of creating films that were unabashedly entertaining and calculated to generate the maximum profit. He observed the success M-G-M had met with *San Francisco* (1936), a romantic epic set against the city's 1906 earthquake and fire, starring Clark Gable, Jeanette MacDonald, and Spencer Tracy. Zanuck decided that he too could produce such a spectacle, which was hardly an original thought. Sam Goldwyn had a similar idea with his South Seas drama *Hurricane* (1937) directed by John Ford, providing filmgoers with a surfeit of natural calamities in the late 1930s. Zanuck, like his competitors, wanted a large-scale sensation and believed that the Chicago fire would provide the ideal back-drop for the massive melodrama he envisioned.

Zanuck set his writers to work on the screenplay for *In Old Chicago,* the working title of which was the truly awful *Mrs. O'Leary's Cow,* in late 1936. He aimed to capture events leading to the birth of the modern city as it emerged, phoenix-like, from the devastation of the fire, but like all Zanuck's historical epics, its plot bore only the slightest resemblance to actual events of the past. By November 14, 1936, Zanuck's writers presented him with a preliminary story treatment. At the story conference a week later, Zanuck's ideas regarding plot and casting had begun to form. For the hero, Dion O'Leary, he wanted "a Gable type," for the heroine, Belle Fawcett, he envisioned "a character like Frances Farmer played in *Come and Get It.*" Delineating the female lead's none-too-attractive character further, Zanuck noted "girl should be a tart...a girl who puts stuff in men's drinks, etc." He then assigned the screenplay to two different writers and told them each to come up with a separate treatment.

Zanuck exerted complete control over script development, a practice that held drawbacks, as many Alice Faye, and later Betty Grable, musicals reflect. Dialogue, plot twists, and even the actors' mannerisms repeat themselves from one film to the next—even when the movies were not out-and-out remakes of earlier productions like *That Night in Rio* or *Hello, Frisco, Hello.* In Zanuck's lexicon, spurned chanteuses abandoned the sites of their early triumphs to find escape (and *always* success) on the London stage. Wrongheaded heroes never accepted help from the women who loved them, preferring instead to sacrifice love to their own pride and endure heartbreaking separation until the final reel. And men and women bickered relentlessly until one kiss revealed their true feelings and turned hate to love. Alice Faye always acknowledged the repetitive aspects of her movies with Fox. "Actually all those films were the same script," *Variety* quoted her in her obituary. "All they did was change Don [Ameche] over here and Ty [Power] over there."

After reading the two versions of the script presented to him in December, Zanuck ordered his writers, "You are to get out another *single* treatment," he said, "combining the two versions and added notes from the conference." He wanted, he said, the same kind of "suspense and pull which was achieved in *San Francisco* where Gable and MacDonald search frantically for each other." The script evolved throughout the spring, reaching its "revised final stage" by May 13, 1937. By this time Zanuck and his writers had transformed the character of Belle to "a great-souled woman in shady surroundings," while Dion became "a ruthless go-getter."

For once casting great-souled women and ruthless go-getters failed to present the usual problem for the talent-starved Zanuck. Early in his thinking about the film he had decided on Clark Gable as Dion and Jean Harlow, then at the pinnacle of her fame, as Belle Fawcett. That Zanuck proposed to outshine an M-G-M movie using M-G-M stars was an irony on which apparently no one commented, even Louis B. Mayer. By 1937 M-G-M had developed its own project with casting problems—the children's fantasy *The Wizard of Oz,* for which they felt the only possible candidate for the role of Dorothy was Fox's number-one star, Shirley Temple. The moguls agreed to trade. The deal looked auspicious as spring of 1937 drew to a close and showed every indication of going through smoothly.

Preproduction on *In Old Chicago* hit its first snag when Zanuck learned that Clark Gable would not be available after all. Henry King, the movie's director, did not regard this as a setback. "I felt he [Gable] was too old to be believable as Alice Brady's son," he said. "Audiences would never forgive him at the end, but they would forgive a headstrong younger man." At King's suggestion, Zanuck reluctantly turned to one of his new actors, Tyrone Power, who had recently starred in the costume drama *Lloyds of London.* Power was a handsome young man with luminous eyes who came from an acting family. Zanuck remained unconvinced about him for some time, even dropping him from Alice's *Sing, Baby, Sing* after Power encountered difficulty with the director. Alice, who had coached Power in the part and participated in his screen test, felt terrible when he lost the role.

"I took him to the Tropics Restaurant," she remembered. "I told him not to let this one setback get him down." She had faith in his talent and knew he would become a star and so worked to convince him that "all the letdown meant was a delay until the day he would find this out for himself." Her instincts proved right. Power worked hard in *In Old Chicago* and the role turned him into a major star.

Plans moved ahead to begin production once Jean Harlow finished filming *Saratoga* at M-G-M, but at the end of May, she fell ill in the middle of shooting. In her absence the company shot around her, and Eddie Mannix, head of M-G-M production, quietly warned Henry King that Harlow's health might prevent her from starting *In Old Chicago*. "We're trying to finish a picture with her and we just hope she'll recover enough to finish it," King remembered Mannix saying. On June 7, 1937, Jean Harlow died from uremic poisoning at the age of twenty-six. The news stunned all of Hollywood, particularly Alice, whose early screen image had been modeled on Harlow. "I felt a strong empathy with Jean because when I started at Fox they tried to make me 'another Harlow'," she said. "When she died I was terribly upset."

Harlow's death left Zanuck in a bad position. He had to find a leading lady for one of the most expensive movies he had yet attempted on extremely short notice. Henry King remembered that "Jean's tragic death almost ended in an indefinite postponement of the picture *In Old Chicago*." Replacing Harlow represented a trickier proposition than replacing Gable, King said, outlining the difficulties: "It had to be someone with fire, not just a pretty face; it had to be someone capable of conveying depth of characterization; and it had to be someone who could sing the three numbers with style." King immediately thought of Alice Faye, but, ironically, the studio brass balked at the idea of casting Faye in a role written for Harlow, despite the fact that they had spent two years, from 1934 to 1936, promoting Faye in Harlow's image. Their concern revolved around Faye's as yet untested dramatic abilities. They ordered a screen test and waited for the results.

Alice wanted the part of Belle and knew it might be one of the best roles of her career. Tyrone Power volunteered to do the screen test with her, in a gesture guaranteed to put her at ease and demonstrate his gratitude for her earlier support. Her screen test, consisting of the words "Get out!" as Power bursts into her room, was, as King put it, "the shortest test of her that anybody ever made." It apparently looked fine and Zanuck awarded her the part on June 18. Harry Brand issued a press release that gave the impression that Zanuck had had Alice in mind for the role all along. "During the past year, Zanuck has been building Alice toward bigger dramatic roles, and the present role, the culmination of this process, is expected to advance her to top rank stardom," the release stated. "The importance of this assignment," it continued, "can be gauged by the fact that *In Old Chicago* is the most ambitious picture from the standpoint of cost and production value which 20th Century-Fox has attempted...the re-enactment of the Chicago fire of 1871...has a separate budget of $500,000."

Alice's good fortune held as the studio assigned personnel to the rest of the picture. In addition to her friend Tyrone Power, Alice would be working with Don Ameche as Dion's brother, Jack, and Alice Brady as their mother, Mrs. O'Leary, as well as Henry King as her director. King respected Alice's potential as a dramatic actress and recognized her sensitivity. "I knew I could inspire confidence in her and bring out that sense of natural accomplishment so important to a really fine actress," he said. "I knew that Alice would deliver a first-rate performance as Belle, but she had to feel I was on her side." By all accounts the cast and crew of *In Old Chicago* worked well together. King, who had been an actor in silent pictures, never raised his voice or shouted orders. Skilled at managing people, Henry King enjoyed a remarkable thirty-year tenure at Twentieth Century-Fox, signing on as a director in 1930 and remaining through the disintegration of the big studio system.

King, who discovered the joy of flying when he scouted locations for the 1930 Will Rogers film *Lightnin'*, decided that Power, Ameche, and

Faye should all take flying lessons, believing that shared experiences formed the basis of friendships. His idea apparently worked, although Power was the only one who fell in love with flying and continued with it. Power and Ameche took turns playing pranks on Alice, and the three of them, along with others, ate lunch in the Gold Room of the studio commissary almost every day. "There was a lot of fun on that set," Ameche said. "Tom Brown and Andy Devine and Alice Brady and a lot of people like that. It was good fun." Faye felt particularly close to Tyrone Power, with whom she shared a birthday. "Ours was always a good friendship, never a romantic one," she said. "He would tell me about his love affairs, and I would tell him about mine. It was a brother-sister kind of thing."

Alice contended with her usual case of extreme stage fright the first day on the set. "This poor gal was so nervous she could barely remember any of her lines," King said. To build her confidence during the first few days of filming, the astute director would call "cut!" after only a few words of her dialogue. Zanuck viewed the daily rushes where King consistently interrupted Faye throughout each part of the scene and questioned King's strategy, but King recalled that within a few days she said, "Oh, Mr. King, I know all this now." He said, "I worked with her that way for two days and she wanted to do it, she wanted to go ahead, she was now getting acquainted and getting more relaxed."

Because of King's care in developing Alice's confidence, she felt perfectly comfortable with her first big dramatic scene. It occurred when Power, as Dion O'Leary, attempts to kidnap Belle Fawcett by bribing her driver and hiding in her carriage when she comes out of the saloon. Alice completed four pages of dramatic dialogue without hesitation. King remembered shooting the scene only three times: for the waist-high shot and the two close ups he would need to assemble the scene at the editing process. "It came out perfectly," he remembered. "I ran the rushes and Darryl Zanuck called in all the brass and announced a new 'actress' at Fox."

In addition to his nervous young leading lady, Henry King had his hands full with *In Old Chicago*. It was a complicated movie on many levels.

The climactic fire scene required a lot of night shooting. "We had, I think, at least two weeks," remembered Don Ameche. "It might have been more, starting to shoot about eight or nine at night and shooting until five or six in the morning, until light came." Studio crews built a special tank of water adjacent to the set where the fire scenes were shot, and as an extra precaution King prohibited women cast members, including Alice, from the filming of the fire, instead using stunt men in dresses. Everything in the sequence went smoothly and no one was hurt. In fact, the only serious injury during the whole film occurred as a result of the costumes rather than the stunts or special effects. In one of the saloon scenes Alice caught her heel in the train of her costume and fell down a flight of steps. When an extra named John Roy picked her up, she fainted from the pain and remained unconscious for twenty minutes. Members of the company rushed her to the studio's emergency room where two doctors determined that she had broken no bones but had bruised her back. King suspended filming briefly while she recuperated enough to return to the set.

In Old Chicago represented a turning point in Alice's career. She felt relaxed and confident working under Henry King's direction, and happy in the company of her costars Ameche and Power. "When I was doing all those romantic things on film, I was single," she recalled. "I just had lots of fun—Tyrone Power, Don Ameche and all those guys...they were so much fun to work with, and so attractive." For the first time in her film career, Alice began to feel a sense of camaraderie. After all her self-doubt about whether she really belonged in Hollywood, Alice started to relax and feel at ease with herself and her work. Twentieth Century-Fox would not release *In Old Chicago* until April 1938, so Alice remained unaware of its impact on her career for at least seven months after she completed work on it. The delay allowed her some time to absorb the newfound sense of professional accomplishment Henry King had instilled in her before circumstances surrounding the film's release plunged her into full-scale stardom.

CHAPTER 6

Treadmill

Before the end of shooting *In Old Chicago* in the summer of 1937, Alice began seeing Tony Martin again. Alice's brother Sonny and her friend Betty Scharf had interceded on Tony's behalf, and Sonny arranged to bring Alice to Sugie's Tropics one night when he knew Tony would be there. Martin had resolved his own qualms and persuaded his mother to overlook Alice's religion. "Now I was in command of myself," Martin said. "We began going out again. It was just like it had been, only more so." Eventually he proposed and Alice accepted. They eloped to Yuma, Arizona, in a chartered plane on Saturday, September 4, during the Labor Day weekend. As one columnist noted, their elopement "climaxed a romance punctuated by many estrangements." Alice's hairdresser, Helene Holmes, and Martin's agent, Nat Goldstone, stood up for the couple, and Judge Henry C. Kelly performed the afternoon ceremony. Tony presented Alice with a square-cut diamond ring, and the *New York Times* reported that the bride wore a powder-blue suit and an orchid corsage. By eight o'clock that evening the newlyweds had returned to Hollywood where Nat Goldstone and his wife hosted a celebration at the Trocadero, where "lilies of the valley and gardenias and a three-tiered wedding cake decorated the table." Within the week Jule Styne, Alice's vocal coach at the time, threw a cocktail party that included Tyrone Power, Harry Brand and his wife, Alice's brothers, and one of the Ritz Brothers.

Henry King, in his position as Alice's mentor, disapproved of her decision. "He tried to talk me out of marrying Tony," Alice said later, not enumerating the reasons for King's objections. King may have felt that Alice and Tony, each twenty-two years old, were too young to settle down. Or perhaps King occupied a better position from which to gauge Tony and Alice's individual chances for success in the movie industry, and he sensed that Tony didn't have Alice's star power. Walter Scharf credited Tony as having a "superb baritone voice and the good looks of a matinee idol" but acknowledged that Tony "never quite made it in films, although numerous producers, notably Howard Hughes, tried to get him to the top." Alice was certainly aware of the inequity of the positions that she and Tony held in Hollywood's pecking order but probably thought that one or two good roles would put Tony on top, just as had happened with their buddy Tyrone Power. Additionally she almost certainly underestimated her own talent and growing popularity. Nor could she know that within another year she would become one of Hollywood's top ten box office draws, which Zanuck would exploit to the hilt. Off by themselves Tony and Alice could ignore the pressures of show business and just be Mr. and Mrs. Martin. But they were naïve in their belief that they could separate their marriage from their professional lives and that the disparity in their status and salaries would not create a strain.

The demands of Alice's career dominated their wedding, just as it would their marriage. Tony and Alice eloped to Yuma over a long weekend because Alice was scheduled to begin filming *You're a Sweetheart* at Universal on Tuesday, September 7. Universal had originally scheduled the start date for Alice's picture for August 27 but postponed it because she was unavailable, finishing her scenes for *In Old Chicago*. A long weekend coinciding with a break between movies gave Tony and Alice the opportunity they needed to get away from her normal six-day workweek, plus the bonus of a brief honeymoon—exactly two days. Alice's work, not Tony's, also colored the media's coverage of the nuptials. A press agent for Universal revealed the couple's plans to a columnist Saturday morning, saying,

"Don't say I told you but please give a plug to the picture Alice is making out here." When the same columnist called Twentieth Century-Fox for confirmation, their press agent said, "You can say for certain they will be married in Yuma; Martin told me himself." The canny publicist added, "But don't plug the Universal picture, plug the last one Alice made for us."

The terms of Alice's loan to Universal placed a particularly heavy burden on the newlyweds. Moguls could loan their contract players at will, without their consent, and at a profit, which the studios pocketed. This aspect of the big studio system was one about which actors most often complained, representing as it did the film industry's equivalent to leasing equipment or hiring out chattel. Fox seldom loaned their top performers because of the demands of their production schedule, and, after *You're a Sweetheart*, they never loaned Alice to another studio again. Universal had financial troubles and needed a hit to bail it out; that they wanted Alice to star indicates how bankable a talent she had become. They negotiated with Fox to borrow Alice for precisely four weeks, for which they would pay Fox $40,000. Various estimates of Alice's salary at the time indicate she earned a weekly paycheck of $1,500 or above, but not as much as $2,500, which was the amount of her raise from Fox in the fall of 1938. Therefore Twentieth Century-Fox earned a net profit of at least $8,000, if not $8,500, a week for Alice's services to Universal.

Universal's contract stipulated that Alice would begin work on August 27 and conclude on September 28, giving them four weeks to film the scenes in which she appeared. When they postponed the start date to September 7, because Fox still needed Alice, Universal faced the problem of running overtime and having to pay Fox an additional fee. Their solution instead was to juggle the shooting schedule and work longer hours. The contract allowed Alice Friday afternoons and evenings off to perform on the *Music from Hollywood* radio show, but the rest of her week was apparently fair game. Delays precipitated by the replacement of a stock character after the first week, and the death of actor William Gargan's father during the third week, forced them to acknowledge by September 24 that they would have to ask Fox to extend Alice's availability beyond the contract's stipulated concluding date of September 28. "It is absolutely impossible to finish with her by this time," they stated in the weekly status report. "The company is working with Miss Faye all Saturday and Saturday night until midnight or later." By working long hours and continuing to juggle the schedule, they felt they could complete the twenty-six scenes and three big production numbers in which Alice appeared by October 16. Universal renegotiated with Fox and bought themselves a two-week extension of Alice Faye's services, for a mere $26,250.

Everybody won from this deal except Alice. Universal got a hit movie that "really saved the place," according to its director, David Butler. Twentieth Century-Fox made somewhere between $54,000 and $57,000 in profit for their six-week loan of Alice. And Alice got to spend the first month of her married life working ninety to one hundred hours a week. Universal managed to complete the film before the second deadline, which they accomplished by "working last Sunday [October 3] and by working Monday night." They had saved the most intricate dance routine until the end, fitting in a minimum of rehearsal time and postponing the long shots, which male lead George Murphy performed with a double at a later date.

The business of making *You're A Sweetheart* is a quintessential example of Hollywood's exploitative labor practices, yet Alice apparently enjoyed making it and formed several lasting friendships, most notably with her costar (later Senator) George Murphy and character actor William Gargan. Director David Butler even named a racehorse after her, in return for Alice performing a particularly difficult dance routine on the ledge of a theater set. The routine involved George Murphy and Alice beginning the dance on stage, then climbing up to the ledge of the balcony stage right, after which they made a complete circuit of the theatre at a great height from the projecting decor before swinging down the stage curtain on the other side. The result was a lighthearted and graceful performance, probably the closest anyone ever came to replicating the breezy sophistication of Fred Astaire and Ginger Rogers. The only drawback was Alice's fear of heights. David Butler, strapped for time, didn't have the leisure in which to humor his acrophobic star. He promised to use a double for the long shots, sparing her the more demanding aspects of the dance, but he needed Alice up on the ledge for the close and medium shots. Butler, who was an avid racing fan, finally resorted to bribery. He had just acquired a two-year-old filly, which he planned to run at Santa Anita. She was, he told Alice, "the most beautiful filly that you've ever seen in your life. If you'll do this, I'll call it Alice Faye," he promised her. Alice finally agreed. As Butler remembered, "We got the shot, and I had to name this filly Alice Faye."

Alice Faye (the horse) debuted at Santa Anita some time later, after *You're a Sweetheart* had wrapped and both Butler and Faye had returned to Fox, their home studio. The odds on the horse were forty-to-one, and Butler remembered everyone in the studio putting money on the race. "Zanuck, Bill Goetz, Schenck and all of them played the horses and they had loudspeakers in their offices where they got the service the same as bookies got," Butler said. "We heard a scream go up, and somebody came running onto the set and said, 'Alice Faye won and paid forty three dollars.'" The entire studio erupted; they had all backed Butler's filly. "The property men, the set decorators, the makeup department, all came running down on the set," he remembered. "Alice started to cry—ruined her make up. They won a fortune on the horse." Zanuck called Butler up to his office to congratulate him, saying he had won a substantial sum himself, but then lowered the boom. "Do me a favor," Butler remembered Zanuck saying, "As long as you're here, please don't name your horses after any of the stars. We've lost two hours!"

Universal rushed through postproduction on *You're a Sweetheart* and released it during the holidays on December 26, 1937. Alice again won accolades from the reviewers, particularly *Variety:* "Miss Faye has added fancy ballroom dancing to her versatile equipment, and Murphy has acquired a rather pleasant singing voice on top of his dancing skill," it noted. "That gives the two a chance for superlative teamwork in every department." Faye won raves elsewhere, even from critics who hated the movie's plot and supporting characters. "She can look the heroine for any kind of romance," said *Dallas Morning News* critic John Rosenfield, "she can deliver a song without ornamenting it out of recognition, and she can work plausibly through the silliest of plots to account for a worthwhile theater visit." *You're a Sweetheart* proved that Alice had evolved into a consummate professional able to deliver a commendable performance in a weak vehicle. She also worked successfully under the pressure placed on her by a studio trying to operate within serious time constraints.

If Alice saw too little of her brand new husband during the filming of *You're a Sweetheart,* she had the opposite problem during her next project, *Sally, Irene, and Mary.* The newspapers reported that Darryl Zanuck's wedding gift to the young couple would be a European tour. In reality, he decided to exploit the publicity value of Tony and Alice's marriage by casting them together in a new movie. It was not a happy experience for either one of them. Too little time together followed by constant togetherness in a work setting strained their relationship. "You can't imagine what it's like," Alice said in an interview a year later, "waking up with a person beside you in the morning as a starter, then sitting across the breakfast table from him, then working together on the set. . . . there were times when I thought if he grinned in just that way again—the way I had always loved before—I'd have to brain him and take the consequences. And he felt the same way about me."

Rumors of sharp quarrels followed by strained silences circulated, as the couple underwent their period of adjustment to married life in the public forum of a movie set. At one point the film's director, Lew Seiler, criticized Tony, saying, "It's too bad you can't sing your part," to which Alice snapped, "It's too bad you can't direct." Tony did not need Alice to fight his battles for him, but recalled that "it felt good realizing I had somebody like Alice on my side." Despite appearances, she was more than capable of holding her own on a set when angry; but she was just as quick to fight with Tony as defend him. He felt worse when, at some point during the production, the inevitable happened and a member of the press referred to him in print for the first time as "Mr. Alice Faye." It wouldn't be the last time. "She was a big star and I was trying to catch up to her," Tony remembered. "They never let me forget that."

Sally, Irene, and Mary was another variation on the theme of the backstage musical. This time it involved three manicurists trying to break into show business by turning an old barge into a dockside supper club. They are guided in this endeavor by radio comedian Fred Allen, Jack Benny's arch rival, as their agent. Allen and the film's supporting actress, Louise Hovick, more commonly known as Gypsy Rose Lee, represented further examples of Darryl Zanuck's penchant for novelty casting, like that of Walter Winchell in *Wake Up and Live.* Hovick had also appeared in Alice's *You Can't Have Everything* and demonstrated an arch comedic quality that worked well in contrast to the lead character's inevitable sweet spunkiness. Alice found working with Gypsy Rose Lee good, earthy fun. "Once on the set," Alice remembered, "Gypsy was wearing a very low-cut gown and one of her breasts popped out. 'Get back in there, you're 3000 miles from home!' Gypsy exclaimed."

Despite the buildup, *Sally, Irene, and Mary* was another tired-plot-with-new-twists film, which film musical historian Ethan Mordden summed up by saying, "Faye sings and romances Tony Martin, Joan Davis performs the big apple, Jimmy Durante clowns, Louise Hovick menaces Faye, Fred Allen hangs out, for catastisis [heightened drama] the boat snaps its mooring during a performance . . . the usual." Critics nationwide, led by Frank Nugent of the *New York Times,* found that the movie fell far short of its advertisements as "Positively the Top Hit Ever Given You by 'Hit Maker' Darryl F. Zanuck." Nugent wasted no time in pegging it for what it was, "a forthright exploitation of the voice, full lips, and other things of Alice Faye and her tenor-husband Tony Martin." The public's reaction proved more positive, having been teased by ongoing studio publicity releases: news that the Hayes Office considered Alice and Tony's first screen kiss far too long was one studio publicity effort. "Our fans were so anxious to see us together," Alice said, "that they made that so-so film a major box office smash."

After *Sally, Irene, and Mary* wrapped, Tony and Alice got down to the serious business of trying to make their marriage work. They concluded that making movies together placed too much of a strain on their relationship and decided never to do it again. Alice said at the time, "Things usually work out better in this profession, I believe, if married people don't work together." One fan magazine phrased their decision a bit more flamboyantly and broadcast it to a waiting world: "In solemn conference, after an interminable period of angry recriminations interspersed by haughty silences, they agreed never again to work in a picture together." Alice had also decided to give up performing on *Music from Hollywood* with Hal Kemp, retiring from the airwaves at the end of December 1937. She cited poor health brought on as a result of a schedule dominated by work. "Some people may be able to do both [making movies and radio broadcasting], but I can't and preserve my health. So I am turning down all air offers from now on," the newspapers quoted her as saying. Some, like the *Providence Sun Journal,* implicated Tony in the decision, with headlines like "Alice Faye Quits Air for Hubby—She Wants Tony Martin to Have All the Radio Glory." Others simply recognized Alice's desire to be free to spend time with Tony at the end of a workday.

Measures like these helped alleviate Tony and Alice's immediate problems and allowed them the luxury of making the more mundane adjustments to married life. Alice met and charmed Tony's grandparents in Oakland. Alice's mother remained unconvinced that Tony was right for her daughter, but she befriended Tony's mother, whom she enjoyed phoning to talk about "the kids." Alice took steps to keep her career in perspective, like giving up the radio show. Tony learned when to try to calm Alice down after a bad day with Zanuck and when to leave her alone. They enjoyed going out for cheeseburgers or Chinese food and getting together with their circle of friends, who didn't let Hollywood intrude on the good times. But sometimes Alice herself couldn't let go of the studio when she was angry, worn out, or frustrated. Tony complained there were times when she came home to a house full of guests whom she would leave Tony to entertain if she were out of sorts. She would greet them coolly, then head upstairs to bed.

Tony and Alice remained at a loss for a model on which to base a solid marriage that fit their peculiar set of circumstances. Alice's parents contended with dire financial circumstances and eventually drifted apart. Tony's parents had stayed together, but any experience Tony gained from years of observing the marriage of an Oakland tailor and his wife simply did not apply to his own situation. "For a while it worked," Tony conceded. "We both tried hard."

The toughest blow, according to Tony, occurred at the opening of *In Old Chicago*. Twentieth Century-Fox premiered the blockbuster in New York the first week in January 1938, although it apparently waited until late March and early April to put it into general release. Fans and autograph seekers mobbed Alice, who required a police escort to the theater. When she entered the lobby, it was on the arm of Fox's chairman of the board Joe Schenck rather than her husband's. Tony said that Alice always paid close attention to his feelings at premieres, and especially at the post-premiere parties. She would make a point, he said, of getting him "a good seat, at a good table, so he could talk with the right people. And we'd always have the first dance together." But the evening *In Old Chicago* opened, as the valets announced the arrival of the stars' limousines outside the theater, he recalled, the inevitable happened: "Mr. Tyrone Power's car... Mr. Spencer Tracy's car... Miss Alice Faye's car." Once they got home, Tony said he told Alice, "I don't think I can make it like this."

Tony remembered that Alice apologized and told him she understood but didn't know what she could do about it. "I think if she could have rectified the situation, she would have," Tony said. "But... there wasn't a damn thing she could do about it." From Alice's perspective, the incident introduced a sour note in what was a major career triumph. As Ed Sullivan remarked, all of the acclaim and frenzy of the opening, occurring as it did on the same street where she had been a chorine only seven years before, must have made her feel grand. Alice acknowledged that it did, adding, "The other night I met George White out here and he asked me if I'd like to do a Broadway show for him—me, the former *Scandals* chorine. That really tickled me," she said. "It's a crazy business at that, isn't it?"

Sullivan's article also indicated that Alice's thoughts that opening night had led her along another track. "I was thinking about my father and how much I would have given if he had been there to see the mounted cops protecting me," she said. Alice must have been even more gratified by the review published in the *New York Daily Mirror,* which had taken the lead in vilifying her over the circumstances of her father's death two years before. "Alice Faye looks ravishing, sings provocatively, acts commendably, [and] wears the tights . . . of the period with fine pictorial effect." To find herself in a position of having to apologize to Tony for the acclaim she had earned through her hard work in *In Old Chicago* might not have registered resentment with Alice right away, but the thought may have eventually seeped into the back of both their minds and introduced another element of tension.

In the midst of working out the challenges of her marriage, Alice discovered that her next assignment would reunite her with her favorite costars. Zanuck planned to assign Alice, Tyrone Power, Don Ameche, and her esteemed director Henry King for another Twentieth Century-Fox blockbuster, Irving Berlin's *Alexander's Ragtime Band.* After working with Berlin on *On the Avenue,* Zanuck realized that Berlin had a host of songs stashed away, none of which had ever been used in movies. He came up with the idea of a super-musical, based to some extent on Berlin's life story, tracing the ups and downs of a bandleader and his singer, using literally dozens of Berlin tunes. Berlin agreed to the project, a spectacular showcase of his music, but came away with two significant concessions from Zanuck. First, Berlin's name would appear above the title in the credits, an uncommon occurrence for a songwriter in films. Second, according to Berlin's daughter, the story would be a fictionalized biography, not "what Darryl Zanuck had originally wanted, a hoked-up version of his own life story." Berlin had not enjoyed the results of other Hollywood versions of various public figures' lives. Over and above these points, Berlin walked away from the negotiating table with a package that included "Alice Faye and Ethel Merman, the best of the screen, the best of the stage, delivering the best of Berlin, thirty years of hits wrapped up in a big, slick, 20th Century Fox package with Tyrone Power, Don Ameche and a cast of hundreds."

One social historian of New York City asserted that Berlin's interest in writing for Hollywood stemmed from the fact that the "more sophisticated adaptations of jazz and blues styles like Gershwin, and lyricists like Lorenz Hart and Ira Gershwin," threatened him and that writing for the movies, which demanded "simpler fare," gave Berlin "the perfect opportunity to ply his artful artlessness." Whatever his motives for adjourning to the west coast, Berlin had found in Zanuck the means of accessing a worldwide audience for a significant amount of his work. *Alexander's Ragtime Band,* noted Walter Scharf, was "the first movie to consist entirely of a writer's catalogue of standards," as both production numbers and as background music. "When the camera went into a nightclub, by some strange coincidence only Berlin tunes were played by the orchestra," Scharf said, an innovation that would be repeated in another Berlin movie *Blue Skies.* Of the more than two dozen Berlin songs featured in *Alexander's Ragtime Band,* only three were new compositions: "I'm Marching Along with Time," "My Walking Stick," and "Now It Can Be Told," the latter written especially for Alice Faye.

Zanuck set his writers to work creating a Berlin biography out of whole cloth. Berlin's daughter, Mary Ellin Barrett, remembered being aware of the efforts that went into preparing *Alexander's Ragtime Band.* It was "something exciting and different, so the word drifted down to the children's level . . . but there were also 'headaches' not unconnected to a name that also drifted down, 'Zanuck,' a name to inspire respect and wariness." She sensed the underlying tension in her father's work for Fox—"cast headaches, money headaches, scheduling headaches, and so many post-ponements." Berlin may not have been accustomed to having so many elements of a project out of his control, which could explain his children's' heightened awareness of the project. "Never before had my father been in quite such a feudal relationship," Barrett said. Nor did Berlin's obligations with *Alexander's Ragtime Band* subside after filming began. Alice remembered meeting Berlin during rehearsals and seeing him on the set frequently. "Sometimes he'd just sit and watch," she said, "sometime he'd play and sing his songs to help me get their feeling." The movie permanently linked the names of Irving Berlin and Alice Faye together in the public's consciousness, so much did the songwriter contribute to the singer and vice versa.

According to another Berlin biographer, Zanuck remained concerned with what he perceived as the script's "lack of genuine honesty" as filming commenced. Alice observed that Zanuck's concern for honesty did not extend to the appearance of his stars. "In *Alexander's Ragtime Band* the script followed the two leading characters—me and Tyrone Power—for a quarter of a century, but neither of us aged a bit through it all," she said. Another point on which the film was less than honest was its reflection of what Zanuck biographer George F. Custen referred to as "Zanuck's complicated nostalgia." Custen cites *Alexander's Ragtime Band* specifically as a typical example of what many critics dismissed as a "lightweight escapist confection," but that he feels was actually something far more insidious. "The films took refuge in a certain 'approved' version of the past," he argued, because they "drew on one ideal by erasing another." The aspiring WASP heroes inhabiting Zanuck's world "ignored the populations who created the ragtime and jazz that were redefining popular culture," Custen said. "Irving Berlin's treatment for Zanuck's 1938 film *Alexander's Ragtime Band* pointedly denied that African-Americans had made any contribution in shaping this music."

How much of the upper-level concerns about the script or the score made themselves felt on the set is difficult to determine. Ameche, Faye,

Power, and King all remembered *Alexander's Ragtime Band* with affection. King referred to the three actors as his "happy trio," citing their marvelous chemistry together. Although they never again worked as one unit, he kept their photographs grouped together on his wall for years. Alice felt secure under King's direction, which was meticulous and well organized, according to Fox producer Otto Lang. "He was a superb director," Lang said. "I mean really, truly, you know, as though it was done with a slide rule, he would know every shot ahead, every angle, how many angles." King also knew how to get what he wanted out of Alice, and he coaxed another outstanding performance out of her. "Like most sensitive, talented people, she needed to feel she was doing it herself, not just aping a director's instructions," he said. "She always took direction beautifully without any show of temperament, and when you were done the character she played came across with a vibrant warmth of personality so many actresses did not possess."

The genuine regard King's stars held for one another and for King transmitted itself to the screen and added an element of real feeling to the film. The rapport of Ameche, Faye, and Power together in one film is what their fans remembered and what made the biggest impact at the box office. Because of the enormous popularity of both *Alexander's Ragtime Band* and *In Old Chicago,* Alice would spend the rest of her life answering the question posed by so many fans: what was it like to kiss Tyrone Power? "I would say 'Like you'd died and gone to heaven,'" Alice said, "but as far as really wanting to go to bed with him, I never really wanted to. I don't think he wanted to go to bed with me—maybe we would have. It just didn't happen." She remembered that "a lot of women sleep with their leading men—lots of them do, but I didn't do it."

Zanuck had allotted *Alexander's Ragtime Band* a budget of two million dollars, about as much as he spent on *In Old Chicago.* Without the expense of a twenty-minute fire sequence, more of *Alexander's Ragtime Band's* budget could be devoted to sets, costumes, and, above all, musical production numbers. "By 1938 the recovery had set in," Alice said, "and money was no object—or as near to being no object as it can be with Hollywood moguls."

The supporting cast included Ethel Merman, to whom the young Alice had confided her ambitions years before in New York, as well as Jack Haley, Jean Hersholt, and John Carradine. It boasted twenty-nine musical numbers, "the greatest number of songs in any one musical," said Henry King. Gwen Wakeling, the costume designer who had frequently earned criticism for her work in previous Alice Faye vehicles, distinguished herself with the elegant, restrained gowns and stylish suits worn by Faye and Merman. Each element of the film reflected a level of quality and attention to detail that previous Twentieth Century-Fox efforts consistently lacked. It represented a turning point for the studio and marked the beginning of an era in which Zanuck committed himself, from time to time, to truly superior productions.

In the midst of filming for *Alexander's Ragtime Band*, Fox released *Sally, Irene, and Mary*. The studio scheduled the opening at Grauman's Chinese Theater on March 4, 1938. They planned to immortalize Alice and Tony with the traditional ceremony of placing their footprints in cement in the theater's courtyard, but the occasion was postponed a week when Alice fell ill. Whether Tony deserved to have his footprints preserved at Grauman's at that stage in his career was a question better left to the studio bosses, who apparently didn't share Tony's qualms about coattailing in on his wife's fame. Alice was enjoying the single most significant year of her career; in the seven months of her marriage to Tony, she had added considerable luster to her already golden image. Unfortunately, *Sally, Irene, and Mary* failed to provide Tony with the breakthrough role he so desperately needed, and their marital tensions continued.

When Alice concluded her work for *Alexander's Ragtime Band*, the couple decided to take their long-deferred honeymoon. It would give them a chance to get to know one another outside the Hollywood pressure cooker and to determine whether they felt equal to facing the challenges posed by Alice's success. Harry Brand's publicity department dutifully announced the couple's plans in a press release dated April 15. That day they departed from San Francisco on the *Lurlene* bound for Hawaii.

The couple intended to spend a month in Hawaii, but barely two weeks elapsed before Fox released another announcement that Tony and Alice were taking the boat back to California. "Alice Faye is homesick and wants to celebrate her birthday (May 5) with friends at home," the statement said. That their trip would coincide with her birthday could hardly have come as a surprise to Alice. Tony Martin wrote in his memoirs that their Hawaiian vacation was "a honeymoon to remember," yet he also said that it took place immediately after their Yuma elopement, not seven months later. Alice said nothing about it at all, either at the time or later. Clearly, something occurred to precipitate their return only halfway through the vacation.

Tony Martin recollected that at some point after the *In Old Chicago* incident, he decided to "make it on my own" and asked his agent, Nat Goldstone, to find him some nightclub bookings in the East. "I had to scratch and claw my way somehow up to her plateau," he said. His radio work and the few films he'd made for Fox meant he could command a fairly handsome salary. Harry Brand's office announced in July that the studio granted Tony a leave of absence to make an extended personal appearance tour. Alice, they asserted, gave him a solid silver baton with her name engraved on it, because this trip was the first time they'd been apart since their marriage. Tony regained some of his self-esteem on the tour; audiences thronged to see him, he earned good money, and he could be his own man. Alice, on the other hand, grew despondent coming home to an empty house every night. She had ascended to the rank of queen of the lot at Fox; their production schedule depended on her. Zanuck was not about to let her join her husband for a tour lasting the same amount of time it took to shoot another spectacularly profitable Faye film. Alice was trapped.

Tony's tour meant that he missed spending their first wedding anniversary with Alice. He also missed the premiere of *Alexander's Ragtime*

Band. He may have regretted the first but probably not the second. The press and the public heaped accolades on Alice. "The film is a triumph for Alice Faye," said *Film Weekly*. "Alice Faye hits the high spot of her acting career," said the *Brooklyn Daily Eagle*. Irving Berlin was delighted with the reception accorded her rendition of his "Now It Can Be Told." Alice missed having her husband at her side during her second triumph of the year, but his presence was a two-edged sword. His support would have meant a great deal, but she had eclipsed him again and the world knew it.

Alexander's Ragtime Band took almost two years to make, from conception to release, about as long as *In Old Chicago*. "I made both of them in one year," recalled Henry King, "which, if it wasn't an achievement, it was certainly a lot of work." The two Zanuck productions constituted an extremely effective one-two punch and catapulted the trio of Ameche, Faye, and Power to the top of the Hollywood heap. *In Old Chicago* garnered six Academy Award nominations, including Best Picture, with wins for Robert Webb as Assistant Director (a category eliminated after 1937) and Alice Brady for Best Supporting Actress. *Alexander's Ragtime Band* also received half a dozen nominations, including Best Picture, winning only for Music—Best Scoring. Both films proved extremely popular at the box office, and everyone involved with them came out shining. After *Alexander's Ragtime Band*, Alice's fan mail jumped to the second highest on the lot at Fox. Radio offers poured in, but mindful of Tony and her time commitments, she declined them. In September Harry Brand announced that Zanuck raised her salary to $2,500 a week.

The year 1938 taught Alice that her life as a star would grow more complicated as her popularity and importance increased. If Alice's voice in the interviews of 1938 sounds a bit bewildered, it was because she found herself caught in a life filled with paradoxes, and she probably wondered how she got there. She had a fabulous career with a spectacular salary, yet in her day-to-day life she worked longer and harder than her mother had during her childhood. She had a handsome husband whom she loved, yet she could only sustain her relationship with him by allowing him to escape the glare of her publicity for months at a time.She was a twenty-three-year-old performer in peak physical condition from ten years of constant dancing, yet she found her health breaking down with increasing frequency. Sometimes an injury laid her low, as it had during *In Old Chicago,* other times a cold turned into something worse—in an era that predated antibiotics.

Underlying all the rest of the conflicting circumstances of her life was Alice's introversion, the greatest paradox of all. She knew she occupied the position of queen of Twentieth Century-Fox Studios, but she had difficulty realizing it inside. Objectively, she wished she derived greater joy from her stardom. "Every girl in the world envied me. The truth is, I envied myself. I wished I could have shaken myself up and made myself more of an extrovert. I wished I could have been more of a party girl. But like the leopard with those damned spots, I couldn't change what I was—or what I wasn't."

Alice seemed to be saying that if she had been a different kind of person, she might have enjoyed her position more. But viewing her situation from a different angle, one wonders if anyone could have enjoyed it. Overwork, a troubled marriage, and frequent illness dampen many peoples' taste for an active nightlife. Instead of wishing for a different personality with which to enjoy the perks of her position, perhaps Alice should have acknowledged the many difficulties with which she was coping so well.

After *Alexander's Ragtime Band,* Zanuck wasted little time in assigning Alice to her next project, *Tail Spin* (a title perhaps reflecting her mental outlook at the time). Her role as an "aviatrix" competing in the Cleveland Air Races constituted quite a departure from the backstage musicals in which her audience expected to see her. Frank "Spig" Wead, the naval flyer turned screenwriter whom John Wayne portrayed in *The Wings of Eagles,* wrote the screenplay—a barely disguised version *Stage Door,* only with airplanes. Like the theatrical soap opera, which pitted Ginger Rogers as the spunky-chorine-waiting-to-make-it-big against Katharine Hepburn as the society-newcomer-with-dreams-of-stardom, *Tail Spin* starred Alice Faye as the spunky-air-racer-waiting-to-make-it-big against Constance Bennett as the society-newcomer-with-dreams-of-victory. Like *Stage Door,* *Tail Spin* was a women's ensemble piece, with wisecracking Joan Davis mimicking Eve Arden's role, Jane Wyman aping Lucille Ball's girl-from-the sticks character, and Nancy Kelly as the emotional Lois who telegraphs her suicidal intentions to the audience with a faraway expression and eerily calm demeanor.

Stage Door received an Academy Award nomination for best picture of 1937; *Tail Spin* fared less well. Critics failed to remark on its resemblance to the earlier film, concentrating instead on its obvious flaws. The *New York Times* noted that "it is constructed on a simple formula: every time the picture is about to crash, Mr. Zanuck crashes a couple of planes instead." The *New York World-Telegram* was more succinct: "*Tail Spin* ... does an inglorious nosedive." Alice fared slightly better with *Photoplay*'s remark that "Alice Faye has a poor role, but managed to survive," and the *New York Daily Mirror's* assessment that "Miss Faye and Miss Bennett ... do manage to stage a nice face-slapping match." It was an incomprehensible sequel to Alice's success in *Alexander's Ragtime Band* and demonstrated the capriciousness of the big studio system's casting system.

Years of steady work as a performer had provided Alice with the knowledge and experience most valued by her studio and allowed her to work through the mixed material the studio assigned to her. Through choice roles and a big publicity buildup, Twentieth Century-Fox had transformed Alice over the course of 1937 from a promising entertainer to the queen of the lot, a foundation stone upon which Zanuck planned to build a more profitable studio. Alice reciprocated with hard work and tractability, the two characteristics management values most in a laborer. Whether through custom or convenience, Alice had fallen in the trap of deferring to the studio on decisions involving not only the roles she played, her appearance, and her salary but also her workload in terms of the number of hours she worked in a day, the number of days in a week, and the number of movies in a year. She realized it at the time, she remembered, saying, "It might have been considered a trap, but if it was, it was that well-known one made of the richest velvet. If it was a cocoon, it was lined in satin. If it was a prison it was the most luxurious prison ever conceived by mortal man." In 1937, she could anticipate neither the heights to which her career would soar nor its eventual effect on her personal life. She would gradually learn that she paid a price for acceding to all of the studio's decisions, but not in time to save herself from a serious heartbreak.

CHAPTER 7

Queen of the Lot

If they are to be believed, stories released from the set of *Tail Spin* by the Fox publicity department reflect a distracted Alice. One stated she found it difficult to throw herself wholeheartedly into her fight scene with Constance Bennett, instead pulling her punches and worrying excessively about any injury she might cause. Another reported that Tony Martin always sent her roses on the days when she sang before the cameras, yet for her only number in *Tail Spin*, "Are You in the Mood for Mischief," they failed to appear. "Alice Faye was visibly nervous and upset . . . until further investigation revealed the messenger was delayed by a road accident," the release said. Finally Harry Brand's department reported that she had a cold and was confined to bed. Typically for Alice, it developed into flu, and the studio announced that it planned to send her on a vacation on a farm for complete rest.

The latter announcement actually proved true. The end of 1938 saw Alice entraining for Detroit where she hoped to catch up with her touring husband in time to celebrate the new year with him. Then she proceeded to a farm in Owensville, Ohio, for a week's rest at the home of Mr. and Mrs. George Bistrain, the parents of one of her California friends, Mrs. Ben O'Kent. On January 7, 1939, Alice made headlines when she and two women friends stopped for cocktails at a hotel bar in Cincinnati to kill time before embarking on the return journey to Los Angeles. Their waiter apologetically announced that he was not allowed to serve unescorted ladies. "Well, then get me an escort," the exasperated Alice apparently said. The waiter produced one of the hotel's auditors, who obligingly assumed the role of host. "She signed the check—but I paid it," he said. Stymied by the awkwardness of having a complete stranger foisted off on her to appease convention, Alice apparently "talked shop," refused to introduce her companions, and gave no autographs other than her signature on the check. Tony Martin's reaction to the ensuing headlines—"Alice Faye Orders a Drink and an Escort," and "Wanted: a Boy Friend"—can only be imagined.

The incident highlighted the ongoing problems that Tony and Alice faced as they pursued their separate careers in separate locations, problems that only seemed to increase as time passed. Alice now realized that Zanuck stacked the deck against Tony at the studio and that his only hope for success approaching hers was radio and nightclub work. One article quoted her, stating that "Alice says it won't do Tony much good to return to Hollywood because the studio doesn't seem to want to give him a break, putting him in B pictures all the time." The same article also said, "Talk around town has Alice and Tony breaking up, but Alice shied away from comment on domestic conditions at the Martin manse. Her official spokesmen at the studio say, without much conviction, they think there's nothing to the rumors."

Tony couldn't get a break in Hollywood, and Alice's contract with Fox meant that she couldn't get away from Hollywood for more than brief periods. For the foreseeable future, the best the couple could do was make a life for themselves between Tony's tours and just endure the separations. "That was another wedge driven between us," Tony said. "She wanted a husband at home, naturally. And I was across the country. I was just a voice on the phone." Alice frequently discussed the possibility of retiring in another five years in interviews, at the same time firmly squelching any speculation about their plans for a family. In the meantime, Tony began to suspect that some of Alice's friends who hadn't wanted her to marry him in the first place began gossiping about him. He also felt that the men who had always admired Alice were taking advantage of his absence to ingratiate themselves to her at his expense. The Martin marriage continued to rock along in this way into 1939.

Upon her return from Ohio, Alice reported to the studio for her next film, *Rose of Washington Square,* in which she costarred with Tyrone Power for the third and last time. Since his days as a Warner Bros. scriptwriter, Darryl Zanuck had kicked around the idea of a movie based on the life of the Ziegfeld comedian Fanny Brice and her relationship with her gambler husband, Nick Arnstein. The idea would later be adapted into the 1960s musical *Funny Girl.* "This is a story," the first script treatment declared, "of a girl who loved a no-good guy and sacrificed everything she wanted out of life to keep that love. Throughout the story runs a heartbreak song, 'I Love That Man.' It should have the haunting quality of that old favorite, 'My Man.'" Zanuck eventually decided to use "My Man," Brice's signature tune, which Alice sang leaning against a streetlight wearing a tight satin skirt and a black beret.

Walter Scharf recalled, "We knew we were in trouble before the film went into production. Miss Brice was going to sue." Zanuck played up the publicity value of Brice's suit, allegedly sending Alice to Peoria, Illinois, to avoid New York process servers, then announcing to the press where Alice was and why he had sent her there. In fact, Fox sent her home from New York by way of Peoria rather than Chicago but, as Alice recalled, "I was told not to show my nose outside the door of my compartment." Eventually Brice sued Twentieth Century-Fox, Alice Faye, Tyrone Power, and their costar Al Jolson for $750,000 for "defamation of character, unauthorized use of her life story, and invasion of privacy." Zanuck settled out of court in December 1940 for somewhere between $30,000 and $40,000. Nick Arnstein, who had also filed suit, received $25,000. For less than $65,000, Darryl Zanuck had purchased several months' worth of national press coverage on behalf of his movie.

The public was anxious to see Alice Faye and Tyrone Power reunited, after the success of their first two outings together. *Rose of Washington Square* did not need the publicity of a celebrity's defamation suit to fare well at the box office. It had Alice Faye "who excels in representing a suffering entertainer," as one review put it, in a role tailor-made for that particular talent. Tyrone Power again played to his strength as the charming ne'er-do-well, Bart Clinton. Al Jolson, in his penultimate movie role, sang all of his signature tunes: "Toot, Toot Tootsie Goodbye," "California, Here I Come," "Pretty Baby," "Rock-a-bye Your Baby with a Dixie Melody," and of course, "My Mammy." In addition to the haunting "My Man," Alice sang the period pieces "I'm Just Wild about Harry," "Ja-Da," and "The Vamp," among others. Sadly, two other popular standards sung by Alice, "I'm Always Chasing Rainbows" and "I'll See You in My Dreams," were shot but eliminated. Darryl Zanuck pulled out all the stops to make *Rose of Washington Square* as commercial a musical drama as possible, and theatergoers everywhere rewarded him handsomely.

Alice did not enjoy making *Rose of Washington Square*. She suffered from comparisons with Fanny Brice such as that made by the *New York Times,* which stated, "Miss Faye doesn't resemble Fanny Brice; she doesn't sing 'My Man' well either." Her habit of allowing her lip to tremble when she sang annoyed some critics, who did not hesitate to express their irritation in print. She did not care for her egotistical costar Al Jolson, who played her character's best friend and shared more scenes with her than Tyrone Power. Years later she would bluntly recall Jolson as "the most awful man I ever met. Every time I go by that cemetery out in L.A. I look at that big tombstone and wonder how it ever keeps him down." Finally, her weeklong Ohio farm idyll did not restore her energy as she had hoped. She admitted shortly after the picture wrapped that she had been ill during most of the shooting. "I felt badly all through the picture and I knew I would have to do something," she said, knowing full well that there was little she could do. Many years later she said, "If I didn't show up for work, the work stopped. It wasn't like a department store, where if one clerk stayed home with an ingrown toenail the store still opened. If Alice Faye stayed home during the shooting of a film starring Alice Faye, the whole thing shut down. So I went to work every day, no matter how lousy I might have felt. That's one of those things people don't think of when they consider the 'glamorous' life of a movie star. With the entire responsibility of a huge production on your shoulders, you jolly well go to work every day."

A trip to New York followed by a sea voyage back to California through the Panama Canal gave Alice a much-needed boost. She also determined to live quietly during her next film, *Hollywood Cavalcade*, accepting few invitations and getting plenty of sleep. "Alice Faye Now a Hermit," the columnists crowed, making much of her self-imposed nine o'clock bedtime. "I have been out only twice, to quiet dinners with friends, since I started this picture and even then I was in bed early," Alice said. Her efforts at limiting her activities while making movies got an additional boost that spring from Darryl Zanuck, when he bought out Twentieth Century-Fox's stars' radio contracts and forbade them to perform on the radio. The *New York Times* announced "Alice Faye Is Banned from Air by Zanuck" on February 22, 1939.

By buying out his stars' contracts, Zanuck was responding to complaints from the Association of Motion Picture Exhibitors across the nation, who perceived radio as a threat to their box office receipts. Allowing movie stars to perform on radio, they reasoned, simply kept their patrons home listening to their favorite entertainers for free. They would use the same argument against television after World War II. Certain factions within the film industry feared radio and, in 1939, as one historian noted, "launched a publicity campaign for movies through advertising 'Movies Are Your Best Entertainment,' spelling MAYBE, which they quickly dropped." Alice's contract allowed her to make eight radio broadcasts a year. Tyrone Power, whose contract Zanuck purchased a few weeks prior to Alice's, had also been a radio regular.

The big studios had resisted allowing their stars to appear on radio in the early 1930s, but toward the end of the decade their attitude began to relax.

Within six months of Zanuck's ban, Alice appeared on *Maxwell House Coffee's Good News* on NBC to sing "So Help Me" and in 1940 made four broadcasts, compared to the five she had done in 1938. The contract that Zanuck purchased may have given Alice the option to do eight broadcasts a year, but she had never fully exercised that option. She found making movies a full-time job and often declared throughout her career that she found life simpler when she could concentrate on doing one thing at a time. Alice called her life as a Hollywood star a "fairy tale," but she understood too well that making movies "was tough demanding work. In those days studio contract players—such as I was—were hustled from one film to another. Today an actor considers himself overworked if he appears in two films a year. We used to do four or five and think nothing of it. It was not unusual for me to finish one film in the morning, have lunch, and start working on another picture that same afternoon."

Alice's single-minded work habits served her well for *Hollywood Cavalcade,* which represented a departure for her on several levels. First, her role as silent screen star Molly Adair presented physical challenges she had never encountered before. Second, this would be the first movie in which Alice did not sing at all. Even her dramatic roles in *Now I'll Tell* and *In Old Chicago* had included musical numbers, but this part demanded she get by on acting ability alone. Finally, Zanuck decreed that *Hollywood Cavalcade* would be filmed in Technicolor, Alice's first feature in the new medium. It was essential that she make every effort to look healthy and rested. Around this time, Alice took up the habit of getting a massage every day, and she found it helped her enormously in preparing for "another long day at the office." It certainly provided her with a healthier means of dealing with pressure than the alcohol and pills many of her peers employed. Every evening after dinner and studying her lines for the following day, Alice remembered that she was visited by "a great strapping hulk of a woman who was a specialist in Swedish massage." The daily grind of the studio and the stresses in her home life were pummeled out of her and she "slept like a baby."

Hollywood Cavalcade was another of Zanuck's pet projects, whose screenplay he spent months shepherding through the creative process. His concept for the movie revolved around the characters and pioneers of the silent picture business in the early days of Hollywood. In the November 1938 conference on the first story treatment for *Hollywood Cavalcade,* Zanuck chided his writers for the lack of punch in the story and the futility of the screenplay's conclusion. He began considering the advantages of recasting the film as a dramatic musical, and noted the points in the script where numbers could be inserted logically.

By February 1939 Zanuck still conceived of *Hollywood Cavalcade* as a musical, but by May 15, with the starting date looming, he considered eliminating all the musical numbers entirely. "Mr. Z. feels that audiences have seen enough pictures opening with Alice Faye singing an old-fashion tune," the minutes of the story conference stated. "There was *In Old Chicago* in 1937, *Alexander's Ragtime Band* in 1938, and *Rose of Washington Square* this year. With a great dramatic story like *Hollywood Cavalcade,* we do not have to resort to the formula pattern of providing a frame-up for a few numbers for Alice Faye. It reduces our picture, pulls it down." At a second conference two days later, Zanuck postponed the starting date for the picture to May 29 on the grounds that since they eliminated the music from the drama, "several elements [are] insufficiently developed. An A picture like this has to have a certain amount of dramatic and emotional violence." He also wanted to change the movie's title to "Falling Star," perhaps to better reflect the male lead's fall from filmmaking grace.

Walter Scharf reacted to the elimination of the musical sequences as any musical director would, calling *Hollywood Cavalcade,* "one of the least memorable films I made with Alice." He disliked working with Al Jolson as much as Alice had in *Rose of Washington Square.* Jolson, who made a cameo appearance in the film to re-create his historic role in the *Jazz Singer,* was understandably proprietary about the way his sequence went. Scharf said Jolson "gave us more trouble than the rest of the movie combined, but [his] enormous talent and presence in retrospect at least made it all worthwhile."

Alice did not share any screen time with Jolson in *Hollywood Cavalcade,* a circumstance for which she was probably grateful. Instead, she enjoyed several scenes with silent screen legend Buster Keaton, including a pie-throwing sequence and a Keystone cop chase. "I never had so much fun in my life," she said. "I guess deep down inside every one of us lurks the urge to smack somebody in the face with a lemon meringue pie." When one of Keaton's pies hit her prematurely and with vigor, she chased him around the set and out onto the street trying to return the favor. Whether it was the sheer fun of playing slapstick or the joy of releasing her pent-up tensions in a maelstrom of pastry, Alice Faye adored working in *Hollywood Cavalcade.* She later claimed that it was the only one of her movies she kept. She never sang a note in the movie, but she got a kick out of several scenes in which "I started out looking glamorous and ended looking like scat." In addition to pies in the face, she sat on a pie, fell off of a motorcycle into a mud puddle, went neck-deep into a puddle of water— once on her own and again with Keaton—and reveled in her one opportunity to perform physical comedy. Like everyone else on the set, she revered Buster Keaton but found him "a quiet, reserved gentleman and not easy to know." She later regretted that her own innate shyness prevented her from getting to know him better. "I was never too outgoing myself, so the result was that we were polite and friendly, but nothing beyond that," she said. "I am sure I could have learned a great deal from him, if only I had tried a little harder to draw him out of his shell."

In spite of her efforts to stay healthy, Alice again took sick during the production. She apparently continued coming to work, where they installed a nurse on the set for her. Eager publicists insisted that the old-fashioned Cooper-Hewitt lamps employed for authenticity caused Alice's one-hundred-degree temperatures; doctors later determined the trouble was a pair of infected tonsils and a run-down constitution. Fortunately,

Technicolor suited her honey-blond hair, deep blue eyes, and creamy complexion and gave no indication that she was not in peak form. (Or perhaps her fever coincided with her hospital scenes, so it didn't matter.) After the initial shock of her appearance in the opening scene, in which she wore a brunette wig and a red tropical-patterned blouse, audiences enjoyed a beautiful, polychromatic close-up of Alice holding a bouquet of yellow roses and wearing a picture hat trimmed in blue and lavender. Technicolor's contract with Fox, as well as the rest of the major studios, stipulated that their advisor, Natalie Kalmus, would orchestrate a production's color palette. While the use of Technicolor meant that Alice "suddenly had to become conscious of what colors were best for me," Kalmus had the final say. The costuming combinations in which Alice appeared worked well for her coloring—deliciously hued pastels, pearl grays, and basic black.

Hollywood Cavalcade proved a solid commercial success, though not of the caliber of *Alexander's Ragtime Band,* and certainly not in a league with other studios' offerings in 1939. That year marked a watershed for Hollywood, with such films as *Dark Victory, Gone with the Wind, Goodbye Mr. Chips, Mr. Smith Goes to Washington, Ninotchka, Stagecoach, The Wizard of Oz,* and *Wuthering Heights,* just to name those nominated for the Motion Picture Academy's Best Picture Award. Critics found Alice's unexpected comedic antics a pleasant surprise and remarked on her ongoing ability to turn in unaffected and creditable performances. They also noted the pleasant naturalness of Fox's use of Technicolor, and many of them indulged themselves in a guessing game of who in the movie was meant to be whom in the pantheon of silent film greats. If Zanuck found the critical response to his brainchild disappointing, he could at least take comfort in the fact that Twentieth-Century Fox's gross receipts in 1939 were second only to M-G-M's, even if it was by about 30 percent less. M-G-M's Louis B. Mayer sat in the catbird seat, able to draw on a roster of talent that included the likes of Clark Gable, Greta Garbo, Spencer Tracy, and Myrna Loy. Zanuck, working from a weaker position in terms of star power, still managed to produce a creditable string of A pictures.

Zanuck demonstrated that he could also turn out some true disasters, as he did in the fall of 1939 when he released Alice's *Barricade*. An ill-conceived vehicle to begin with—Alice played a café singer on the lam for killing a mandarin in war-torn China—it suffered from sloppy editing. Filmed in 1938, Zanuck closed down the project before shooting was complete. Nevertheless, he decided to throw it together and release it in the fall of 1939, probably in the hope that it would return a profit on the weight of Alice's name. Surprisingly it did, but it remained a "piece of liverwurst" Alice preferred not to discuss. "They changed the story after we shot it, splicing bits of film together in the editing room," she said. "What finally was shown in the theaters made no sense at all. My hairstyle changed within the scenes because of that haphazard editing."

Alice's upcoming picture fared much better, enjoying a large budget and stellar cast. Another historical drama, *Little Old New York* costarred Fred MacMurray, Richard Greene, Brenda Joyce, Ward Bond, and Andy Devine. Directed by her favorite, Henry King, the story centered on Robert Fulton's development of the steamship—a subject that leant itself neither to musical treatment nor alluring costumes. Nevertheless it allowed Alice to display, if nothing else, her emerging comedic abilities, for which she won high marks from the critics. The *New York Times'* Frank Nugent, for example, stated, "She begins to realize the comic possibilities latent in a pair of blue eyes of high batting average and a mouth that was never meant for Lady Macbeth." Yet Alice continued to seethe over the *Barricade* fiasco. She understood that it was the kind of production that, had it been released earlier in her career, could have ruined her, and she must have deeply resented Zanuck's attempts to capitalize on her name so shamelessly. "As it was, since I had already achieved some degree of fame and reputation, I was able to ride out the storm and move ahead," but *Barricade* remained "a genuine botch," she asserted.

Alice soon had more than a bad picture to occupy her attention. In the five months between October 1939 and February 1940 she would live through a succession of highs and lows that would leave her emotionally drained and would begin to alter her outlook on her life and her career. It began simply enough with the decision of Tony and Alice to give up on the rented houses they had occupied since their marriage two years before and buy their first home. They chose the eleven-and-a-half-acre estate of Jack Haley in the San Fernando Valley community of Encino. It fulfilled as nearly as possible Alice's childhood dream of owning a house with a big lawn and fruit trees, since the property boasted orange, peach, and walnut trees. She and her husband, who in keeping with her childhood fantasy was a man of elegance who habitually wore tuxedos, took possession of the nine-room house on October 1. Alice had achieved all three of her childhood dreams: stardom, husband, and place in the country. Having to maintain an uneasy coexistence between her husband and her stardom was a scenario that she had never envisioned, but the grown-up Alice seemed prepared to continue to do it, at least for the foreseeable future. The new house was the frosting on the cake, an oasis to which she could easily escape from the studio, and a refuge where the Hollywood comparisons from which Tony suffered could not penetrate. "Tony and I have celebrated our second wedding anniversary and I guess we will be able to weather the storm," Alice told Louella Parsons. "I believe we are happier now than at any time since our marriage."

Twelve days after they moved in, a fire gutted the house, leaving Alice with only the clothes she'd worn to the studio. The cost of the damage was estimated at $25,000, in an era when a man's suit cost $25 and a new Dodge sedan cost $815. Newspapers assured anxious readers that her furs and jewels were locked in a safe and undamaged. Their failure to mention Tony in any of the coverage may have indicated that he had again left town on tour. Alice had no option but to check into the Beverly Hills Hotel and await delivery of a trunk of clothing the studio assembled from her old movies. Builders anticipated that it would take at least three weeks before she could return to the house. In the days that followed, she authorized the contractors to rebuild, shopped for clothing and personal items to replace those that were lost, and probably wondered if all of her dreams were destined to be fulfilled so imperfectly.

Alice's circumstances seemed to improve by Christmas, as she headed for New York to spend the holidays with Tony and promote her new movie. Later she arrived at an interview for *Little Old New York* sporting a large star sapphire, Tony's Christmas gift to her. She assured another columnist that she much preferred spending her New York sojourn accompanying Tony to Madison Square Garden sporting events to seeing the shows on Broadway. By January her professional fortunes took another leap forward when she placed seventh in the Motion Picture Exhibitors' poll of 1939's top ten most popular stars at the box office. Her career was soaring, her home repairs continued, and her marriage looked secure. Then on February 22, 1940, Alice took the world by surprise when she announced her intention of divorcing Tony Martin.

Alice took Tony by surprise as well, knocking him flat. He maintained in his memoirs that the night before the news broke she called him at the Royal Palms in Miami and they had had a warm and loving conversation. The divorce came out of "darkest left field," just as his salary had jumped to two thousand dollars a week and he found himself "flying all over the map" to fulfill engagements. Alice cited Tony's long absences as the cause, though they were nothing new. When Louella Parsons pressed her for a comment, she issued one that sounded like her lawyer had drafted it for her: "Tony is a grand person, but it was inevitable that we should part, since our careers have kept us from each other...He has been very successful, but our long separations have not been conducive to permanent happiness." The question of why Alice filed when she did is probably best answered by Tony, who wrote, "I am convinced [her friends] were telling her that I was running around in Florida. I'm no saint, and I guess I flirted a little and responded to the flirtations of others. But, on my honor, I didn't have a serious romance while we were apart." Such a statement does not, of course, rule out casual romances. Rumors of Tony's extramarital affairs must have gotten back to Alice at a point in her life when she was fed up with trying to keep her marriage going. She had always been capable of quick, incisive action, and this time she took it.

Judge Samuel R. Blake granted Alice's divorce petition on March 22, 1940; under California law the divorce would become final a year later. She told the judge she blamed their breakup on career differences and long separations, estimating that they had only spent about eight months together in "short visits," throughout their twenty-eight-month marriage. She also cited Tony's indifference, stating that on her last trip to New York "I saw very little of him because he played cards most of the time and spent most evenings at the ice hockey games." Inevitably, press coverage of the proceedings also included a detailed description of what any well-dressed movie queen would wear to court: a gray tailored pencil-striped suit, a large turn-back brim picture hat, and fox furs—adding as an afterthought that she appeared nervous and distressed.

In an interview with *Photoplay*'s Katharine Hartley in April 1939, Alice stated that she believed in divorce "if it's necessary for the happiness of both people." Alice had watched her mother and father's marriage fail and, from that standpoint, knew what she was talking about. She was equally familiar with the pain of separation, having endured it in one form or another beginning with the first month of her marriage to Tony. No doubt she divorced him to escape from the marital limbo that their bicoastal careers imposed on them and the sense of betrayal over Tony's alleged high jinks. The opinions of people concerned for her well-being, like Henry King and her mother, must have finally prevailed as well. Once she had made her decision, Alice acted unequivocally. Yet she refrained from unburdening herself either to her close friends, like Betty Scharf, or to the press. Her only comment regarding her relationship with Tony in later years was "the marriage simply did not work out."

People throw themselves into their professional lives following a defeat in their personal ones, and Alice was no different. Her next project,

Lillian Russell, was one she had looked forward to and from beginning to end it was hers. She always considered it her best dramatic part. "Playing Lillian Russell was a challenge, but I was helped immeasurably by the director, Irving Cummings, who had been an actor and really made the picture for me," Alice said. "He had known the real Lillian Russell, a great of the Gay '90s, and was able to advise me on her sense of humor and the way she worked." Zanuck conceived the vehicle as a way to "convey to modern-day audiences just why terrific attention was showered upon her [Lillian Russell]," and crafted the script in which he placed Russell "in the center of it all."

Zanuck's notes reflected his usual ambitions. He wanted "a big picture like [M-G-M's] *Ziegfeld*" but found that the star "who will probably be Alice Faye needed some added spark (outside of singing which we know Alice can do so well)." He felt his writers had yet to realize the story's "glamorous, romantic, and dramatic possibilities." He wanted to reflect Lillian Russell's reputation as a woman who "made men fall at her feet and give her gifts." Whether Alice Faye, or any other actress at the time, was equipped to realize Zanuck's fantasy is a question best left to the psychoanalysts. Critics noted that Alice had the face, the figure, and the voice, and as one of the top box office attractions of the late 1930s, Alice enjoyed a popularity that approached Lillian Russell's. Zanuck's script hampered Alice's performance, however. He never completely eliminated the wooden, portentous quality that afflicted many of his historical re-creations.

To better emphasize Russell's devastating effect on the opposite sex, Darryl Zanuck assigned Alice not just one leading man but several. "It was my fifth film with Don Ameche, who was always fun," Alice said, "and I was thrilled to have Henry Fonda as my other leading man." Henry Fonda, fresh from his critically acclaimed role as Tom Joad in John Ford's *The Grapes of Wrath,* was less than thrilled with the assignment. "Well the first film after *The Grapes of Wrath* Darryl F. Fuck-It-All Zanuck had me make was *Lillian Russell* with Alice Faye," Fonda said. "Now I've got only good things to say about Alice Faye. But shit! I was only one of ten men in that picture! I swear it. Count 'em. Don Ameche, Nigel Bruce, Eddie Foy, Jr., Weber & Fields, Edward Arnold, Warren William, Leo Carrillo, and Ernest Truex."

Unlike Fonda (whose frustration was understandable), Alice reveled in her role, regretting only that Fox chose not to film the extravagant production in Technicolor. Director Irving Cummins had indeed worked with Russell, appearing as her leading man at the age of twenty-one in Russell's last legitimate play in 1910, *In Search of a Sinner.* He fed Alice the kind of personal details about Russell that allowed her to tackle the characterization with a minimum of her usual anxiety. Alice found the dresses designed by Travis Banton also helped her portrayal enormously. Zanuck did not stint on period costuming for his pet projects. For *In Old Chicago,* for example, Alice performed in one saloon sequence wearing a pair of hose trimmed with sequin butterflies and lace, costing two hundred fifty dollars a pair; later in the same film she wore a twenty-five-hundred-dollar pair inlaid with a dozen diamonds. The costumes for *Lillian Russell* were equally luxurious. "Everything was handmade," Alice remembered. "We used to say that it was a pity that the audience never got to see those undergarments, because they were things of remarkable beauty. I remember one corset I wore in Lillian Russell that was trimmed in the finest lace and really was a work of art. But nobody ever saw it except me and the wardrobe department. Still," she added, "it made me feel special, and perhaps that was the whole point."

Alice exhausted herself again during the filming of *Lillian Russell,* and a studio press release announced that they made the unusual provision of giving her a singing-dancing stand-in. Certainly the strain of her divorce and its aftermath did not enhance her condition. Her next feature film would be a splashy Technicolor musical with a Latin American theme called *Down Argentine Way,* scheduled to begin shooting in July. Alice spent the intervening time pulling herself together and making a few appearances. In March, just a few days after her divorce hearing, she had purchased a parcel of four acres adjoining her Encino property, with the intention of expanding her citrus orchard. On June 3, 1940, she performed on *Lux Radio Theater*'s presentation of *Alexander's Ragtime Band,* reprising her role as Stella Kirby with Ray Milland as Alexander and Robert Preston in Don Ameche's role of Charlie Dwyer.

Alexander's Ragtime Band constituted Alice's *Lux* debut. She remembered enjoying her performances on the program. "The way it went," she said, "was Lux soap had a deal with different actresses—I was one—and then when they'd give you all this publicity, you know—so and so uses Lux soap blah blah blah, you'd have to do so many Lux shows. They'd ask if you wanted to do certain ones." For *Alexander's Ragtime Band,* Alice sang seven of the movie's Berlin tunes, including the title song and "Now It Can Be Told," in addition to the songs Ethel Merman had sung in the movie, like "Blue Skies" and "Say It With Music." Fox song-and-dance man Dan Dailey remembered that the *Lux* program, hosted by Cecil B. DeMille, kept movies alive after their initial releases in an age that predated television.

As Alice caught up with herself, Zanuck moved headlong into the production of *Down Argentine Way.* The script, intended to showcase New York's newest nightclub sensation, Brazilian singer Carmen Miranda, had been in development since the previous fall. As Zanuck said, "Our idea is to make a disguised version of the [horse racing] picture *Kentucky,* but to lay it in South America today, particularly the Argentine and Buenos Aires. We want to fill the picture with humor, a little drama, a lot of romance, and the South American-Portuguese Samba music." One film historian credited Zanuck with perfecting the formulaic remake, developing it to "almost an exact science." *Down Argentine Way,* according to Zanuck's outline, would feature the usual suspects in addition to Carmen Miranda, who would play herself. It would be a small part giving her an opportunity to sing a couple of her songs.

Zanuck intended to capitalize on the magnificent stir Carmen Miranda had created in Shubert's *Streets of Paris* revue on Broadway in the fall of

1939. Alice had seen it, found Carmen enchanting, and persisted in drag-
ging Tony Martin to the show, since he had made a highly successful recording of Ary Barroso's "No Tabuleiro de Bahiana." The Bahiana music Carmen
and her band popularized became a national craze, and Carmen earned a
reputation as the girl who saved Broadway from the New York World's
Fair.

Carmen Miranda's mere presence in *Down Argentine Way* earned the
picture a big publicity buildup well in advance of filming. It earned still
more when Alice Faye suddenly announced to the studio that she refused
to do the movie. Walter Scharf, who had returned to Fox from Paramount
specifically to work on *Down Argentine Way,* remembered that "I was on
the lot only four days when Alice told Zanuck she didn't want to make
the picture. It sent the studio boss into near hysterics. He had not only
gone to a great deal of trouble, at her request, to bring me back to Fox,
but her own costumes had been designed and made and some of the pre-
recording in which I was involved had already been done. Alice then went
into the hospital. She said she needed an urgent operation. Zanuck was
furious."

The *New York Times* reported on June 8 that Alice had undergone "a
major abdominal operation at Cedars of Lebanon hospital last night," having been "taken suddenly ill at her Encino home." The general public assumed the star had been stricken by appendicitis. Alice later admitted, "It
has been written that I had appendicitis, but it wasn't that. And no, it
wasn't an abortion. It was just one of those things." Betty Grable biographer Doug Warren attributed the surgery to hemorrhoids. Whatever the
surgery was, no evidence exists to suggest that it was a lifesaving procedure. Nor is there reason to believe that Alice opted for elective surgery at
precisely this moment as a negotiating tactic to win improved terms in
her contract. It is unlikely, given her films both before and after 1940,
that she objected to the script for *Down Argentine Way* for artistic reasons.
Nor was Alice's temperament of the sort to harbor professional jealousy
against a highly publicized newcomer like Miranda.

Alice's reason for balking at *Down Argentine Way* remains obscure, but a likely scenario suggests itself. After her recent divorce, and years of performing in poor health, she was worn out. Musicals were physically demanding and she had just completed the exhausting *Lillian Russell*. She and her doctor may have decided that it would be better for her to undergo the elective surgery right away and get some much-needed rest. Rarely did she undertake a movie role without succumbing to a cold. The cases of flu or pneumonia her colds often developed into were dangerous diseases in a pre-penicillin age. Rarely did Alice get enough time to fully recover. As she stated many times, if she did not show up for work, the studio had to shut down production. She lived under tremendous pressure to perform. But this time she opted not to, calling it quits before the production was too far along. This time Alice decided her health would come first.

Walter Scharf remembered the aftermath of her announcement: "His [Zanuck's] number one girl was giving him the kind of trouble other stars were sometimes expected to give, but Alice never." Perhaps she realized that the only thing Hollywood expected from its docile, hardworking performers was more hard work, performed with the smooth dependability of an automaton. She had grown impatient with living her life in fits and starts, a few weeks here or there crammed in between productions. Her divorce from Tony illustrated the consequences of a life lived in that way. She was tired and resented the fact that the inexorable tide of the studio's schedule could not accommodate her need for a couple of weeks to recover from an elective surgical procedure. She recalled in her memoirs, "I used to have temper. Not a terrible one, but still I could blow my top occasionally. It happened most often when I was at work." After the stresses and fatigue of her recent life, Alice blew her top.

Walter Scharf remembered that Alice backing out "was the talk of the lot. No one knew what would happen next, if the film would even be made." Zanuck moved with the swift expedience typical of Hollywood's moguls. First he dispatched Walter Scharf to New York to audition a new

Fox actress currently starring in Cole Porter's Broadway hit *DuBarry Was a Lady*. Second, he placed Alice Faye on suspension for the first and only time in her career, negating the rumor that an emergency appendectomy caused her sudden hospital stay. The *Spokesman Review* of July 14, 1940, reported on "this oddest of all studio-actor altercations," stating that Alice was "off pay for failure to appear 'able, willing, and ready' for the star role" and that the studio felt that "Miss Faye could have postponed the surgery and that she used it as a means to escape a role she did not relish." The article went on to predict an early settlement for "Miss Faye . . . one of the ten leading money making stars on last years official tabulation . . . is the best feminine star on 20th-Fox's [sic] card and is badly needed at this particular time in as many pictures as it is possible for her to produce."

As the *Spokesman Review* pointed out in Alice's case, Zanuck was in no position to wait out the predicament Alice created. The studio's cash flow demanded that Alice work as much as possible. Don Ameche said they all knew that Fox exploited them, but he didn't blame the studio. "The banks owned the company at the time; they were so much in debt. And they had no one else to go with." How Alice Faye and Darryl Zanuck resolved their differences went unreported in the press. Alice may have served her suspension and reported back at its conclusion. Zanuck may have lured her back with some kind of incentive, perhaps promising not to force her into the kind of punitive roles other studio heads assigned their wayward performers. Whatever their agreement, Zanuck probably preferred to keep it quiet. Otherwise he would expose a weak spot in his studio's structure that other performers and their agents might exploit. Alice quietly returned to work sometime at the end of the summer of 1940 and, for the time being, apparently all was forgiven.

Alice Faye was beginning to hold Twentieth Century-Fox responsible for the stresses of her recent life. Zanuck would not have noticed the change in his leading actress right away. It took her time to recover from the heartache of her divorce, the fatigue, and the ill health. Zanuck would find in the months to come, though, that Alice was no longer complacent. She might continue to have difficulty asserting herself, but she would resist much more tenaciously when she felt imposed upon. Her star would continue to rise over the next few years, but she would value it differently. In deferring to the studio's priorities she also began to consider her own.

CHAPTER 8

So This Is Harris

At the beginning of June 1940 Darryl Zanuck had an Alice Faye Technicolor extravaganza on his hands and no Alice Faye to star in it. His solution to the problem, typical of Hollywood in that era, eliminated the short-term problem of replacing Alice in *Down Argentine Way*. It also solved the long-term question of how to prevent Alice Faye from causing this kind of problem again. Zanuck brought in the girl he sent Walter Scharf to New York to see. Building up another blue-eyed, blonde singer-dancer who could succeed Alice Faye at a moment's notice would insure that Alice would think twice before balking at future assignments. Actress Celeste Holme later asserted that "Zanuck always ran the studio by having actors afraid of somebody else." The new girl was, as Gregory Peck described her, the kind of actress Zanuck seemed to favor, a "dishy" sort of girl, just like Alice. Her name was Betty Grable.

Grable had knocked around Hollywood for several years, landing contracts first with RKO, then Paramount, but never ascending into the ranks of A pictures at either studio. She was performing in an act with Jack Haley at the San Francisco World's Fair when a Twentieth Century-Fox talent scout spotted her. The studio signed her to a long-term contract, which they agreed to defer when she landed the ingenue's part in *DuBarry Was a Lady* on Broadway. "There was no guarantee that *Du Barry Was a Lady* would be solid hit or that I would get good notices in it," Grable said, "but both things happened." Nevertheless, Grable knew from experience that she could still misfire on the screen, regardless of good stage notices. *Down Argentine Way* gave her "a once-in-a-lifetime opportunity," she said, putting her over the top with movie audiences. "Alice's misfortune was my good luck . . . with the same opportunity that *Down Argentine Way* afforded me, many another still unknown girl struggling in Hollywood could have reached the top."

On Friday, June 21, 1940, exactly two weeks after Alice underwent surgery, Betty Grable reported to work on the picture. Her costars, in addition to Don Ameche and Carmen Miranda, included veteran character actors Charlotte Greenwood, J. Carrol Naish, and Leonid Kinskey. Kinskey replaced Cesar Romero at the last minute, when Romero contracted a typhoid-like illness and found himself in the same hospital as Alice Faye. Romero's absence from *Down Argentine Way* reduced the number of Latin American cast members by fifty percent, leaving only Carmen Miranda to lend a sense of authenticity to the first of Twentieth Century-Fox's famous Latin American cycle. Technically, even Miranda was not a native South American. She had been born in Portugal to a family that immigrated to Brazil when she was a child.

Zanuck's development of the Latin American musicals stemmed only in part from his desire to showcase the popular Miranda. Central and South America represented important new markets for Hollywood to tap in order to maintain their international revenue stream should Europe fall to Hitler. Unfortunately, none of Zanuck's minions, or anyone else in Hollywood, questioned the assumption that the only kind of movies a Latin American audience could appreciate were those that took place in Latin American settings, with Latin American themes, punctuated by the rhythm of Latin American music. By underestimating both the sophistication of Latin American audiences and the diversity of the cultures they represented, Zanuck created quite a stir south of the border, but not of the kind he had envisioned.

When *Down Argentine Way* played in Buenos Aires, Argentines took offense at the way the film depicted them, including as it did typical clichés of Hispanics as shady characters running crooked race tracks or fat, somnolent, burro-riding peasants; while the Americans, as always, played the good guys.

Despite a sour reception overseas, *Down Argentine Way* proved phenomenally successful for Betty Grable, who eventually earned a place as one of the top ten moneymaking stars between 1942 and 1951 and became Fox's longest-term leading lady. Zanuck had what he wanted, another dishy blonde, and he lost no time in putting her in the role he had developed with her in mind when he gave her a contract, *Tin Pan Alley* with Alice Faye. Grable's biographer referred to the combination of Grable and Faye as "a dangerous piece of casting in that one might be reckoned to spoil the show for the other" but admitted that that proved not to be the case. The combination of Alice Faye and Betty Grable worked well in part because Zanuck delineated their characters in *Tin Pan Alley* as complementary opposites. For Grable's role as Lily, he envisioned "a flighty girl who just naturally falls into success with little effort on her part." She was, he said, "the glamorous type—she wants success and lots of men—she is ambitious and would pick up with anyone who can do her any good." Alice Faye's Nellie, later renamed Katie, he perceived differently. "Make her conservative, [a] practical type . . . level-headed, who sees ahead," Zanuck ordered his writers. "She will retain her practical slant—and coupled with it is the basic idea that she does not care for show business. It's just a means to an end to her—it pays more money than other kinds of work, and way down deep what Katie really wants is the love of the right guy and a home and kids."

Pairing Faye and Grable also worked well because the two women hit it off so well together. Alice's daughter, Alice Regan, remembered how close they were, although "they were total opposites." Harry Brand's publicity department initially attempted to cast them as natural adversaries, since they would compete for the same roles, but the purported feud between them "was just something that the Fox studio publicity department dreamed up to draw attention to our film," Alice said. For her part, Betty recalled being completely awestruck by Alice, a big star whom she had greatly admired. She remembered how nervous she felt at their first meeting. When she finally worked up her nerve to approach Alice, all she could think of to say was "Alice, you've got eyes just like a cow's." Betty remembered, "She gave me kind of a strange look and said, 'That will get you a cup of coffee and a piece of stale bread.'" But Alice recalled, "The truth was that we liked each other very much and became good friends, and stayed good friends until the day [Betty] died."

What drew the two performers together probably rested in their commitment to hard work, their tenacity, and their honesty. Like Alice, Betty took her work very seriously. According to Cesar Romero, "She was a hell of a good performer and she worked hard." Like Alice, Betty could also be stubborn. And like Alice, Betty showed zero tolerance for Hollywood phonies. Her frequent costar Dan Dailey said, "Betty was such an on-the-level broad herself. If anybody tried to con her, well look out. No matter who it was, a director, or another actor, or a boss, or a publicity man—mostly publicity men—she really let loose on 'em."

In Betty Grable and Alice Faye, Zanuck found two musical stars who excelled in conveying energy, good humor, and a dash of vulnerability all wrapped up in sparkling blonde packages. Grable executed dance numbers with a jazzy vivacity, while Faye delivered ballads with a stirring voice and haunting eyes. Film historians have accused Zanuck of assembling a stable of bland stars, but if Betty Grable and Alice Faye did not demonstrate the histrionic range of Katharine Hepburn or Bette Davis, neither did they possess those actresses' more grating qualities. They wore well over time. Main Street may have admired the exoticism of Hedy Lamar or the mystery of Greta Garbo, but they understood Alice and Betty. Like Ginger Rogers, Alice and Betty represented a glamorized version of the girls everyone knew; the ones who climbed trees and played sandlot baseball with the neighborhood boys until the day they discovered lipstick. A nation stumbling out of a worldwide depression and standing on the brink of a world war responded to these "bland" actresses, who seemed to epitomize hard work and fair play, yet retained a sexy, lighthearted appeal. Americans took them to their hearts, named their babies after them, and made them the box office successes they were.

The two women's chemistry raised *Tin Pan Alley* out of the realm of just another Zanuck retread, which in almost every other respect it was—a fact of which Zanuck himself was well aware. In a May 25 story conference, his secretary jotted down that Zanuck "feels that no matter how we tell this story we are going to run into the formula groove of *Alexander's Ragtime Band,* particularly from the war on." Audiences did not seem to mind. Instead, they found many elements of the picture captivating. Alice and Betty put over an especially unforgettable sequence, in which they performed "The Sheik of Araby" with the rotund character actor Billy Gilbert. Wearing sequined brassieres and sheer harem pants, they sang and shimmied across the stage with a superabundance of sex appeal. In 1992, film historian Doug McClelland asked the rhetorical question, "Who can forget the pantalooned pair, Alice in big bra, Betty in small, singing and dancing 'The Sheik of Araby'?" It is an iconographic image and remains one of the most commonly used film segments when classic movie channels discuss either Grable or Faye.

The costumes for the routine appalled Alice at the time, however. "*Tin Pan Alley* was famous for the authenticity and stylishness of its pre-World War I costumes, and I enjoyed wearing them, even the hobble skirts," she said. She made an exception for the transparent harem pants and skimpy top, which violated her sense of personal decorum, challenged her negative self-image, and opened the door to her innate insecurity. "I begged Fox executives to let me wear costumes that would hide God's generosity," she remembered. "But of course Darryl Zanuck and the rest of the Twentieth Century-Fox brass tried to show as much of me as the standards of those days would permit." She recalled many occasions where censors objected to her costumes and insisted the studio reshoot the scenes in which she wore them.

Loretta Young remembered reporting to Wardrobe on one occasion and being asked to wait by David Levy, who ran the department. "Alice Faye is in here and she's upset, so we'll be a little late for your fitting," he said. A few minutes later he returned to ask if Loretta would go in and speak to Alice. "She's always upset at fittings because her bosoms are so large," he confided. Young said, "Well, little flat-chested me . . . I couldn't believe it. Here I am, stuffing Kleenex in my . . . I thought he was kidding me. Here was a girl, her body was one of the most beautiful things about her. And she hated it." Alice admitted to envying Betty Grable's less-enhanced figure, while Betty preferred Alice's because Alice didn't have to wear padding. Alice said, "She could wear dresses I never could and vice versa." As for "The Sheik of Araby" costumes, Alice remembered that they "had boys and men all over the world drooling . . . yet I was so busty and so embarrassed about it that I wore a shawl over my costume until the last possible second."

By the fall of 1940, when all of this took place, Alice gave every appearance of riding high. She seemed to be recovering from her divorce and enjoying her career and the friendships it brought her, especially with Betty Grable and Jack Oakie. No evidence remains to judge exactly how she felt about the direction her life was taking at this point, yet she must have felt excited and pleased both personally and professionally. Never an introspective person, nor one given to confiding in friends, Alice kept her private life under wraps with remarkable success. Achieving such a degree of privacy seems even more remarkable because *Showman's Trade Review* named Alice the nation's outstanding female box office star in 1940, placing her in the number three position behind Mickey Rooney and Tyrone Power but ahead of both Myrna Loy (fourth) and Bette Davis (fifth). Filling out the remaining top ten positions, in order, came Alice's old costars Spencer Tracy and Shirley Temple, then Clark Gable, Fox's figure-skating darling Sonja Henie, and, finally, James Cagney.

The article announcing the list provided the context by which the significance of Alice's coup can be measured, stating, "theatremen operating showhouses in big towns and small all over this country can . . . tell to a scientific nicety exactly who really rates as a public attraction and who does not. . . . The standing of screen stars as measured in the exacting terms of the box office draw is something which Hollywood well might find more interesting and important than much of the comment and estimation over which great concern is expressed throughout studio circles." So while Hollywood insiders may never have considered Alice Faye the most prestigious singer/dancer/actress of the day, exhibitors across the nation knew her true value. Alice contributed enormously to Twentieth Century-Fox's balance sheet, generating an income stream larger than every other Fox star except Tyrone Power, and more dependable than that of Shirley Temple, whose age precluded success beyond the onset of adolescence. Queen of the studio since 1937, Alice was now queen of the industry.

Since her divorce from Tony Martin, the press had linked Alice's name with a number of bachelors, including a Texas millionaire named Charles Wrightman and radio announcer John Conte. Conte, who worked on the *Burns and Allen Show* and *Maxwell House Coffee Time,* had met Alice through Tony Martin the year before. He had spent some months in New York but had returned to Hollywood where he pursued Alice seriously. Throughout the spring of 1941 the press considered him the odds-on favorite in her life, completely overlooking a dark horse who had entered the race. News of the interloper would not break until the spring of 1941. In the meantime, Alice prepared to work on her first Carmen Miranda movie, *That Night in Rio,* in which she costarred with Don Ameche for the last time.

Twentieth Century-Fox took a bit more care with *That Night in Rio* than it had with *Down Argentine Way,* submitting the script to the Brazilian embassy, which cut several scenes. Like *Down Argentine Way,* it boasted a recycled plot in a new setting. This time Zanuck transferred the action from Paris, where Maurice Chevalier's 1935 version, called *Folies Bergere,* took place, to the colorful Rio de Janeiro, which, one critic noted, was currently out-frolicking the "no longer light-hearted" Paris. Events in Europe had moved quickly, rendering Latin America an even more critical market than before.

Zanuck intended to win back those South American countries alienated by *Down Argentine Way* with a typically American show biz "more-and-better" strategy, grabbing and holding the audience with a lavish—even by Hollywood standards—production. His selection of a screenplay with a plot revolving around the "seduction" of a married woman (Alice Faye) demonstrates just how out of touch he was with the social mores of the predominantly Catholic continent he was attempting to win over. Despite his words to the contrary, Zanuck clearly thought only in terms of what an English-speaking public might enjoy.

Alice enjoyed less than two weeks rest between the conclusion of her work on *Tin Pan Alley* and the beginning of *That Night in Rio*. Fortunately her role as the Baroness Duarte did not demand much of her. The picture really belonged to Don Ameche in the double role of Baron Duarte and his look-alike, an American nightclub entertainer named Larry Martin. Alice had only one song-and-dance routine to learn (which was later cut from the film), did not appear in at least a third of the movie's scenes, and sang only two of the movies songs, both ballads. Carmen Miranda, in her first acting role, drew the livelier samba numbers. These she delivered uninterrupted, as one clause in her contract stipulated. The camera was not allowed to cut away for the "reaction" shots typical in most nightclub scenes, a perk that the studio never extended to Alice. What Alice did relish was another set of stunning costumes designed by Travis Banton, including a gold lamé evening dress that the studio announced had cost twelve hundred dollars. With it she wore an elaborate jeweled necklace from Joseph of Hollywood that cost the studio six thousand dollars to rent and insure. Perhaps the most lustrous ensemble Alice ever wore in films—"a scandalous dress [she] fills to overflowing," one critic wrote—it nevertheless imparted a regal quality that she carried off quite well.

Alice had yet another episode of poor health during the filming of *That Night in Rio*. She missed three days of work in December after contracting the flu, and director Irving Cummings had to shoot around one of her biggest scenes.

Nevertheless, Alice appears at the peak of her form in *That Night in Rio*. She was, as the *Hollywood Reporter* noted, "a lovely figure in Technicolor." She looked relaxed, confident, and happy, both in the film and in a set of candid photographs taken on the set. She enjoyed the usual jokes with her costars, playing along when Tyrone Power, visiting the set of his two friends Ameche and Faye, sat in as an extra during the nightclub scene without revealing himself to the director until after the shot was in the can. Early in 1941 Alice signed a new two-year contract with Twentieth Century-Fox, which celebrated her status as the longest-term player on the lot. Since 1934 she had appeared in twenty-six major productions. She knew that she was not just another "pretty young thing whose only talent was looking beautiful." She had grown in confidence, just as her reputation had grown in stature. The latter still outdistanced the former, but her innate shyness was about to get a big boost. Alice had fallen head over heels in love with one of the most unlikely candidates in Hollywood's pool of eligible bachelors. Typically, Alice had gone for yet another bandleader, but otherwise her choice of comedian Phil Harris, the brassy musician from the *Jack Benny Show*, floored her friends and fans alike.

Alice and Phil's low-profile courtship astonished everyone when the news broke at the end of March 1941, four days after the court awarded Alice her final divorce decree and she and her mother boarded the SS *America* for a trip to New York. The story gained currency over the next couple of weeks, yet even those who knew the couple took a pessimistic view of their relationship's chances for survival. On April 20, columnist Jimmy Fidler stated that "the boys are laying nine to five that Martha Raye and Neil Lang never reach the altar... And much longer odds on the Alice Faye-Phil Harris merger." Louella Parsons wisely refrained from making book one way or the other, confining herself to the brief statement,

"There never has been a more whirlwind courtship than that of the popular Alice and Harris. Alice met the very good-looking Harris about two months ago."

In truth, Rudy Vallée had introduced Alice to Phil at the Pennsylvania Hotel many years before, but both had been involved in busy lives revolving around successful careers and less successful marriages. It took a chance meeting at a San Fernando Valley nightclub with Jack Oakie acting as a catalyst to set things in motion. "One night while I was shooting *That Night in Rio,* I was dancing at the old Charlie Foy's Supper Club when Oakie danced by and dragged me over to introduce me to his old buddy Phil Harris..." Alice said, "but nothing happened for awhile." Their dogs finally brought them together. Harris owned a home on Encino Avenue close to Alice's property, and they both allowed their dogs to run loose. The dogs engaged in a tussle one day and Alice's Doberman beat up Phil's Doberman. When he saw his dog, Phil telephoned Alice to chew her out and she bit back, as she usually did when put on the defensive. "It was quite a lovely argument," she remembered, "because we both have a way with words." He suggested that she keep her dog penned, while she countered that if his dog couldn't take it, perhaps his was the one that should be penned. With that, Harris apparently asked Alice out on a date and she accepted. What followed constituted a full-scale assault by Phil. He remembered that for the next three weeks they were together constantly, "one mad round of bridge, visits to each other's homes, fishing, parties, walks about Encino, and a hundred other things that few people associate with Hollywood romance, but that [they] point to in a Main Street love affair."

In very little time, the two had allowed their relationship to develop into something serious. They quietly announced their engagement on May 5, Alice's birthday, but the national press, according to columnist Nate Gross of the *Town Tattler,* remained skeptical. "Theirs was one of the most talked of romances in movieland and writers from California to New York speculated as to whether it was the real thing or just another publicity stunt," he said. Alice, who was in New York shortly after the announce-

ment, wrote Phil a series of letters reflecting how smitten she was, referring to him by the nickname "Fresno." Realizing how much she missed
him, she determined to return to California as quickly as possible, writing, "I think mother will stay on. Her energy is out of the world, so I decided to leave her here. I can't stay on any longer and pretend I'm having
fun without you." Phil told columnist Gross that "I wanted to go to New
York and join her last week, but we couldn't make it as we opened a two-
week engagement at the Los Angeles Paramount Theater. So she came
home and is keeping me company back stage."

On May 12, 1941, three days after the release of Alice's new film,
The Great American Broadcast—a serviceable amalgamation of *Tin Pan Alley*
and *Alexander's Ragtime Band* set against the pioneering days of radio—Alice and Phil, with Phil's friends Mr. and Mrs. Sam Maceo, eloped in Ensenada, Mexico. Alice described the event as a wild, impromptu affair, very
spur-of-the-moment and completely silly. "Nobody remembered the bride's
bouquet, so one of our friends ran across the street to a vegetable patch
and picked a head of cauliflower and a couple of carrots and some lettuce
leaves and made a bouquet out of all that," she said.

In the midst of such a personal whirlwind, one wonders if Alice had
any real sense of who this man was. Just as with her marriage to Tony,
friends warned her away from the guy who seemed so completely her opposite in interests, temperament, and background. Wonga Philip Harris
was born in 1904 in Linton, Indiana, the only child of circus musician Harry
Harris and his wife, Dollie Wright. The name Wonga, which Phil used
through a good portion of his childhood, honored a performing Indian
chief who became one of Harry's good circus friends. Phil spent his form-
ative years in the tiny midwestern town, enjoying most of the things Alice missed growing up in Manhattan: trees to climb and pick fruit from,
open fields and woods where he could hunt, and lakes in which he fished.
The rough-and-ready child became an inveterate outdoorsman, and Phil
spent most of his adult years living from one sporting adventure to the
next. Since Phil's parents continued traveling with the circus and various

tent shows, the boy spent his earliest years living with his maternal grand-parents in a little house on Linton's "E" Street, occasionally spending school vacations on the road with his folks.

Phil's interest in music began early. He took up the drums at the age of nine or ten and never looked back. After the ninth grade, he left Linton to live with his parents in Nashville, and in short order had formed his own band at Hume-Fogg High School. He eventually took to the road himself and spent the next fifteen years traveling all over the world. One of his first bands, the Dixie Syncopaters, joined the Ruth Stonehouse troupe on tour, eventually playing the Princess Theatre in Honolulu. By the late 1920s, Phil had taken his orchestra from California to Hawaii to Australia. In Sydney, he met and married an actress named Marcia Ralston, nicknamed "Mascotte." His marriage did little to detract from his "ladies' man" image, and rumors circulated via various publicity ploys, including that he installed a telephone on his drum stand so he could take calls from admirers while he worked.

By the early 1930s, just as Alice broke into show business, Phil and Carol Lofner—his partner at the time, landed a spot as the house orchestra at the St. Francis Hotel in San Francisco. During their three seasons there, Harris became a star attraction. In May 1932, after dissolving his partnership with Lofner, Harris traded his drumsticks for a baton and took up a successful run at the Coconut Grove in Los Angeles's Ambassador Hotel. That year he also starred in an RKO comedy short called *So This Is Harris,* the "plot" of which turned on Phil's extraordinary appeal with women. It became the surprise hit of the year, winning the Best Short Subject Oscar at the 1933 Academy Awards and cementing Harris's position as a national name.

Over the next several years, Phil Harris's star continued to ascend. In 1933 he and his orchestra headlined in New York, Chicago, and the summer season in Galveston, and he made a second hit film, the feature-length *Melody Cruise.* The next year, he returned to the Coconut Grove as a replacement for Bing Crosby. By 1935 Phil had not only affiliated with the

National Hotel Chain in a deal to play each of their establishments across the nation, beginning with their flagship enterprise, New York's Waldorf-Astoria, but also signed a radio deal with Cutex Nail Polish to broadcast a show that ran for seventy-eight weeks. The "broad-shouldered Max Baer of the bandleaders," as one columnist described him, had worked hard at success and it had come to him over the course of many years. He earned a reputation as a stellar entertainer as well as an astute businessman and knew a good opportunity when he saw one.

Phil Harris was playing a four-month stand at the Palomar Ballroom in Los Angeles in 1936 when the best opportunity of his career approached him. Comedian Jack Benny had a problem with his two-year-old radio program. His sponsor, Jell-O, found the overall format successful, but had determined that his bandleader, Johnny Green, did not reflect the comedian's style. Green, in the meantime, had received an offer from Fred Astaire to join his radio show for Packard.

What the Benny show needed, the pundits decided, was a foil for Jack's character who could introduce some excitement to the program. They envisioned a brash, confident man and hit on the idea of using Phil Harris. Phil debuted on the *Jack Benny Show* on October 4, 1936. In introducing him, Jack Benny described Phil to the listeners as tall, good-looking, and "the kind of a guy you could trust with your best girl . . . if you can trust your best girl." In contrast to his character's extreme behavior in later seasons, the novice Phil came across as confident, polite, and a bit hesitant, although he and everyone else in the cast lost control when Benny, in attempting to call Phil the "romantic type" mistakenly referred to him as the "romantic tripe." Nevertheless, he was off to a good start in a role he would continue to play for sixteen seasons. (Coincidentally, among the popular tunes Phil and his orchestra played in that first program was their rendition of the Alice Faye hit "Sing, Baby, Sing.")

Over the next few years, the Jack Benny troupe, with Phil Harris, grew into one of broadcasting's best-loved and longest-running comedy ensembles. By 1938 Phil had delineated his character's persona as a hard-living, self-loving womanizer, presenting quite a contrast to his elegant predecessor Johnny Green. In his memoirs, Jack Benny attributed the popularity of Phil's character to his complete outrageousness. "Among our mainstays," Benny said, "was the brassiest, most worldly character, played by Phil Harris. He was loud-talking, illiterate, rude, alcoholic, arrogant, boastful, preening himself on the clever ripostes he uttered and never hesitating to compliment himself openly on his bon mots, which he thought superior to my dreary quips. He didn't even pretend to be polite." Such a character presented radio audiences with a respite from the usual stock characters. Phil, Jack Benny, and their writers created something entirely new, completely different. "With all the crassness," Benny continued, "there was a quality of sophistication, or worldliness about the Phil Harris character that made him different not only from every other character on our program, but from every other character of radio. He was completely immoral...Harris radiated vitality, joie de vivre, immorality and a sheer gusto in animal pleasures that made him unique among all the characters is radio."

The contrast between Phil Harris's aggressively hedonistic radio persona and Alice Faye's sweet, low-key sensuality rendered their real-life relationship difficult for the public to comprehend, let alone digest. The suddenness of their elopement to Mexico enhanced the shock value. One publication, the *Radio and Television Mirror,* had even done an extended piece on the Alice Faye-John Conte affair entitled "Alice Faye's Secret Radio Romance," which named Conte as Alice's "second love." It hit the newsstands at the time Alice and Phil headed south of the border. (Conte rebounded quickly, involving himself in an affair with Fanny Brice, whom Alice had portrayed in *Rose of Washington Square.*) Those who knew Phil understood that the radio image was just that. "Phil Harris in his personal life was not like our imaginary Phil Harris," said Jack Benny, "although the character grew out of mannerisms of his natural style, because by nature Phil is a happy-go-lucky, self-confident guy with a zest for experience and plenty of self-esteem." Alice, who must have found these characteristics exceptionally appealing after her years of dealing with Tony Martin's insecurities, put it less analytically. "Phil is not a kid," she said. "He's old enough [eleven years her senior] to know what he's doing and wise enough."

Yet for all his age and experience, Phil may not have realized just what he was doing when he swept Alice off her feet and into the office of Mexican judge Jaime Pardo. Both Phil and Alice realized that their Ensenada elopement was not legal, since Phil's divorce from Marcia Ralston had not become final. They told the press of their plans to "re-marry" in September before they had even left Ensenada. Yet in the midst of the flurry of congratulatory telegrams from industry honchos like William Goetz, Joe Schenck, and even Darryl Zanuck, it became clear that they had misjudged the public's reaction. Columnist Jimmy Fidler took the first shot in an article that appeared a week later: "Mexican 'Wedding' of Alice and Phil Is Meaningless." In it Fidler stated that the couple had two options: either they were not married, which made the attendant publicity silly in his view, or they were married and Phil was a bigamist. Whichever it was, Fidler intimated that it looked like a cheap publicity gimmick to him. "Alice and Phil say they're going to 're-marry' in September," Fidler concluded. "How much nicer, how much more beautiful it would have been had they waited until then. Instead of making a spectacle of an institution that most of the country's millions still hold sacred and important."

Phil and Alice had miscalculated. They may have regarded their Mexican elopement as a lighthearted romp that affirmed their regard for one another, but some members of the public took a different view. Many Americans remained unwilling to tolerate such typically "Hollywood" disregard for the institution of marriage, even from their box office favorite. The backlash became apparent even as Jack Benny's writers incorporated the news into the last two shows of the season. On May 18 announcer Don Wilson identified the orchestra's opening number as "I Tied the Knot in Ensenada," which drew a large laugh from the studio audience. The rest of the show's action centered on Jack Benny's day as he starred in the Twentieth Century-Fox production of *Charlie's Aunt,* which left plenty of room for references to other Twentieth Century-Fox personalities, most notably the polo-playing Darryl Zanuck, heard galloping by on his horse. At the mention of Alice Faye's name, Phil Harris feigned innocence as he asked, "Alice who?" to the audience's delight. Additional references to the couple's marriage followed in Jack Benny's last show of the season, which aired on June 1.

In the meantime, however, studio spin doctors went to work with a series of articles with headlines like "Alice Faye Writes Husband Daily and Plans Wedding." While Phil and his orchestra were on summer tour, the columns stated, Alice worked on *Weekend in Havana,* "but she's also redecorating a house, writing three letters a day to husband Phil Harris, and making plans for her wedding." Another article opened with the fact that actress Alice Faye was in love with her husband and "in two more months the law will let her live with him." Throughout the summer, the studio released stories stressing the fact that despite the couple's love for one another they were living apart until September. "Blonde Miss Faye, Ork Leader Harris Are Marking Time," the stories ran.

Correspondence addressed to columnist Hedda Hopper indicated that the studios did not overreact as they assessed the public's depth of feeling on the subject of Alice and Phil's "wedding." In July, one woman in Kansas wrote to Hopper after hearing her broadcast on the subject, "I wondered if you really know what we think of her [Alice]." She urged a boycott of both Jell-O, which sponsored Jack Benny's radio program, and Alice Faye's films, stating that Alice and Phil had "no right to go to some other country, get married and then come back expecting the public to take it and like it." Hopper responded by pointing out that "in every state in the union except California, they are considered legally married. However, there is a law in the state of California which prohibits a person divorced within this state to be married within the state until one year has elapsed from the date of divorce." Hopper felt, however, that such a technicality did not excuse their actions. "I think the whole matter of remarriage after divorce is taken entirely too lightly," she said.

Ironically, Phil Harris did not take his first marriage any less lightly than Alice had hers. His marriage to Mascotte had lasted almost ten years, and, according to those who knew him, the divorce came as a complete shock to him. Songwriter Sam Coslow, who worked with Phil on an RKO film featuring radio personalities Lum and Abner called *Dreaming Out Loud,* recalled how unprofessional Phil seemed on the day of his big scene. He played a fast-talking city slicker but could not get his lines out. "We thought [Phil] would breeze through his part like an old hand, after years of being featured on Jack Benny's radio show," Coslow said. Instead, Phil flubbed his lines and cost the production half a day's work before the director broke his dialogue into small parts and got the take that way. Neither Coslow nor the rest of the company realized that Mascotte had walked out on Phil that morning. "Phil's musician [later] told me that on the morning of Phil's big scene with us, he awoke to find his wife gone, leaving only a short note to say she wanted a divorce," Coslow remembered. "They hadn't even had an argument the night before. Phil had gone to bed with no inkling of what was to come. Until he saw her note, Phil was still under the impression that he was a happily married man. Phil arrived at the studio in a state of shock."

The article describing the divorce hearing provides no further insight into Mascotte's real reasons for leaving. In fact, except for the difference in names, it reads almost exactly like the article describing Alice and Tony's divorce hearing. Mascotte charged Phil with subordinating his personal life to his career, citing various instances when he refused to take her out in the evenings and declined to include her in his vacations. In the days when women were still raised to be considered ornaments, it would have required an intrepid lady indeed to enjoy Phil's favorite vacation activities, hunting and fishing with the guys. Over the years, the only people who accompanied him regularly in these expeditions were cronies like Bing Crosby. Before many years of their married life had passed, Alice learned that when Phil headed for the wide-open spaces, she could opt instead to spend her time at Elizabeth Arden.

Alice proved gung-ho at first, though. As the couple marked time during the summer of 1941, she spoke glowingly of the outdoor life, comparing herself with fellow actress Carole Lombard, who learned to share her husband Clark Gable's passion for roughing it. "This outdoor business is opening up an entirely new world for me," Alice declared. "I never knew it existed." She asserted that Phil had taken her horseback riding and fishing and she had loved them both. Alice's behavior at the outset of her engagement to Phil contrasted dramatically with her demeanor during her marriage to Tony Martin. The cautious statements, the deferred plans, and the overall reserve had vanished. In a statement that positively gushed, she announced, "I sleep at night. I don't worry about anything, and the whole world looks different." Everything about Alice radiated the fact that she had found the man she wanted.

Alice prepared to give her second marriage her all, hoping to avoid the pitfalls she encountered during her first. She knew exactly what troubles distance and long working hours introduced into a relationship. Fortunately, Phil's role on the *Jack Benny Show* would keep him in Los Angeles for large portions of each year. "If he also can play in some local night clubs he may do that," Alice said. "But he does not intend to go touring with his band. What we want to do is live a normal kind of life. It may be difficult to arrange it, but we're going to make a real try." Children figured largely in Alice's plans for a "normal life," and she also contended that a movie set was not conducive to the health and well-being of a mother-to-be. "I think it is bad for an expectant mother to be working in pictures. Bad for the baby, I mean—pre-natal influence. An actress," she said, "is under a strain and nervous when the arcs go on and I wouldn't want any child of mine to get that kind of start." She expressed her hope to begin a family in the near future and indicated her interest in renegotiating her contract with Fox. "What I am hopeful of," she said, "is getting my contract adjusted so that I'll only have to make one or two pictures a year."

Alice had worked steadily half of her life to provide for her family's needs and reach the pinnacle of her profession. Only she understood what her success had cost her, and only she could decide whether it was worth maintaining. The evidence suggests that it had begun to pall for her even before she thought of remarrying. Now with the prospect of the husband, family, and home she had always wanted, the appeal of making movies diminished even further. She still enjoyed her career and wanted to continue with it. She simply refused to accept the consequences of the pace she had allowed the studio to set for her. The next few years would introduce extraordinary changes into Alice's life, some of them cherished, others wholly unexpected. None of them undermined her determination to create a personal life of her own with a husband she planned on keeping. Phil was now her top priority. Whether Darryl Zanuck knew it or not, Alice's willingness to dance to the tunes he called had just evaporated.

An early photo of Alice in tap shoes.
PHAFC, Linton, Indiana.

A Chester Hale chorus girl. PHAFC,
Linton, Indiana.

Rudy Vallée's vocalist. PHAFC, Linton,
Indiana.

After the car accident, 1933.
Roy Bishop Collection.

The Harlow-style Alice, seated. Author's collection.

Harlow-style close up. Author's collection.

Poor Little Rich Girl. Author's collection.

Tyrone Power and Alice, from *In Old Chicago*. Author's collection.

Alice, Tyrone Power, and Don Ameche, from *Alexander's Ragtime Band*. Author's collection.

Alice, Bill Faye, and Rudy Vallée. Author's collection.

Alice and Tony on their wedding day, 1937. Roy Bishop Collection.

Alice and Tony at a premiere, 1937. Roy Bishop Collection.

Alice and her family, left to right: Sonny (Charles), Alice, Mama Faye, and Bill, 1938. Roy Bishop Collection.

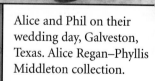

Alice and Phil on their wedding day, Galveston, Texas. Alice Regan–Phyllis Middleton collection.

June Havoc, Alice, John Payne, and Jack Oakie in *Hello, Frisco, Hello*. Author's collection.

Impatient with the routine?
PHAFC, Linton, Indiana.

Alice with Dana Andrews in *Fallen Angel*.
Author's collection.

The Jack Benny troupe on the Orient Express,
1948. PHAFC, Linton, Indiana.

Publicity for the radio show at the Encino house: Alice, Jr., Alice, Phil, and Phyllis. PHAFC, Linton, Indiana.

Cast of the Phil Harris–Alice Faye Radio, sponsored by Rexall.

Autographed Pfizer publicity photo, dual image, 1984. George Ulrich Collection.

CHAPTER 9

Movies and Motherhood

Weekend in Havana, shot during the summer in which she bided time between weddings to Phil, became one of Alice's happiest movies. It showed. She found herself surrounded with her favorite costars, including John Payne, Carmen Miranda, and Cesar Romero. Zanuck also assigned director Walter Lang, with whom she worked in *Tin Pan Alley,* to the project. Alice also felt confident in the role she played. "It gave me another comedy role, that of a slightly common Macy's salesgirl," she said. "I was born in New York, so I was familiar with the lingo. She refers to her travel 'brochoor' and is constantly using her hands like many of the people I knew from my girlhood in Manhattan."

Alice's comfort level on the film had nothing to do with Darryl Zanuck. He crafted the script for *Weekend in Havana* with Betty Grable in mind, only assigning the role to Alice in the final story conference. Further demonstrating his attitude about the interchangeability of stars is the fact that he directed that the leading man's role be written for Henry Fonda, changing it a month later to Don Ameche, then finally assigning it to Payne. Zanuck's real preoccupation with the project centered on authenticity, which experience had finally taught him was key to avoiding the derision of Latin American audiences. He sent a Technicolor crew to Havana to shoot local settings, stating "we want to get all the wonderful atmosphere we can get... to give us an atmosphere of authenticity and color."

Zanuck's newfound desire to avoid the pitfalls of cultural representation set *Weekend in Havana* apart from the preceding Latin American romps in a small way. Otherwise there was little to distinguish this film from any of the others beyond the ongoing popularity of its stars. Alice Faye remained Fox's top musical star, while Carmen Miranda had achieved sixth place in the lot's rankings by 1941. The assets of both were set off to good advantage by a series of vibrant costumes designed by Gwen Wakeling. Each also enjoyed a monochromatic moment in the film. In a supper club scene, Miranda wore a dazzling white dress dripping with fringe, while Faye played a scene in the casino in an elegant black lace gown and mantilla. In the same way that Scarlett O'Hara's mourning dress leapt off of the screen in *Gone with the Wind*'s Technicolor Virginia Reel sequence, Faye and Miranda's ensembles kept them firmly in the viewers' eyes as they moved across the lush tropical color palette of pre-Castro Cuba.

Alice had every reason—and more so as it turned out—for looking as well as she did in *Weekend in Havana*. Toward the end of filming, she discovered she was pregnant. "Some people have said that I looked better in that movie than in any other," she said, "so maybe pregnancy agreed with me." What also agreed with Alice was the prospect of putting an end to the matrimonial limbo she and Phil had occupied throughout the summer. On September 20, California Superior Court Judge John Beardsley signed the final decree granting the Marcia Ralston-Phil Harris divorce. That evening in Galveston, Texas, Justice of the Peace James A. Piperi remarried Alice and Phil before a small group of friends at the Hotel Galvez. Maceo acted as best man for Phil and Alice, just as he had in Tijuana the preceding May.

A week after their Texas wedding, the Harrises released the news of Alice's condition to the press. Jack Benny and his writers made a great deal of on-air hay from the fact that their show's resident hedonist was about to become a father. Twentieth Century-Fox received the news less enthusiastically, accompanied as it was by the additional statement that Alice planned to spend at least a year away from the rigors of filming. "I have always felt that motherhood is infinitely more important than any career," Alice said. "Now I expect a baby, I have decided to drop my screen work." This news threw a monkey wrench in the studio's plans for a Gay Nineties costume piece called *My Gal Sal*, which they had already publicized as an Alice Faye vehicle. Louella Parsons estimated in her column that Alice's decision cost the studio three million dollars, but just as they had for *Down Argentine Way*, Fox recast the film, awarding the role to another up-and-coming star named Rita Hayworth.

Alice clearly intended to continue working but just as clearly intended to make marriage and motherhood her main priorities. How she would bend the studio to her way of thinking over the long term remained to be seen. "Definitely and absolutely I am continuing my career, as soon as my baby is old enough for me to leave," she told Louella Parsons. "I am the restless type and I know I won't want to be idle long... my only thought now in retiring is to give the baby every chance. I was so tired and nervous and making a picture takes so much out of an actress." Parsons questioned Alice's decision to pass on *My Gal Sal*, which she could have completed in four months. Film historian Roy Hemming asked the same question, suggesting in his book that Alice was simply fed up with costume musicals. Alice's response to Parsons was that she was far too worried that something might go wrong: "I felt if anything happened just because of a movie I would never forgive myself. In addition to keeping myself well I didn't want to let the studio down... but I just didn't feel right about it." Alice's motives might have been more mixed than she let on either in print or to herself. She might actually have wanted to dodge *My Gal Sal*, but there was little the studio could do about it. For the duration of her pregnancy Alice occupied an unassailable position.

As a result, the circumstances following Alice's September wedding to Phil could not have contrasted more sharply with those following her marriage to Tony Martin. For the first time in her career, Alice's time was her own. Instead of racing back to the studio and plunging into her normal work schedule, Alice actually had time to honeymoon. She was free to rest, to arrange her new home, and to travel with Phil, yet her hiatus from films did not keep Alice out of the limelight. In October she accompanied Phil and the Jack Benny troupe to New York, where they broadcast the season's opening shows. She even became part of the program's story line. In one episode Jack's parsimony leads him to arrange for his cast to share berths as they traveled by rail between Los Angeles and New York. He finds himself in a dilemma, however, when Phil reminds him that Darryl Zanuck, upon whom Jack fawned at every opportunity, would not be pleased to hear that Jack forced one of his biggest stars to travel in such conditions.

Jokes notwithstanding, Alice fully enjoyed the freedom to travel with her husband. "I have never been so happy in my life," she told Louella Parsons. "Phil is so sweet and thoughtful and I am determined that we will never be separated." Her pregnancy did little to deter her from accompanying him. "I am a little worried now because the Jack Benny show may travel this year, and if the Bennys travel it will mean that Phil will have to go to Florida," she said. "Naturally I will go with him, but I would prefer to remain in Los Angeles, where my mother lives—and where I will have the baby, but you can depend on it—if the Benny show emanates from Florida, I will be there with Phil." Alice also indulged in a little radio work herself as she awaited the arrival of her baby. On February 9, 1942, she appeared in *Lux Radio Theater's* version of "City for Conquest," based on the boxing drama that had starred Jimmy Cagney and Ann Sheridan.

Otherwise Alice differed very little from other expectant mothers around the nation. This was especially true after December 7, 1941, when the Japanese attack on Pearl Harbor changed the personal plans and expectations of the entire United States. Hollywood mobilized almost immediately, but there was little Alice could do in her current condition. On the other hand, Phil, as a member of the cast of the nation's top radio show, could participate in war bond sales and visits to military bases. Eventually, he and his band enlisted en masse in the Coast Guard, forming an entertainment unit for the men stationed out of Catalina Island.

Alice stayed quiet throughout the spring of 1942, as world events shook the foundations of ordered society, Alice stayed quiet. She made one radio appearance and otherwise awaited the arrival of her child. In the second half of May, well past her presumed due date, Alice underwent a caesarian section at Los Angeles's Cedars of Lebanon Hospital. Dr. Stanley Imerman delivered Alice Faye Harris Jr. at 2:38 A.M. on May 19, after a difficult session in which he nearly lost both the mother and the daughter. The baby's umbilical cord had been wrapped around her neck. Phil, described by the newspapers as "very much on edge" as he played an engagement at the Biltmore Hotel, arrived at the hospital and had to wait another hour before the attending physician allowed him a glimpse of his new daughter.

News of her baby's birth allowed Alice briefly to resume her place in the spotlight, receiving congratulatory telegrams from studio friends and associates. Newspapers heralded the news, giving stories of Alice Jr.'s arrival a patriotic spin. "Alice Faye Fan Mail Trebles," wrote columnist Bill Wickersham, who attributed the increase to the interest of servicemen around the globe. "Many of the soldiers, sailors, marines and flyers were solicitous in offering [Alice] advice as regards names for the little stranger, how to take care of herself, and frequently assured Alice that she's still their favorite star." But if the GIs (or studio bosses) thought that the baby's safe arrival meant Alice would hotfoot it back to the studio, they were in for a disappointment. Alice had other ideas.

Alice later wrote in her memoirs that she didn't accept any movies for a year so she could be with her baby, but either her memory proved faulty or she deliberately chose to revise the fact that she chose to spend the first three months of her new baby's life away from home. In 1942, Phil had arranged to go on a three-month national tour during the *Jack Benny Show*'s summer hiatus. Alice accompanied him, leaving the baby in Hollywood, in the care of a nanny and Mama Faye. At the beginning of August, Louella Parsons briefly mentioned in her column that Alice planned to return to Fox to begin shooting her next film, *Hello, Frisco, Hello*, in early September. Shooting had to be postponed until November, however, when Alice suffered some sort of birth-related relapse and nearly died while she, Phil, and the orchestra were in New Orleans.

When Alice had recovered sufficiently to return to Twentieth Century-Fox late in the fall, she found a studio undergoing abrupt changes. Sidney Kent, who acted as president of Fox Film Corporation and played a key role in its reorganization during the Depression, died of a heart attack in 1941 at the age of fifty-six. The same year, the Board of Directors of Twentieth Century-Fox named Spyros Skouras of Fox Metropolitan Theaters as head of the company. Skouras's appointment filled the vacuum at the top of Fox's East Coast operations, but shortly thereafter a vacancy occurred in California. Darryl Zanuck, patriot and enthusiastic veteran of World War I, asked for a leave of absence from Fox to serve in the military. The board granted his request, and he left for his stint in the European theater of operations in the middle of 1942. Bill Goetz, customarily the least involved of the three Twentieth Century partners, assumed Zanuck's role as head of production for the duration.

Alice returned to the lot in November, greeted with an impromptu gathering on the soundstage of her new project, *Hello, Frisco, Hello,* a thinly disguised remake of her previous film venture *King of Burlesque.* Her reaction—"Everybody seems to remember me. I didn't think they would"— might have sounded a bit guileless in peacetime, but her eighteen-month leave had seen major changes in personnel. Alice found herself surrounded with a host of new faces, and, had she delayed her return much longer, she might not have even known her costars. As it was, the celebration heralding her return also served as a farewell party for John Payne, Tyrone Power, and Cesar Romero. As quickly as the three men could complete work on their current films (Payne with Alice in *Hello, Frisco, Hello*) they would report to their bases: Payne as an Army private, Power as a Marine pilot, and Romero as an ordinary seaman in the Coast Guard.

Senior members of the cast and crew of *Hello, Frisco, Hello* greeted Alice warmly, happy that one of their favorites had returned to work.

She remembered, "I was beautifully treated by everybody, especially the cameramen [Charles Clarke and Allen Davey] and the costume designer [Helen Rose]." She was reunited not only with her customary costar John Payne but with her old friend Jack Oakie as well. Oakie behaved true to form, keeping the set lively and the company in stitches. "Jack Oakie was a riot," Alice recalled. "When we were on *Hello, Frisco, Hello,* we got word from on high that 'a new young virgin' named Jennifer Jones was on the lot to play in *Song of Bernadette* and we were all to behave ourselves. I can't imagine what they thought we'd do," Alice continued, "but you know Oakie. He went around saying, 'Okay, let's gedda loada dis virgin!'"

Darryl Zanuck, who had been developing the script for *Hello, Frisco, Hello* with his usual fervor just before his departure for the army, had conceived the notion of using one exceptional song to carry the movie along. The remaining numbers, for the most part, would be old standards from the turn of the century. He even toyed with the idea of purchasing the rollicking title number from the Clark Gable–Jeannette MacDonald film *San Francisco* from M-G-M. After his departure, negotiations for the song continued. One studio executive, conducting a story conference on *Hello, Frisco, Hello* for Bill Goetz, stated why it was "important that we buy the song 'San Francisco' from M-G-M. We want to use it as the theme song throughout, but we will hear only the *music*. The words will probably be sung under the main title but nowhere else."

The music would have to carry *Hello, Frisco, Hello,* which had little else in terms of innovations of plot or dialogue to recommend it. Still, viewers could rely on the sheer entertainment value of the film's musical selections. Lionel Newman, the head of Fox's music department, knew Zanuck's fondness for nostalgia pieces and over the years had conducted extensive research into the popular tunes of bygone eras. Staff composer Harry Warren, who helped in the selection of numbers, remembered that all but one of the dozen or so pieces that made it into the final cut of the movie represented Newman and his department's skillful reorchestrations of such old favorites as "Silvery Moon," "Grizzly Bear," "Sweet Cider Time," and

"Why Do They Always Pick on Me?" Newman's artful reliance on musical memory, combined with the lush costumes of Helen Rose and the charming performances of Faye, Oakie, and Payne, resulted in an above-average period piece ideally suited for audiences facing the early, anxious days of America's involvement in World War II.

The exception to *Hello, Frisco, Hello's* reliance on old standards was a new number composed by Mack Gordon and Harry Warren called "You'll Never Know." The poignant ballad, sung in what *Variety* called Alice's "quieter, more composed, very effective" new style, became an instant classic forever associated with Alice Faye. Rarely has a song's message combined so effectively with its singer's interpretation to strike a chord in the emotional life of a nation. Its timeliness was profound, reaching audiences in the spring of 1943 as America's citizen soldiers continued to head overseas in ever-increasing numbers. Alice's tender, almost plaintive, rendition of tune and lyrics epitomized the sentiments of an entire generation of young people sacrificing their personal desires to the exigencies of war:

> You went away and my heart went with you.
> I speak your name in my every prayer.
> If there is some other way to prove that I love you,
> I swear I don't know how.
> You'll never know, if you don't know now.

"You'll Never Know" spent twenty-five weeks on *Your Hit Parade* and became Harry Warren's biggest sheet music seller. The Motion Picture Academy awarded it the Oscar for Best Song of 1943. Ironically, many of the accolades heaped on the song did not extend to Alice, presumably owing to Twentieth Century-Fox's preference that their stars not record. Alice never made a commercial recording of "You'll Never Know" in the 1940s—not even a V-disc, the 78-rpm records created especially for distribution among the armed forces. Her association with the number that became her signature extended only to a few radio performances, her rendition in *Hello, Frisco, Hello,* and a second film performance during her cameo appearance in the 1944 release *Four Jills in a Jeep.* These few performances, however, apparently cemented the connection between Alice and "You'll Never Know" in the minds of the public. Even after her death in 1998, it remains the song for which Alice Faye is best remembered. One can hardly invoke the tune without mentioning the performer, and vice versa.

After *Hello, Frisco, Hello,* Alice began work on one of the most interesting, and certainly the most thoroughly examined, films she ever made, *The Gang's All Here,* directed by Busby Berkeley. Originally entitled *The Girls He Left Behind,* it provided wartime escapist fare at its most extreme. The patriotic dialogue—"Mr. Mason, if you had a beard, you'd remind me of my two favorite people: Santa Claus and Uncle Sam"—is contrived to the point of pain in many spots, while the plot provides only the thinnest of excuses for the lavish musical numbers.

The meager plot line remains a minor point in an extravagantly entertaining production that, if profits are any indication, sated the public's appetite for delicious girls, tuneful music, telescoping sets, and beautiful costumes. Some Faye fans have argued that "essentially it is not good Faye. Pregnant with her second child through much of the shooting schedule, she did not feel well, and at times seemed almost bored." Others have cited *The Gang's All Here* as one of Faye's most memorable performances. She moves through the film with a decided twinkle in her eye, as if she knows what director Berkeley is up to and finds it pretty darn amusing. Her air of camera-consciousness, from her knowing wink in the opening number to her cocked eyebrow in the final sequence, serves a dual purpose. It enhances the air of unreality Berkeley sustains throughout the film as he moves in and out of production numbers, and hints that none of this nonsense should be taken seriously. Her poise and detachment also provide the viewer with a welcome respite from the film's surrealistic elements. Alice's calm beauty (rarely did she look lovelier in films) is the counterpoint against which the rest of the film's frenzied activity plays.

The Gang's All Here differed from Alice's previous films in that, because it was made in 1943 under Bill Goetz, it did not undergo the intense scrutiny to which Darryl Zanuck subjected all of Twentieth Century-Fox's big budget projects. In fact one wonders what might have become of Berkeley's innovations had Zanuck had a hand in the film's development. Initial drafts of the script elicited only a cursory inspection and apparently resulted in only two significant changes. The first involved casting. Executives initially assigned the ingenue role of Vivian Potter to Fox starlet Linda Darnell, but reassigned the part to Sheila Ryan.

A second, more significant, change affected the movie's grand finale. Film buffs will remember that the conclusion of *The Gang's All Here* represents an almost psychedelic production sequence, done to "The Polka Dot Polka" and a reprise of "A Journey to a Star." In it chorines wield chartreuse and pink disks one moment and red neon hoops the next as they maneuver through Berkeley's contemporary vision of patterned color and motion. Its excitement stems from what Martin Rubin calls, "one of Berkeley's furthest excursions into unfettered abstract spectacle, ending with a total breakdown of spatial and realistic restraints." During the penultimate moments of the sequence, in fact, the screen is devoid of human beings. Berkeley reduces it to a giant kaleidoscope, in which Alice's face appears several times against a background of blue lamé cloth. A quick turn of the lens, however, eliminates her from the screen completely, after which a fantasia of polychrome geometry holds sway.

In contrast, the original conclusion, conceived by Fox screenwriters, represented a nod to the war effort, and a not-very-innovative one at that. It revolved around a "spectacular patriotic number, presenting a glorified military wedding," according to production notes. "The backdrop a colonial type of church with a broad flight of steps and columned portico, soldiers form a canopy of crossed swords, the bridesmaids coming through as the curtains part. They wear red, white and blue costumes, and carry bouquets that can be used to form a flag for the finale." Clearly, Berkeley, who thrived on cinematic innovation, was not about to mar his vision of the possibilities of Technicolor by filming something so banal.

The Gang's All Here constituted Berkeley's first foray into Technicolor, excepting the two-strip Technicolor process used on his very first film, *Whoopee!* It was also his first film for Twentieth Century-Fox. Because he was new to the studio, Alice remembered, "I wasn't as close to him as Henry King, Irving Cummings, and Walter Lang, who were my pet directors at Fox." Calling him "that master of outrageous production numbers," Alice said, "Berkeley had a problem with alcohol, but he was very clever, had a lot on the ball." *The Gang's All Here* contained at least two of Berkeley's most remarked-upon sequences. *New York Times* critic Theodore Strauss commented, "Mr. Berkeley has some sly notions under his busby. One or two of his dance spectacles seem to stem straight from Freud and if interpreted, might bring a rosy blush to several cheeks in the Hays Office."

Film students everywhere will immediately recognize the number to which Strauss referred. It was Carmen Miranda's rendition of "The Lady in the Tutti Frutti Hat," which featured a titillating routine in which several dozen chorus girls, in tropical shorts and halter tops, created unusual patterns by waving a collection of papier-mâché bananas, "as big as canoes," as Alice put it, along with some equally oversized strawberries. On one level, the use of the giant fruit merely exploited to good advantage the Technicolor process. On another level, one indulges in analysis at one's own risk.

Just as Alice's screen persona contrasted with that of her flamboyant costars, so too did her solos provide a break from the climate of excess pervading much of the rest of *The Gang's All Here*. Berkeley presented her ballad "No Love, No Nothin' (Until My Baby Comes Home)" with unusual restraint, creating a showcase for the singer that benefited from an absence of distracting camera movements or outrageous imagery. Similarly, Alice's initial rendition of "A Journey to a Star," set against a moonlit sky and framed by the protective railing of the Staten Island ferry, succeeded as a result of the performer's talent and style rather than her director's. More than any other actor in *The Gang's All Here*, Alice emerges as a three-dimensional human being rather than a caricature. Berkeley uses Alice to anchor the rest of the film's action, which critics and audiences noted with approval.

Fans hungry for feature-length Faye would have to make do with *The Gang's All Here* for the foreseeable future. Sometime in the course of the film's seven-month shooting schedule, Alice discovered she was expecting another baby. She waited until filming had concluded before making the news public. Around the same time, Alice also disclosed another piece of news. On August 31, 1943, Louella Parsons's column carried an item stating that Alice intended to retire from the screen. Parsons noted that Alice's decision came at a particularly bad time for Fox, because Gene Tierney and Betty Grable—who had married trumpeter Harry James in Las Vegas on July 5 of that year—were already out on maternity leave. Studio bosses found themselves in a bind. As if the loss of their top male stars to the war effort had not wreaked enough havoc within Twentieth Century-Fox's production schedule, along came an outbreak of pregnancies to decimate their ranks of female talent. As later events proved, the timing of Alice's announcement was undoubtedly intentional and worked as a potent threat. Within weeks, the press alerted concerned moviegoers to the fact that Alice had just concluded negotiations on a new contract with the studio.

Alice's new deal could not have been more to her advantage. It provided for her performance in one motion picture a year, with the option for a second left entirely to her discretion. She maintained to the press that she had to threaten the studio in order to win more time at home with Phil and the fifteen-month-old Alice Jr. Rosalind Shaffer reported that month after month of 6 A.M. calls for work on *The Gang's All Here* left Alice little time to see either her child or her nightclub-performing husband. Alice admitted to feeling not only miserable but fearful that the pattern of her marriage to Tony Martin might be reasserting itself. Nevertheless, when Shaffer asked Alice if she would prefer to devote her time exclusively to home life and children, Alice apparently responded, "Heavens, no; on the baby's days with me, when the nurse is off, I go limp and my knees tremble, I'm so nervous with her. She's so energetic I get completely worn out, so that I can hardly crawl upstairs with her when bedtime comes." Alice asserted that she had worked too hard to get where she was in films and that she could never give it up. Making movies was too much a part of her. Clearly, then, what Alice was looking for was some kind of balance as she worked to maintain the career and the marriage and family that were all so important to her. Limiting her screen work seemed to offer the best solution.

Another advantage the new contract offered was leaving the choice of any subsequent films, after she fulfilled her one-picture-a-year obligation, up to Alice. She had become increasingly interested in doing dramatic roles, for two very good reasons. The first, of course, was that it typically took only eight to ten weeks to shoot a drama, whereas musicals, like *The Gang's All Here,* which took seven months to film, required enormous time commitments as dance routines were blocked, songs were recorded, and elaborate scenes requiring large numbers of people were staged. She based her second reason on some very sound advice her mentor, director Henry King, had given her. "I was getting more mature [Alice turned twenty-nine nine days after her second child's birth]," she said. "Henry King—who *was* Twentieth Century-Fox as far as I was concerned—whispered in my ear that I should ease myself into other kinds of roles." Alice remembered King telling her, "It's time now for you to do something more serious: you're growing up." As a Fox veteran of eleven years, Alice knew all too well that droves of fresh, beautiful talent arrived in Hollywood everyday and that continued performances in musicals would only accentuate her age. If she wanted to extend her career, she needed to diversify the kind of roles she undertook. It is entirely likely that she hoped that her new contract would allow her to do just that.

Of course, the point was moot in the winter of 1943 and the spring of 1944, as Alice awaited the birth of her second child. Phil was away on a Victory Bond Tour in Victoria, British Columbia, when the baby arrived by caesarian section at St. John's Hospital in Santa Monica on Wednesday, April 26, 1944. Only after Phil returned and was able to see his new baby girl did the Harrises decide on her name: Phyllis Wanda. In the meantime, Alice, whose best friend, Betty Scharf, had seen her through the delivery, could not have felt lonely from the sea of communications that began washing in. Jack Benny, Harry Brand, Joe Schenck, and Darryl Zanuck all cabled their congratulations. Alice's brother Bill and his wife, the Scharfs, Harry Brand, Joe Schenck, Bill Paley of CBS, and Phil Harris's orchestra all wired flowers to Alice.

Two messages that arrived during Alice's hospital stay stand out. One was a birthday card from Joan Blondell saying, "To the sweetest in the world from Aunt Sissy." Blondell had won the role of Aunt Sissy in the dramatic classic *A Tree Grows in Brooklyn,* after the studio determined that it could not delay filming long enough for Alice to play the part (Alice's copy of the final shooting script was dated May 1, 1944). She took the loss philosophically, at least according to Hedda Hopper, who quoted Alice as saying, "There'll be another part any day now." It is hard to imagine, however, a character more ideally suited to Alice, whose own impoverished childhood as the daughter of a New York city policeman made her a perfect fit. Such a sympathetic and highly visible character could have provided Alice with exactly the right transition to dramatic roles she was looking for, as well as provide her fans with a portrayal they could relish despite the fact that she did not sing. Instead, it was Blondell who reaped the rewards of an outstanding portrayal for which she will always be remembered.

The second noteworthy message delivered to the hospital came from a studio employee named Rufus Le Maire, who announced, "We can now begin immediately production of *The Dolly Sisters,* with your two children playing the star parts." How Alice reacted to this jest regarding her next film assignment is unknown, but subsequent events indicate she couldn't have been entirely pleased. *The Dolly Sisters,* which was scheduled to begin in June 1944, constituted yet another one of Zanuck's nostalgic musicals.

Zanuck, who had returned from the armed services in June of 1943, re-sumed his role as creative guru with his usual vigor. He immediately went to work on *The Dolly Sisters,* a film loosely based on the lives of the famous identical twins Jenny and Rosy Dolly, theatrical and nightclub performers in the 1910s and 1920s, "one or the other [of whom]," as the story confer-ence notes reveal, "was always reported marrying a millionaire, or break-ing the bank at Monte Carlo, or winning half a million francs, or auctioning off a million dollar collection of jewels." Invoking, inevitably, his successes with *Alexander's Ragtime Band* and *Tin Pan Alley,* Zanuck forged ahead with the usual plot devices and characterizations that had served him so well in the past. Alice Faye, he decided on August 26, 1943, would be very good for the part of Jenny.

Alice had other ideas. Although the studio announced that she would play the role opposite Betty Grable, a column in July 1944 hinted at trou-ble. "Somehow there's a feeling that Alice won't be on hand when the bell rings," it stated, attributing her reluctance to a "case of another ac-tress gone completely domestic." Louella Parsons stated flatly, "There is one thing I do know—and that is that you fans need never expect to see 'The Dolly Sisters' with Betty Grable and Alice Faye! Neither Betty nor Alice believe it is wise to make a picture together." While Parsons quoted Alice as saying, "I think Betty should have her own pictures and I should have mine. We can do much better that way," Alice later admitted that was not her reason. Obviously acting on Henry King's advice, she said, "I wanted to do more mature things. I refused to do *The Dolly Sisters.* June Haver did that, and it was the first time I was persnickety. In those days you did as you were told." She said that she remembered asking Darryl Zanuck about expanding the kind of roles she undertook but that he "turned her down with a polite but patronizing air, and argued that you have to give the public what it wanted and it wanted Alice Faye singing and dancing." Zanuck had good reasons, of course. Alice Faye and Betty Grable musicals generated extraordinary revenue for the studio, and he was not about the jeopardize Fox's most dependable income stream just to humor what he considered an actress's whim. Nevertheless, Alice said, "After all those years of light and flimsy musicals—pleasant enough and good entertainment, but hardly anything you could call meaty—I longed to sink my teeth into a script that had some bite to it." Clearly Alice and Zanuck had reached an impasse. The studio recast *The Dolly Sisters* and began production, fans wondered if they would ever see Alice Faye in films again, and Alice quietly went about the business of introducing a new baby into her home in Encino in what she referred to as a state of "semi-retirement."

Over the next several months, the press dutifully kept the public informed about Alice's plunge into domesticity. Hedda Hopper wrote in her memoirs that "the catastrophe that the studios invited was the death of glamour, which had filled the air we breathed," yet she participated fully in that process. Hopper blamed studios for the fact that "stars were asked to stop wearing the golden glow of gods and goddesses and look like plain folks, as homey as apple pie and lawn mowers. You couldn't pick up a magazine without coming across publicity shots of Betty Grable out marketing, Bette Davis washing dishes, or Alice Faye changing diapers." It was quite a charge for someone who in September 1944 crafted a story for *Modern Screen* based on the domestic life and habits of the Harris family, complete with photographs of baby Phyllis and the toddling Alice Jr. In the piece, Hopper described the house and its grounds, the decor of the nursery, and Alice's choice of lullabies to sing to her daughters. Hopper painted a picture of domestic bliss that anyone might find it difficult to tear away from, concluding her article with the prophecy that "you'll be seeing Alice again when the studio can sell her an idea. She'll have to be roused out of the contentment and happiness which is apt to make her feel there's no hurry about picking up a career again. If it weren't for the fan letters that keep pouring in . . . I think she might never go back at all."

Fans eager for a different version of what was going on with Alice had only to look across the newsstand to September's *Photoplay,* where Hedda Hopper's arch rival Louella Parsons had published her own story, "You Wouldn't Know Alice Faye." In contrast to Hopper's spin, Parsons described a vibrant Alice eagerly looking forward to resuming her career. "I know now, Louella, that I will never give up my work. I told the studio I would make only one picture a year, but if I get another good story, don't be surprised if I make two or three." Reiterating this theme, Parsons also ran a piece in her column stating that Alice had no trouble with the studio. Parsons quoted her as saying, "I had a nice satisfying talk with Darryl Zanuck and he agreed that it would be foolish for me to make a picture until we have a good story. I won't object to a drama or musical just so I feel it's right. I really want to wait until January before I return to work. I'm enjoying the babies and I couldn't see Phil if I was busy."

Alice and Zanuck apparently resolved their standoff by the end of 1944, when the studio released the news that Alice had signed a new contract. Fans could expect to learn of her newest "important story" assignment once she returned from a bond tour with Phil and Jack Benny. Another six months elapsed, though, before the studio finally announced that Alice would step before the cameras again, a delay Alice insisted was their own fault. Of the dozens of scripts the studio had sent her for consideration, none contained the breakthrough role she desired. "I read every one," she said. "But it was the same old story: singing and dancing and a final clinch and that's all." Alice was determined to win her point: she would either appear in a drama or not at all. "I was tired of being a Technicolor blonde in musicals that didn't even pretend to have a plot," she said. She and the studio, as she put it, "settled down for a friendly suspension, and I settled down at home and had a wonderful time."

Alice enjoyed her domestic hiatus in Encino while her fan mail poured into the studio. It acted as a constant reminder to Twentieth Century-Fox that public interest in Alice continued unabated. In fact in the two years since she appeared in films, it had actually grown. By December 1944 the number of fan letters Alice received doubled from 1943—an increase attributable to the number of lonesome servicemen eager to see her return to the screen. Betty Grable's famous over-the-shoulder cheesecake pose won her the title of queen of the pinup girls in the hearts of

American soldiers and sailors. Alice symbolized something less saucy but perhaps more significant. Millions of men torn away from their young wives and babies took an active interest in Alice's domestic life. Columns describing her home in the suburbs, its fruit trees and chickens, the children's pink and blue nursery, and her contentment as a housewife seemed tailor-made for the war effort. Pictures of the pretty young mother with her two charming babies reassured Americans scattered across the globe that the "normal" life they were fighting for still existed.

CHAPTER 10

Goodbye Fox

America would win the war in Europe before Alice Faye won her war with Twentieth Century-Fox. Faced with the prospect of losing his Alice-based revenue altogether, Darryl Zanuck ultimately conceded. In mid-July 1945, word trickled out through the columns that Alice had returned to Fox. She had chosen to appear in a modern drama directed by Otto Preminger called *Fallen Angel*. Preminger had scored a huge hit the year before with the now-classic mystery drama *Laura*. The combination of *Laura's* popular appeal and critical acclaim apparently acted as the catalyst prompting Alice to select *Fallen Angel* as her first dramatic role. Fox producers were hoping for a successor to *Laura*, which cost just over one million dollars to film and grossed more than double that. Alice must have been swept along by their optimism when she stated that *"Fallen Angel* was just what I had hoped for."* Everyone's expectations for the film ran high. In addition to Preminger, the film's company boasted actors Dana Andrews, Charles Bickford, Anne Revere, Bruce Cabot, John Carradine, and the luscious young Linda Darnell. Behind the camera was the same crew that worked with Preminger on *Laura*, award-winning cinematographer Joseph LaShelle, assistant directors Sam Wurtzel, George Schaefer, and Tom Dudley, art directors Lyle Wheeler and Lee Fuller, and stylist Bonnie Cashin.

Zanuck originally considered Olivia de Havilland, Jeanne Crain, or Anne Baxter for the role of June Mills. He demonstrated the flexibility with which Preminger credited him, however, when Alice expressed interest in the role. Presumably he was prepared to do anything it took just to put her back to work. He gave Alice carte blanche not only on the choice of scripts (she had turned down thirty-five, according to one studio press release), but in other matters as well. For example, Zanuck allowed Alice her choice for a leading man. She opted for Dana Andrews, who had met with stunning success in *Laura*. "She had seen *Laura* and she liked me in the part," said Andrews. "She said, 'I'll do this one if you can get Dana Andrews.'" She was also allowed to choose the film's theme song. It would be played repeatedly on the jukebox in the diner where much of the film's action took place, and Zanuck inserted a scene in which she sang a complete version along with the radio in order "to justify Alice Faye" in the part. Songwriter David Raskin, who wrote the theme song to *Laura,* recalled arriving on the film's set with a selection of three or four compositions, which he played for Alice. She selected the tune that came to be known as "Slowly" once Kermit Goell wrote a lyric.

In their headlong pursuit to re-create the circumstances that had contributed to the success of *Laura,* everyone at Fox, including Alice, seemed to overlook one essential ingredient—the script. The story of *Laura* gave moviegoers a fascinating view of Manhattan's now-extinct café society. Not all of the characters presented were attractive, but they were sophisticated, affluent, and glamorous. They drank cocktails in the afternoon, smoked incessantly, read and wrote the columns, radio programs, and advertisements that drove modern American life. Propelling the action was a nicely conceived mystery revolving around the death of a beautiful and successful "career woman," whose professional and romantic adventures are detailed as the story unfolds.

In contrast, the story of *Fallen Angel* takes place in the tawdry environs known to every denizen of small-town America: the wrong side of the tracks. The reviewer for the *Los Angeles Times* summed it up best by calling it "a somber murder story with repellant characters." Dana Andrews played Eric Stanton, an out-of-work publicity agent who washes up in small-town California. At a roadside greasy spoon, he encounters and becomes obsessed with a beautiful waitress with her eye on the main chance, Stella, played by Linda Darnell. He is not the first. The diner is inhabited by a collection of faded lotharios ogling her every move, including a vending machine salesman, a retired New York detective, and the diner's owner. Stella agrees to marry Eric if he can come up with enough of a bankroll to give her the respectable life she desires. Eric decides, improbably, that the easiest means to his end is to woo, marry, and then bilk June Mills (Alice Faye), the almost-past-her-prime daughter of the town's wealthiest citizen. Before Eric can ditch June, however, Stella is found bludgeoned to death in her rooming house, and Eric must find the real killer before he is wrongfully accused. In the course of solving the mystery of Stella's death, Eric is redeemed by the love of June and commits himself in earnest to their marriage.

The drifter, the tramp, the old maid, the dirty cop—the people inhabiting this drama were as familiar to moviegoers as the headlines of their local newspaper, and provided little of the escape, glamour, or sophistication audiences required from their weekly trip to the movies. Gritty film noir productions would become increasingly popular in the postwar years, but it was not a genre in which anyone expected to find Alice Faye. A more plausible choice for her transition to dramatic roles would have been the one that got away, Aunt Sissy in *A Tree Grows in Brooklyn*. (*Hollywood Reporter* had suggested Alice play the mother in that film, Katie Nolan, the part that went to Dorothy McGuire.) Films produced by other studios in 1945 included several gently dramatic characters, Jimmy Stewart's wife in *It's a Wonderful Life* and the Virginia Mayo part in *The Best Years of Our Lives* among them. Had these been available to her, such roles might have offered Alice the challenge she sought in the context of a more promising script.

Years of working in movie musicals probably did little to hone Alice's skills as a critical judge of dramatic screenplays. Her experience could have qualified her to give graduate courses in song plugging, dance, and general showmanship just a few miles from the studio at UCLA. It may have been her very lack of experience, combined with her keen desire to broaden her skills, that led her to choose *Fallen Angel* above all other scripts. Dana Andrews, who seemed to move with ease between musicals (*State Fair*) and dramas (*The Best Years of Our Lives* and *Laura*), hated *Fallen Angel* from the start. "When the script was sent to me, I said 'no,'" he remembered. Preminger called him in to discuss it. "He didn't understand why I didn't like it," Andrews said. "I said, 'In the first place, I don't think it's a picture for Alice Faye, but beside that, I don't like the part for me. I don't like the picture, It's terrible. It's in bad taste, it's unbelievable. I just can't see it at all.'" Eventually Fox threatened him with suspension. "My agent said, 'You won't work for a year, probably, or six months anyway. It can't be that bad.'" Left with such a choice, Andrews reluctantly played the part.

Alice, in contrast, eagerly awaited the beginning of filming. She must have found the lure of working with Otto Preminger irresistible. The prestigious director, a protégé of Max Rienhardt's, had come to America from Vienna at the request of studio head Joe Schenk in 1935. He promptly fell out with Darryl Zanuck, who fired him, and spent the next several years working on Broadway. *Laura* was one of the first films he completed upon his return to Hollywood. Preminger was a taskmaster with a reputation for brutality. Alice's *Fallen Angel* costar Linda Darnell found him "stubborn, humorless, and terrifying on the set," according to her biographer, Ronald L. Davis. But Alice seemed to relish the challenge. She had told several columnists that she hoped to create something with *Fallen Angel* that her daughters could be proud of. She seemed to have faith that Preminger could help her achieve that goal and willingly submitted to his demands.

How Preminger reacted to the news that he had been assigned a musical star for a film noir thriller is best left to the imagination. His previous encounters with the big studio system left him with a good grasp of Hollywood reality. "Freedom of choice was in rather short supply at Twentieth Century-Fox under Darryl Zanuck," he said. "I was turning out a string of films following rules and obeying orders not unlike a foreman in a sausage factory. I went from picture to picture, usually taking with me a band of regulars on whom I had come to depend: *A Royal Scandal* was followed by *Fallen Angel*, which was followed by *Centennial Summer*." Preminger understood, as he wrote in his autobiography, that the demands for "product" in large volume required "a certain practical adjustment to the realities of budget, shooting schedules, and available talent, all of which had to be attuned sensitively to the personality of the studio head." Zanuck, for example, struck him as someone with "no empathy for women in film. He liked women and was happily married, but women's problems and feelings bored him totally."

Alice arrived on the set for the first day of shooting with her usual case of jitters. She was not scheduled to perform but explained that she was there "just to get the feel of how movies are made again." The next day she fumbled around a bit, stumped by a simple scene in which she closed a door, but quickly adjusted to the routine. As filming progressed, a studio release indicated she particularly appreciated Preminger's style of rehearsing a scene as a whole, as one would do on the stage, then filming the whole sequence in one take. She later admitted, "Preminger was very tough to work for. He didn't care what he said or how he hurt you. He got a lot out of me, though; I was proud of the performance I turned in." Alice maintained her sense of optimism throughout filming. Dana Andrews, still disgruntled over the assignment, remembered having long conversations with her in which he would ask why she was doing the movie. "Oh, you wait and see," he recalled her saying, "this is going to be great. It's terrific."

Alice had faith in *Fallen Angel's* director, its cast and crew, and especially her own performance. She felt confident that her decision to follow Henry King's advice to hold out for more diverse roles was the right one. She may even have believed that Zanuck's tacit endorsement of her choice of *Fallen Angel*, its leading man, and its theme song reflected his support of her decision. Her ability to handle more mature roles meant, at least to her, that she could vary her performances and no longer endure a steady stream of labor-intensive musicals. It meant, too, that she could extend her career beyond the age limit imposed by ingenue and songstress roles. Additionally, her new contract with the studio guaranteed the balance of work and home life so important to her. She looked forward to entering an entirely new phase of her career; *Fallen Angel* would mark its beginning. The delicious sense of anticipation that this line of reasoning produced would have sped Alice along her way to the screening room when she finally got word that the final cut of *Fallen Angel* had been assembled and was ready to view. She settled herself into a chair and took a deep breath as the lighting dimmed and the film began.

Some time later, Alice emerged, stunned, from the studio screening room. Her heart pounded in her ears as she grappled with an overwhelming sense of betrayal and rage. The edited version of the movie on which she had pinned so many of her professional hopes was a travesty. More than that, it was a vendetta, one in which Zanuck had clearly had a hand. It didn't necessarily surprise her that Zanuck had chosen to recut the film in order to build up Linda Darnell. Favoring younger talent in the editing process was a ruthless but common practice in the big studio system. That he did it at her expense rendered it a bit harder for Alice to swallow. Why had he bothered to lure her back to the studio at all if that was his attitude? And beyond that lay the one aspect of the whole situation that Alice found the most incomprehensible. Zanuck had obviously decided to eliminate as many of Alice's scenes as possible, to the detriment of the movie. More than a dozen scenes, most of them essential to the exposition of the story line and the delineation of the characters' motives, were gone. Two more had been drastically cut. In its current state, the movie made no sense whatsoever. Yet Zanuck intended to release it.

As she stood there Alice realized that somewhere on the cutting room floor or in a Twentieth Century-Fox dustbin rested her rendition of "Slowly." That did not directly impact the way the story unfolded, but taking a mental inventory, Alice counted among the missing episodes those in which she and Eric meet, her character's personality and motives are revealed, and their relationship unfolds. They were important scenes that she felt contained her best work. It was pure butchery. What would an audience make of a film that contained dialogue referring to action that was not there? Did Zanuck resent her that much that he would confuse and alienate the public just to humiliate her?

Alice Faye's Irish was as up as it had ever been in her life. "If that's what Zanuck is going to do to me, I'm not going to stay around and be slaughtered," she thought. Alice realized then that Zanuck would never give her a chance. "I couldn't see myself staying there and coming in every day at 6 o'clock in the morning and staying all day long doing one picture after another that I wasn't happy doing," she said. "I knew I was capable of doing something better and they wouldn't give me a chance... because Zanuck wasn't going to give." Dana Andrews remembered that "when she saw the picture, she made the statement, 'I'll never do another picture.'"

Squaring her shoulders and lifting her chin, Alice turned her back on the screening room and walked to her car. She paused for a few moments to gather her thoughts and scribble a note to the studio head. She later said that she would take the secret of the contents of that note to the grave with her. "That goes with me," she told *American Movie Classics* interviewer, Richard Brown. Alice proved as good as her word. She never revealed what she had written to Zanuck, although many years later she indicated that it was unprintable "even today." One can only imagine, given the raw state of her emotions, what Alice wrote. "I was terribly upset," she said. "I felt the film had been ruined." She took a few more minutes to rummage around in her handbag for the keys to her dressing room, taking a few deep breaths as she did so. As her car turned toward the entrance gates, she told the driver to pause while she asked the security guard to deliver her note to Zanuck in the morning. Alice then tossed him the keys to her dressing room. "I drove right out through the gate and I didn't even go to my dressing room to collect my personal belongings," she said. As her car slid slowly out of the studio gates and into the flow of traffic, Alice slid out of the studio cocoon and into the flow of real life. She would not make another movie for sixteen years.

When Alice Faye walked out on Darryl Zanuck and her contract with Fox in 1945, neither her life nor her fame came to an end. She simply ceased appearing in films. She had money in the bank, besides which Phil made more than enough to provide for their family. Her maternity leaves had prepared her for life apart from the studio. She felt more capable of coping with real life than many stars she knew. If no other studio would use her, and she suspected that Zanuck would convince them not to, then her husband and daughters generated enough activity to keep her occupied. What many perceived as the end of her career seemed to represent to Alice a host of new beginnings. "It wasn't hard at all to walk away from movies because I walked into a new way of life," she later recalled. The loss of a career in films often proved too daunting for Alice's peers in the industry to deal with successfully, and many would founder when they discovered themselves adrift as the big studio system broke up in the fifties. Alice, however, remained true to the memory of the spunky heroines she had depicted in films. She moved into her new life with determination, learning about housekeeping, cooking, driving, and generally how to manage her own life. Simply coping outside of the studio environment, one calculated to foster almost total dependency among its star performers, proved a challenge. "We were protected and coddled so much," Alice said. "Our every whim was catered to by studio employees. We didn't have to lift a finger, except to do our jobs in front of the cameras." Alice acknowledged that many actors, including herself, had found the "star" treatment oppressive and struggled to find an outlet, "something, anything to keep themselves from going crazy."

In her 1990 book *Growing Older, Staying Young*, Alice described her transition from films to real life in the following terms: "So the end of

Alice Faye, movie star, marked the beginning for Alice Harris, housewife and mother. I segued from one career to another without missing a beat." Yet by presenting it in such cut-and-dried manner, she undervalued what a massive change it must have represented. Her tendency to forget the details of her past led her to sum up this period in her life as one she "struggled with, but survived." Alice employed those scant four words to convey a shift in lifestyle that led many of her counterparts to drink, divorce, and occasionally total ruin.

The key to Alice's successful adjustment to life outside of the studio limelight was twofold. First, she not only initiated her change in circumstances—firing the studio rather than being fired—she embraced it. Grief and frustration over *Fallen Angel* acted as the catalyst. "I just couldn't see where I was going. I couldn't see anything coming for me but the same old dumb things, while I wanted to do something more ambitious," she explained to a reporter in 1985. "I left and I didn't care. I really didn't." Alice's underlying sense of what she wanted from her life led her a step further. "It's probably hard for outsiders to understand, but all that glamour is just veneer, coating to a pretty hard life," she wrote in her book. "It was a fairy tale in that my every wish was granted and I seldom had to lift a finger, and all around me were handsome men and beautiful ladies. But it was also hollow, repetitious, and confining, and you really never could be your own person." For the remainder of her life Alice expressed publicly only one regret about her abrupt decision to leave Fox, wishing she had been more astute about financial matters. Otherwise, she said, "I once heard Bette Davis say her career was all she had left. I'd hate for that to be true for me, and if I stayed, it might have happened."

The second component of Alice's adjustment to her new life was, paradoxically, encountering and dealing with her own fame. Once she walked out of the studio gates, she ran headlong into the Alice Faye of the publicists' creation; the buffer separating Alice from her public ceased to exist. "I never realized until I got out of movies that I was anybody different," she stated. "Up until then I had spent all my time with the folks in the industry working." She felt she did not deserve the fame she had achieved, and among her peers she tended to be retiring. She cherished the sanctuary of her dressing room at the studio and preferred to remain on the outer fringes at parties, finding it difficult to circulate. Her friend Judy McHarg remembered talking with Alice's mother at a Hollywood party when Alice and Phil arrived. Mama Faye said, "Watch and see where Alice sits," and sure enough, Alice made a beeline for her mother and stayed by her side for the rest of the evening.

Away from movies and learning to run her own household, Alice came face-to-face with members of the general public in everyday settings for the first time in her adult life. "Once I learned to drive and could go to the market on my own, why people would crowd around me . . . I had no idea other people felt that way about me," she remembered. Such tangible demonstrations of her popularity acted as a double-edged sword. On one hand they reassured Alice that she remained a popular performer in the minds of the public, validating the fame she remained unsure of. Yet Alice also admitted that her encounters with people's perceptions of who she was, perceptions manufactured by industry publicity machines, often rattled her. "People at the market would ask me for my autograph and scare the living hell out of me," she recalled. "But I weathered it. I got to talking to everybody and the first thing you know it all worked itself out."

Also reassuring to Alice, in the wake of her departure from Fox, were Zanuck's attempts to lure her back into the fold. Zanuck learned, to his dismay, just how valuable an asset Alice remained. Letters flooded the studio demanding more Alice Faye films, just as the reviews from *Fallen Angel* began to appear in print. In December 1945 the *Los Angeles Times* generally panned the film but remarked that Alice's first performance in a dramatic assignment was "rich with promise." Another reviewer praised Alice while simultaneously criticizing the script, "Alice does not sing in this picture, but her speaking voice is as richly husky as ever, even though she doesn't have much to say." Only Louella Parsons disagreed, possibly to curry favor at Fox. Adhering to the party line of the studio bosses, Parsons asked in her column, "What is it with our musical comedy darlings like Miss Faye, Judy Garland, and Deanna Durbin that they want to do drama?" She accused Alice not only of jeopardizing her natural appeal in such a role but also of photographing poorly. Parsons concluded her piece by pleading, "Dear delightful Alice, please come back in a musical comedy quick. That's where we love you and where you are enchanting."

Zanuck had wasted no time in showering Alice's Encino home with scripts he hoped would lure her into reconsidering her decision. Believing that he could win her over, he sent copies of screenplays for *The High Window, Kitten on the Keys,* and *Mother Wore Tights.* At one point, he even sent Alice a car, a truly extravagant gesture since automobiles remained a rare commodity in the months immediately following the surrender of Japan. She returned them all, politely but firmly, and resisted the temptation to rebut in the press such items as Louella Parsons's October announcement that she would definitely return to musicals. "A fling is all right," said Parsons, "but Alice belongs in those great big Technicolor musicals with tight-fitting dresses and big picture hats." Alice thought otherwise.

Alice made her decision and demonstrated that she intended to keep it, much to the bafflement of Hollywood at large. "It wasn't that my career was finished or that I was over the hill or that nobody wanted me anymore," Alice said. "It was simply that I was tired of it all." Eliminating movies brought Alice the freedom to explore her world and consider her options, without jeopardizing the well-being of her mother and brothers, whom she continued to support. In the absence of a six-day workweek at the studio, Alice now had the leisure to craft a life that would guarantee the control she needed to hang on to what was dearest to her. Phil headed her list. "I was never really wild for a career," she reminded a reporter in 1959, "and after I married Phil it became a rat race. When I wasn't working, he'd be out on the road with his band. When he came back, I'd be making a picture. He'd sit around and not know what to do with his time.

We couldn't go out at night because I had to get up early to go to the studio." In their four years together, Alice repeatedly demonstrated her marriage took priority. Now she intended to focus on it earnest.

But first she had to learn to function outside of the Twentieth Century-Fox cocoon. Describing herself as "this dumb broad who'd been working in the dark all these years," Alice set out to become a housewife. The first step involved learning to drive, which, in turn, meant overcoming her long-held anxiety about automobiles. Two road accidents with Rudy Vallée, one resulting in serious injuries and the other a less traumatic plunge into a ditch in Maine, left her nervous about driving. Phil bought her a car, which she approached with understandable trepidation and mastered with mixed results. "I drove right through a neighbor's gate," she said. Eventually she grew skilled enough to get around a bit, but never grew entirely comfortable with driving.

Alice concluded that learning to market would be the next step in her transformation. Nothing in her impoverished urban childhood, or her subsequent pampered career, prepared her for the task of facing down wily grocers fully aware of her inexperience. Neither did her lack of familiarity with most aspects of cooking. "There weren't big markets like Safeway in Encino then," she recalled. "They were all privately-owned markets and they'd sell me the stuff they couldn't sell anybody else. I had one heck of a time." Unfamiliar with the volume of produce many meals required, Alice bought too much of one thing and not enough of another, arriving home with unusual quantities and combinations of foodstuffs.

Once the war ended and domestic help became available again Alice's family did not suffer unduly from her awkward attempts at managing a home. They eventually employed a staff of four to look after themselves and the property. There was a series of nannies, beginning with Sissy and ending with Bea, to look after Alice Jr. and Phyllis, as well as a cook, a houseboy, and a groundskeeper. Alice came to enjoy marketing and, eventually, cooking. She appears to have given up, however, on the more pedestrian aspects of housekeeping. Phyllis remembered kidding with her about laundry. "I used to say 'Mother, why don't you go put the towels in the washing machine,' and she'd say, 'Where is it?'"

Simply supervising the kind of household the Harris's enjoyed in Encino would have proved absorbing work. After so many years on the road, Phil had become a property owner with a vengeance. "For seventeen years I played one-night stands, slept on buses, never voted, never belonged to a club, or participated in community activities," he said. Once he landed the spot on the *Jack Benny Show*, he could put down roots. "Suddenly I was a citizen," he remembered. The Harrises' sprawling property in the still-rustic San Fernando Valley boasted a fully occupied duck pond, chicken coops, fruit trees, a stable for two or three horses, a ram named Clyde, and a Malaccan Cockatoo. The bird tended to speak in profanities and didn't care for Alice. "It liked men," Phyllis remembered. "It would whistle at mother whenever she went to the pool, and would say 'Goddammit, Phil's home!' whenever Daddy came by." The house sat at the top of a long drive that wound past the stables, then the pool and cabaña area, and a cookout area with an immense barbecue. The bottom of the pool was decorated with tiled fishes and a large octopus just at the point where it began to get deep. "Where the octopus lived was as far as we were allowed to go," Phyllis remembered. Jack Benny's daughter, Joan, wrote in her memoirs of a similar creature at the bottom of the pool of her parents' home in Beverly Hills, which is perhaps where Phil got the idea.

At this time, before any additions, the Harris home consisted of a main floor with a living room, dining room, kitchen, and playroom with a guest bedroom. The children's room was located on this floor at the end of a hallway with a view that overlooked the property. The master bedroom and dressing rooms for both Phil and Alice were upstairs, over the playroom. Phyllis remembered that her mother's dressing room was done in a flesh-toned pink. "I used to sit in her dressing room when she was getting her hair and makeup done when she would go places," Phyllis said. "It was very feminine, just like you would envision in a movie of that era of a lady's dressing room. Her dressing table had a skirt, her chair had a skirt. Very feminine."

In 1948 Phil decided to add a wing for the children, although it really constituted a totally separate house connected to the main house by a catwalk over the driveway. He devoted the first floor to a music room, which included space for his 3,000-volume record collection. The second floor included rooms for the girls, their nanny, and another kitchen. Phil designed a catwalk, with flower boxes affixed to the sides, leading from the children's house to a small sitting area outside Phil and Alice's bedroom in the main house. "It was neat when I think back on it," said Phyllis. "At the time I didn't think it was so neat and I used to run across it as fast as I could go." Phyllis recalled that, as a rule, the girls ate with their nanny in their quarters, and didn't go over to the main house too often. "It was separate," she said.

Alice worked to overcome the issue of her helplessness and met housekeeping challenges as they arose. She also began to relax and enjoy the freedom that came with her new status as an ex-movie star. In what she later admitted was probably an overreaction, for example, Alice stopped wearing makeup for a while. "When I walked off the Twentieth Century-Fox lot for the last time, I got home and washed all of it off my face, and said 'No more!'" she remembered. She eventually returned to makeup but kept it light. She found herself rich in free time and luxuriated in average day-to-day diversions that most postwar wives and mothers took for granted. "We'd go shopping a little bit, or go to the market, or just do little things around, go out to lunch. Whatever," said her friend and neighbor Betty Scharf. "Nothing drastic or big or anything. Just being together was the important thing for us."

Alice and Phil enjoyed entertaining, for the most part preferring to gather with close friends for a quiet dinner. Phil's friend Eddie McHarg, who had been a member of Alice and Phil's Ensenada elopement party, had recently married, and he and his wife, Judy, were frequent guests. "I got a kick out of Alice," Judy remembered, "but I was nervous when I first met her, around the time she was pregnant with Phyllis. Alice said, 'Phil, doesn't Judy look like Mascotte?' I thought, who's Mascotte? When I found out she was Phil's ex-wife I thought, 'Uh oh, I'm in trouble.'" Alice apparently overlooked the resemblance, because she arranged for a screen test for Judy at Fox and provided practical advise for dealing with Zanuck. "If you wind up in Zanuck's office," Judy remembered Alice telling her, "Just keep moving around the desk and asking about his wife, Virginia."

Since neither Alice nor Judy cooked—"opening a can of Franco America spaghetti was about our speed," Judy said—Eddie and Phil took over in the kitchen. "They would call each other and ask what they were cooking for dinner that night," Judy remembered. "The boys would work in the kitchen and we'd sit in the living room drinking cocktails." Phil's specialties included noteworthy black-eyed peas and a finely textured corn bread that those lucky enough to taste it always compared to layer cake. The Harrises also hosted parties occasionally, and Judy remembered one that included Peter Lorre, who arrived with his own pitcher of absinthe martinis. Mostly, though, Phil and Alice tended to keep things simple, and at both their Encino and later their Rancho Mirage homes people from Bing Crosby to the housekeeper always entered through the back door.

Probably the most liberating factor of Alice's new life away from the movie screen was her ability to travel with Phil. The peripatetic bandleader may have established some deep roots in Encino, but the nature of his profession demanded a lot of time on the road. Both Alice and Alice Jr. had joined Phil and the Jack Benny troupe for a bond and hospital tour in the spring of 1945. The toddler managed the trip as far as Chicago, then returned home with a nurse while her parents did a series of one-nighters that lasted two months. Two year's later, in April of 1947, Alice and Phil joined Jack Benny, Phil Silvers, and Frank Sinatra in helping their friend Sam Maceo stage a benefit for the victims of the Texas City disaster, the explosion of a French freighter loaded with ammonium nitrate fertilizer, in which six hundred were killed and four thousand injured. Such excursions gave Alice everything she wanted: she could enjoy the company of her husband and reap the rewards of her fame without recommitting to the treadmill existence she had known at the studio. Because of Phil's career in radio and music and the opportunities it afforded, Alice established a pattern in which she neither occupied the spotlight nor strayed too far from it.

Alice apparently enjoyed an open invitation to accompany the *Jack Benny* radio show on its frequent personal appearance tours in the east. "Two or three times a year, the show would be broadcast from New York," Benny's daughter Joan remembered. "They took the Santa Fe Chief, using an entire Pullman car for the cast, the writers, the director and producer." Alice joined the group in the capacity of spouse rather than performer, but the show's writers, still delighted at the contrast in personalities the Harris marriage presented, often worked her presence into the script in some form or another. Jack Benny's junkets eventually afforded Alice her first opportunity to visit Europe, something she had never been able to do while tied down to the studio. In the summer of 1948, Benny assembled a troupe to accompany him to London, where he played the Palladium, and then cross the channel to Europe to entertain American troops still stationed there.

The Benny troupe left New York on the *Queen Elizabeth II* on July 1, 1948. Joan Benny remembered this as something of a honeymoon trip for the Harrises. "After throwing confetti and waving good-byes to our friends on shore, the tugs backed us out of the pier, and we all went up on deck as we sailed out of New York harbor past the Statue of Liberty," she wrote in *Sunday Nights at Seven*. "Then Phil and Alice disappeared below to their cabin, never to be seen again until we docked five days later."

Ingrid Bergman and Joseph Cotten were among the notables in attendance when Jack Benny opened at the London Palladium after their arrival. Alice, who intended to stay in the background as was her habit, spent her time shopping for china and silver with which to decorate her home. On opening night at the Palladium, though, she wound up performing impromptu versions of "You'll Never Know" and "Alexander's Ragtime Band," after the audience spotted her and applauded thunderously until she took the stage. "They were crazy about her in England," said her daughter Alice Jr., who remembered a later trip to London with her father when the public assumed Alice Faye had accompanied them. "They were lining up down in the lobby of the hotel and banging on the door all night. Dad kept saying, 'I know this isn't for me,' and I said 'I know it's not for me either,' and we found out they thought Mom was there. She loved England and went often, and they loved her."

Jack Benny closed at the Palladium at the beginning of August, and the troupe departed for Germany. Benny's manager and agent Irving Fein wrote that "on this trip, which was my first Army tour with Jack, he brought his wife, Mary Livingstone, Phil Harris and Alice Faye, Marilyn Maxwell, and the left-handed guitar player Frank Remley, who achieved fame on the radio show as Phil Harris' hard-drinking buddy." Phil and Alice compiled a scrapbook of candid snapshots taken during this portion of the trip, and the photos reveal a happy, relaxed group enjoying such lighthearted moments as photographing the star of the production standing out in a field by the Autobahn minus his trousers.

Their itinerary was a tight one, outlined by orders from a General Clay, who placed them on "temporary duty not to exceed seven days for the purpose of entertaining troops," as they traveled from Frankfurt to Kronberg, Wurzburg, Grafenwohr, Nuremberg, and Munich. They stayed for two nights at Kronberg Castle and crammed as much sightseeing into their schedule as rehearsals and performances allowed, then spent the remainder of the trip doing one-night stands. On Saturday, in Nuremberg, the trip turned somber as they toured the Palace of Justice, where the famous war crimes trials were held. Photographs, captioned, then later removed from the book, indicate that the group undertook a side trip to Dachau as well. By Sunday, August 8, their whirlwind tour concluded as they boarded the Orient Express bound for Paris and a refreshing stay at the Hotel George V.

The press inadvertently supported Alice's ability to enjoy her celebrity in small doses while traveling and looking after her home, by continuing to publish stories about her. In November 1947 the nation awoke to the news that Alice had broken her arm playing charades in the Encino home of radio writer Dick Chevillat. In August 1949, the *Saturday Evening Post* ran the not-so-newsworthy information that *Alexander's Ragtime Band* was the role Alice Faye liked best. The real fuel driving the continued interest in Alice's activities, however, was the ongoing possibility of another screen appearance. The tension created by Alice's unresolved relationship with Twentieth Century-Fox fed these rumors, and columnists seized upon them gleefully through the rest of the 1940s and on into the 1950s. Many of these rumors had a basis in fact, as the pile of scripts in Alice's collection attests. Over the years Zanuck, as well as a handful of hopeful but minor independent producers directed a steady stream of screenplays to Alice in the hopes of luring her back and cashing in on her evergreen box office appeal. In 1948, for example, Fox still received more than fifteen hundred fan letters a month addressed to Alice or to the studio pleading with them to use her in another film. In 1950, Louella Parsons announced that Fox had sent Alice a screenplay entitled "Jackpot" but that Alice had turned it down in favor of returning to Europe with Phil and Jack Benny.

Alice enjoyed her freedom too much to consider a comeback in these films or even more dubious vehicles such as "Stars in Their Eyes," the story of a musical star who retires from the stage to be a real wife to her orchestra–leader husband, to name only one of the story treatments in her collection. Alice knew she deserved more than just to grow old in a perpetual cycle of musicals. It had hurt her badly to see what Zanuck had done to *Fallen Angel,* and she was not interested in repeating the experience under any circumstances. She wanted to live her life away from movies and discover what it might hold. In the years to come, she would do just that.

CHAPTER 11

Return to Radio

As Alice forged her new life, she discovered that through Phil and his work a new niche awaited her in a medium with which she was entirely comfortable: radio. She and Phil had begun performing together on *Fitch Bandwagon,* sponsored by Fitch Shampoo. The program was initially conceived as a Sunday afternoon bandstand series on NBC to showcase popular music and feature newcomers in the summer months. In 1943, the show shifted its format, dropping the summer band formula and instead signing a big name for an entire season. For the two seasons between September 29, 1946, and May 23, 1948, it featured Alice and Phil and gradually evolved into what would be the Harrises' own radio show.

A family-based sitcom along the lines of *Ozzie and Harriet,* the *Phil Harris-Alice Faye Show* endured a rough start. It paralleled the real lives of the two stars, with characters such as Alice's brother Bill, played by Robert North, and the Harris daughters, played by Jeanine Roose, who had portrayed Alice Jr. on the *Jack Benny Show,* and Anne Whitfield as Phyllis. The cast also included a streetwise grocery boy named Julius, played by Walter Tetley, a veteran of the long-running *The Great Gildersleeve.* Alice and Phil played their public selves, just as they had done on *Jack Benny.* But they quickly learned that the hedonistic character Phil had created for *Jack Benny* did not adapt well to a domestic comedy. Phil eventually fired the show's first two writers because their jokes, based on *Jack Benny's* version of Harris, skirted too close to the edge of propriety for a family show. Writers Ray Singer and Dick Chevillat succeeded them and resolved the problem to a certain extent by building up the character of Frank Remley, the left-handed guitar player in Phil's band who accompanied Phil and Alice and the Bennys through Europe in 1948. Audiences knew Remley, who had been with Phil's band since at least the early 1930s, through years of jibes directed at him by Jack Benny. Benny's agent Irving Fein remembered that "Remley became so famous on the Benny radio show that when Phil Harris started his own radio program with his wife, Alice Faye, the writers created the character of his sidekick Frankie Remley. Remley had the best laugh I've ever heard and was even a better audience than Jack," Fein said, referring to Jack Benny's well-known appreciation of a good joke. The only problem was that the real Remley couldn't play on both shows, nor was he a professional actor, so Phil cast actor Elliott Lewis in the role of Remley.

Shifting the role of reprobate from Harris to Remley did not constitute a 100 percent solution, as one radio historian noted, because "as a settled-down husband and father, Harris lost some of the comic vinegar on his own show, where he was portrayed as a semi-literate stumblebum." But it worked well enough. The character of Frank Remley, as writer Ray Singer recalled, "was the backbone of the show—he spoke for us. He became in effect Phil Harris on the Harris-Faye show—a crude, hard-drinking guy that Harris, now a family man with two young daughters, could no longer play on the air." Together the Harris and Remley characters created by Singer and Chevillat provided a solid comedic foundation of the program. "Elliott and I were like clockwork," Phil recalled. "It was so easy—it just used to flow." Jeanine Roose, who portrayed Alice Jr. on the show, remembered Elliott Lewis as a "totally extroverted wild man. He and Phil would play off each other all the time, they had such good rapport, and a genuine liking for each other."

Alice, who critics agreed was pleasant enough but did not possess the comic flair of Gracie Allen or Marian Jordan (of *Fibber McGee and Molly*), acted as counterpoint to the mayhem created by Harris and Remley. Her role in the program's various situations was to introduce the voice of reason into her husband's preposterous high jinks—and to sing. Audiences who clamored for Alice's return to the movies could now tune in once a week and hear, if not see, their favorite star give voice to such popular standards of the day as "Buttons and Bows" and "Baby, It's Cold Outside," as well as various numbers she had introduced in the movies. Phil and Alice brought in their old friend Walter Scharf to act as musical director. He selected the tunes, sometimes creating new arrangements, and guided Alice to the best of his ability, vetoing numbers he thought inappropriate. For example, one week Alice elected to sing "You Make Me Feel So Young," an idea Scharf promptly quashed on the grounds that she was not old enough to sing it.

Alice's image as the glamorous movie star who gave up her career to be a housewife and mother became firmly established throughout the span of the radio show, and was reinforced each week with the credit line "Miss Faye appears through the courtesy of Twentieth Century-Fox." Within each show references to her "former" stardom abounded. Her purported wealth, depicted as separate from and far greater than Phil's (who, after all, worked for the parsimonious Jack Benny) served as fodder for constant gags and plot lines, as did various components of her famous background. At one point, for example, when Alice and Phil learned that Rudy Vallée had reached a low point in his fortunes, they invited him to appear on the show to re-create the story of Alice's discovery. Magazine profiles of Alice throughout this period also reinforced the notion of Alice's contented domesticity, devoting the majority of space to news of her children and her progress with cooking, and making very little of her radio work. Alice perpetuated the notion that she was simply a housewife, downplaying to the point of practically ignoring her new career. In one article alone she talked about having quit work, referred to her place as being at home, and gave herself the title of "Alice Faye Harris, Housewife," all despite the fact that the interview was conducted at the radio studio, during rehearsals, immediately prior to a promotional tour she planned to take with Phil.

The widely publicized notion that Alice's only profession, once she left films, was as a homemaker, seemed to reflect not only the postwar nation's view of what was appropriate behavior for a former working woman but Alice's as well. By pursuing a career as a radio entertainer within the context of her husband's work, she pulled off a neat trick, whether she realized it or not: she continued to perform professionally without seeming to, garnering extra points for being a good wife and mother. This theme served the radio show well. Alice playing a movie-star-turned-housewife provided the writers with a host of potential story lines, and diametrically opposed the premise of another classic comedy, featuring Lucille Ball. Much of the humor of *I Love Lucy* turned on the idea of the title character plotting and conniving to gain a toehold in show business, only to be thwarted by her traditionally minded husband, who refuses to consider the notion of his wife with an independent career. Alice Faye's character willingly chose to forgo her career in show business. That she was free to resume film work anytime she chose introduced an underlying element of tension into the program, which the writers carefully avoided exploring.

The show introduced the idea that Alice might return to films only once, in an episode entitled "Movie Star," which aired in April 1949. The story deals with a scheme hatched by Darryl Zanuck and Spyros Skouras to lure Alice back into pictures by offering a small part in the film to Phil. Alice, who has read the script and likes it, nevertheless promises Phil that she will not return to pictures unless he asks her to. Declaring that he will never ask her to, Phil steps away to answer the ringing phone and the audience overhears Phil's side of the conversation:

Hello. Yes, this is Phil Harris. Oh, Twentieth Century-Fox. I was about to call you. Look, Bub, I want you to stop sending scripts to Alice. I don't care who you want to put in a picture . . . Who? . . . Little old mass of ringlets, me? . . . Oh, Darryl, this is so sudden!

Alice, recognizing the ploy for what it is, attempts to save Phil from an inevitable letdown by talking him out of doing the screen test. He insists, and the rest of the program presents the comedic possibilities of a ham like Harris trying to maximize his one-line part, with the underlying subtext that ruthless studio moguls will do anything, even hire Phil Harris, to get Alice back. Indignant at the studio's treatment, Phil decides against a screen appearance, he and Alice return home, and the audience has had a good laugh at the expense of Twentieth Century-Fox.

Alice seemed to subscribe to the belief that, having given up her screen career, she no longer worked, regardless of the fact that Phil produced the radio show, she starred in it, and both of them were obliged to maintain national profiles and work hard to promote it. "As a kid, I remember that they were very busy," said her daughter Phyllis, "always coming and going. I was too little to know the difference, but they were doing something all the time." Alice's work on the show itself was limited to Friday and Saturday rehearsals, followed by Sunday's final dress rehearsal and broadcast, three not-so-full days, compared to the six days of up to twelve hours apiece that films demanded. Perhaps the contrast led her to feel sincerely as if she were not working. "I am crazy about radio," she told Louella Parsons in June 1949. "It's so much easier." Easy or not, the radio show was still a job, which depended on Alice as much as any other member of the cast. The extracurricular promotional work it required demanded even a larger portion of her time. Between 1946 and 1954, Alice and Phil appeared at charity functions supporting Boys Town, the March of Dimes, and the Red Cross, rode on their own float in the Hollywood Santa Claus parade, endorsed a number of household products, including Scotch Tape, and took annual trips to New York to meet with sponsors.

Possibly the highlight of all Alice and Phil's personal appearances occurred in January 1949, when they participated in the gala celebrating Harry Truman's inauguration, along with such entertainers as Abbott and

Costello, Jack Benny, Edgar Bergen, Lionel Hampton, Dick Haymes, Lena Horne, George Jessell, Gene Kelly, Margaret O'Brian, Jane Powell, and Phil Spitalny and the Hour of Charm All-Girl Orchestra. They broadcast their radio show from the East Coast, building the story around the celebration. Walter Scharf remembered an electric evening, the first inaugural gala to be televised, with an immense program of twenty-four acts requiring an intermission at 11:00 P.M. and the grand finale, "The Star-Spangled Banner," taking place sometime after 2:00 A.M.

Regardless of the work, excitement, and demands the radio show placed on her time, or the fact that it was a serious job, Alice clearly considered herself neither a "working woman" nor a "star." Jeanine Roose remembered her as "just a genuinely nice, centered human being ... a very caring nurturing woman," who asked after Jeanine's bumps and bruises, gave her lovely Christmas gifts, and otherwise maintained a certain reserve, preferring to stay in her dressing room. "She wasn't a star in the sense of putting on airs or demanding special privileges," Roose said. "She was just one of the cast. I think she was basically introverted and was much more comfortable in small groups in her own private space."

Alice deferred almost completely to Phil regarding the actual business of running the radio show—the producing, writing, sponsorship, and so forth—maintaining veto power. "She would make no bones if Phil did something on the show that displeased her," Roose said. "She had no compunction about telling him. She was very clear, and he listened." Otherwise she wisely left the management of the program to him. Contrary to his persona, Phil Harris was an astute and experienced businessman. Clarinetist Artie Shaw wrote about the logistics of fronting a band in his memoirs, describing the scope and volume of problems an orchestra leader contended with regularly: personality clashes, tardiness, drunkenness, hiring, firing, transportation, lodging, meals, musical arrangements, contract negotiations, theater and dance hall managers, agents, payrolls, percentages, and so on. To meet and overcome such problems while traveling constantly doing one-night stands, year after year, required energy, stamina, and acumen. Phil Harris had done just those sorts of things from the time he left home at sixteen. Producing his own radio show, therefore, fell well within his wide-ranging capabilities.

The *Phil Harris-Alice Faye Show* was the most successful spin-off from the *Jack Benny Show*, which also launched independent but short-lived programs by Dennis Day and Mel Blanc. As those shows proved, the august comedic parentage of Jack Benny only helped so much. Making the Harris-Faye enterprise a solid success rested entirely on Phil's shoulders, and he had his work cut out for him, contending with not only the quality of the show he produced, its cast, and its writing, but also with sponsors, the network, ratings, and the problems arising from ongoing combinations of all of the above. Phil also had his work for Jack Benny and his own orchestra to consider. John Crosby, a critic for the *Miami Herald*, summed up the first few seasons in a review written in 1950, when the show finally seemed to have found its stride: "Probably no show on radio started out less auspiciously than the Phil Harris-Alice Faye operation back in the fall of 1946," he wrote. "Radio critics everywhere shuddered in rare unison...even as late as 1948 I found myself complaining that the Harris show was loud, crude, and in decidedly questionable taste." Initially the show followed *Jack Benny* on NBC, which may have provided a brief boost but did not sustain it for long. Phil managed to appear in both since it was simply a matter of stepping across the hall at NBC from one show to the other. From time to time, the *Phil Harris-Alice Faye Show* would even pick up and continue the story from that evening's *Jack Benny Show*. *New York World Telegram* critic Harriet Van Horn, who did not care for the program, nevertheless praised Phil's showmanship, saying, "It must be said that Phil Harris reads his lines with the kind of brassy magnificence they demand. His sense of timing is superior as is his handling of comedy songs... for them as likes this kind of humor, this is a great show. Me, I find it flat, tasteless, and much too loud." After two seasons, Fitch apparently felt the same way. The corporation called it quits, and the *Phil Harris-Alice Faye Show* found itself in the market for a new sponsor.

In 1948, the show returned to the airwaves with a new sponsor, the drug company Rexall, and a new character, Mr. Scott, the Rexall sponsor, played by Gale Gordon. At $14,500 per episode, less than half the price paid by the sponsors of the Jack Benny and Bing Crosby shows, Rexall got a bargain. Introducing the character of Mr. Scott enhanced the real-life basis from which the show was derived, eliminated the need for the middle commercial break, and expanded the show's plot potential. It also neatly circumvented the strict broadcasting rules regulating how much time could be devoted to commercials. Writers Singer and Chevillet adhered to one rule, "never knock the product," but otherwise took tremendous license, usually exploring the potential for humor of pitting Frank Remley against Rexall, with predictably chaotic results. The show's volume remained a point of contention with the critics. Acting on the principle of contagious laughter, the same concept that gave television the laugh track, Phil placed the audience microphones directly overhead, rendering the program one of the loudest on radio. Extending the idea a bit further, he arranged for the orchestra's absence during rehearsals. The musicians did not see or hear the script until the program aired, so their laughter was genuine and spontaneous. The show and its rating began to improve steadily. "About midway into that year, they felt better about ratings," Jeanine Roose said. "Then the reviews improved."

Phil might even have breathed a sigh of relief at that point, had CBS mogul Bill Paley not chosen that particular moment to stage one of the most startling coups in broadcasting history. Radio comedians like Jack Benny and Phil Harris owned their own shows, which they produced and sold to sponsors at a per-episode price. The profits they made by doing so inevitably placed them in the nation's highest tax brackets. Paley's CBS and the talent agency MCA, which represented many such entertainers, determined that these programs could be considered property, which could be sold and taxed at the lower capital gains rate. Paley, who was at that time in a position to make capital investments of this sort, figured that if

CBS could convince the comedians to sell their shows, in return for lower tax rates and regular salaries, he could not only buy successful, proven programming for CBS but also gain control of key talent for future television broadcasting. Acting on this idea, Paley bought most of NBC's Sunday night lineup, which included not only Jack Benny but Edgar Bergen-Charlie McCarthy, Burns and Allen, Amos & Andy, and Red Skelton. In one fell swoop, Paley hijacked NBC's top talent.

Why the *Phil Harris-Alice Faye Show* did not join the exodus to CBS is not clear. Existing articles in the trade journals indicate that the deal Phil might have cut with Paley was complicated by questions of sponsorship. Clippings entitled "Phil Harris Can Have Post-Benny Spot on CBS If He'll Shake Rexall" and "Phil Harris Has Chance to Shaft Radio Network" indicate that he might have done so had he abandoned Rexall and opted to cut some kind of a deal with another sponsor, Lever Brothers. What kind of contractual and ethical complications influenced Phil's decision to stay with Rexall and NBC remain unclear. The bottom line is that he did decide to stay, and that decision held tough implications for upcoming seasons.

The most immediate was that in the fall of 1949 Phil and Alice cut their Sun Valley vacation short by two weeks to be back on the air by September 18, in the 7:30 time slot now sandwiched by *Hollywood Cavalcade* and *The Adventures of Sam Spade*. Following the former, one critic noted, was "somewhat like starting from scratch" and did not help them against the new 7:30 P.M. competition from CBS, *Amos & Andy*. The logistics of Phil performing both for Jack Benny and in his own show were complicated as well, since the two studios were now separated by a large parking lot instead of a small hallway. Jack Benny generously arranged for Phil to appear in the top half of his show so that by a quarter past the hour he could race from CBS to NBC and warm up his own audience in time for going on the air at half past. At one point, he also did a guest performance on *Hollywood Cavalcade*, complicating things still further and prompting one columnist to ask, "Did you detect a breathless quality in Phil

Harris's voice when he sang on NBC's *Hollywood Cavalcade* last Sunday? He had just run two blocks from Jack Benny's CBS show, then after he sang, he was whisked across the hall to his own *Phil Harris-Alice Faye* show."

Midway through the 1949–50 season the *Phil Harris-Alice Faye Show* had slipped in the ratings, despite the improved quality of the program. "For a goodly portion of last season," the *New York News* wrote in the fall of 1949, "the *Phil Harris-Alice Faye* show was a clinker. Then at the end of last season, the script became livelier, the characters more real, and some of the jokes actually produced laughter. If the standards set by the premiere are maintained, this should be one of the outstanding entertainments of the year." The show endured for another four years, but the competition posed by *Amos & Andy* threatened Rexall, and the drug company ceased sponsoring the program after June 1950. Conferences with New York executives, which meant moving the whole show across country for a few weeks, eventually resulted in a direct deal with NBC, and later one with RCA. But it is not surprising that Phil, when presented with the opportunity to take the show to television, opted out.

Many fans assumed that Alice prompted the decision not to move the *Phil Harris-Alice Faye Show* to television. In fact the decision was Phil's, as Alice pointed out in a televised interview in the 1980s. He understood that producing a television program entailed all of the same problems that a radio show did, but demanded a great deal more in terms of staging and rehearsals. Guest stars and cast alike had to block out days in their schedules for run-throughs, costume fittings, light cues, and memorizing dialogue. Television also meant pulling double duty. Phil watched Jack Benny make the transition gradually as CBS tested the waters of television. Benny broadcast two shows his first year and gradually increased the number until 1954 when he televised his program every other week—all while continuing to produce a thirty-nine-show radio season. Alice later maintained that she would have liked to do it, although one wonders how her nerves could have tolerated the rigors of live broadcasting. Phil, on the other hand, was apparently not interested in television on any level. He not only declined to televise his own show, he became one of the casualties, along with Mary Livingstone, of the *Jack Benny Show's* move to the new medium. It is interesting to speculate on what the future might have held had he launched a *Phil Harris-Alice Faye* television show. Given the power of syndication, Phil and Alice might have become as well-known to the Nickelodeon generation as Lucy and Ricky, Ozzie and Harriet, or Wally and the Beaver. As it was, said Alice at the time, "Television is not for me. I'll stick to keeping house and buying salty bacon. There's enough work around here taking care of Phil and the girls to keep me busy. Besides radio is hard enough work."

By the early 1950s Phil was intent on pursuing another line entirely. He had apparently always dabbled in real estate, for example, investing with Clark Gable and a few others in a forty-six-acre tract in the then-agricultural community of Northridge in the San Fernando Valley, near the intersection of Balboa and Nordhoff. A self-described golf bum, he became interested in the early development going on in Palm Springs. There a dude rancher named Frank Bogert decided to enhance his operations by adding a golf course at his Thunderbird spread. "We were the first golf course to put houses around the fairways," Bogert said. "I was having a hard time selling the lots, but when Hope and Crosby bought, everybody came. Desi and Lucy built a house, Leonard Firestone built a house, and Phil Harris was one of the first houses there." Phil became involved in the Thunderbird enterprise as one of its founding members, maintaining his home there with Alice for the rest of their lives. Their friend Kay Gregory, who moved to Thunderbird in 1956, remembered that Phil and Alice were a big part of the club. "Every night after the parties, all the celebrities who lived here, and there were many, would entertain, sort of a jam session," she said. "My husband and I were always the audience. In those days we would stay at the club until two in the morning with all this carrying on and it was perfectly wonderful. And Phil and Alice were big numbers in this."

Alice and Phil intended their house in the desert as a weekend getaway, but in 1952 they sold their Encino property to George Gobel and moved to Palm Springs for good. The transition apparently agreed with them, and they began to live more simply, according to Alice. "It's a three-bedroom house, all on one floor, furnished in early American, which always seems to startle people in the desert," she said. It featured a large living room-dining room combination, and white paneled master bedroom with white rug and deep wine-colored curtains. Alice had difficulty sleeping if there was any light, so they generally drew the drapes tightly, but left the windows open to the cool evening air.

After the move, Alice and Phil commuted to Los Angeles for the radio broadcast on weekends and let the television revolution play out without them. "While many of his fellow artists are knocking themselves out with weekly T.V. shows, Phil spends most of his year in the comfortable confines of Palm Springs, lumbering up to Hollywood to assist in NBC Spectaculars a few times a year," wrote one columnist in a piece entitled "Phil Harris Knows How to Live." Alice knew how to live as well. The move to the desert, combined with the cancellation of their radio show in 1954, completed her transition from working performer to lady of leisure. Throughout the 1950s, Phil combined hunting, fishing, and golfing expeditions with occasional television appearances. He also took over the duty of being the movie star of the family, performing in half a dozen feature films, including *Wabash Avenue* with Betty Grable and *The High and the Mighty* with John Wayne. Alice for the most part stayed home and indulged her long-dormant tendencies. "She liked to be at home," Phyllis remembered. "She was a homebody and loved to putter and play in her closet. She would rather clean her closet than do anything." Alice provided the anchor to the Harris household and steadied her peripatetic husband, who, having traveled most of his life because of the nature of his work, now traveled equally zealously because of the nature of his hobbies.

With the radio show concluded and their daughters now attending boarding school in Arizona, Alice and Phil's marriage evolved into a unique arrangement that seemed to provide them with the space they needed as individuals and to allow their marriage to thrive. From the outset of their relationship people had remarked that they had very little in common. Alice's quiet reserve contrasted with her husband's nervous extroversion. "Phil is nervous, always 'on the jump,'" Alice often said, and inevitably such divergent personalities clashed. "Alice and Phil argued all the time, but their arguments were funny," said Judy McHarg. "They'd say funny things and it would make me laugh." Their Palm Springs neighbor Nancy Whitaker described it as "a funny kind of relationship, kind of love/hate, but you couldn't say a word about either one of them to them or they'd have killed you." In their semiretired state Alice and Phil had the leisure to indulge their interests but found few in common. "I know they loved each other very deeply," said Phyllis, "but I don't think they always liked each other. They were very, very opposite. Daddy used to sing that song about how he was racetrack and she was polo. He was barroom and she was afternoon tea. He used to sing that song to her sometimes when he was performing somewhere, because they were such opposites. She loved the elegant and he loved the down and dirty."

Alice's interests were as feminine as the pale pink decor in her dressing room. Bing Crosby's nickname for her, in fact, was Pastel. She enjoyed clothes and jewelry, dressing up and looking her best. "I always thought Alice was quite stylish," said her friend Kay Gregory. "She always knew what to wear and she had a great figure. I remember in summer how smart her cottons always looked." After years of feeling physically run down by movie work, Alice loved having the time to take care of herself. She walked and swam, and treated herself to semiannual trips to Main Chance, the Elizabeth Arden spa in Arizona. She also studied painting for many years in a class taught by John Morris. Phil, in contrast, disliked wearing tuxedos after a lifetime of performing in nightclubs, and he hated to wear a tie. "They didn't entertain and go to dinner a lot because Mother liked elegant parties and Daddy didn't like to dress up," Phyllis said. "He was definitely a man's man and he liked to be with men," she said. "He did a lot of *American Sportsman* shows for television and he went hunting a lot with Mr. Crosby. He'd go hunting at the drop of a hat with anyone."

Phil's interests took him all over the world. "He used to say he wasn't going to let the rocking chair get him," Phyllis said. "He just kept moving." Alice traveled too, but her preferences led her to Europe, especially England, with friends like the Swansons of frozen food fame, Kay Gregory, and others.

One unusual aspect of Alice and Phil's relationship was the fact that they eventually maintained two separate houses in Palm Springs. Their home at Thunderbird had been intended for use as a weekend house and was surprisingly small, only three bedrooms. "We had had a huge place in Encino, so it was an adjustment," said Phyllis. "The thing that was the real adjustment was that Mother and Daddy were in the house. That was just real strange. You didn't know whether to tiptoe and you didn't want to get in their way. Everybody was on top of each other. But then Alice went away to school. I stayed home for one year then I followed her, and after that we were never home again. I think they planned on building a bigger house, but after we left they just never did." Phil ate and slept at the Thunderbird house, but spent his days at a house he acquired at nearby Ironwood Country Club. "Daddy got up every morning and he and Mother had breakfast together, then he got in his car and off he went," Phyllis said. "He went there every single day and had his friends and his secretary up there, conducted interviews, did all his business. Then about four in the afternoon, he would leave there and go to Thunderbird to play cards and have a couple of drinks, then he would come home about 6:00 P.M. So they were never under each other's feet. I think they survived nicely because he had other places to go."

Many who knew them agreed with Phyllis. The wide berth Alice and Phil gave each other helped them endure as a couple. "Alice and Phil simply couldn't be together too many days in a row," said their friend Judy McHarg. Alice Jr. concurred, saying, "I think that's probably how they survived. They both did their own thing and it worked for them for fifty-five years. Imagine. But they had nothing in common, except for us, I think. They didn't like the same things at all. They didn't even have the same friends, really, with a few exceptions. It's funny when you think about it." Yet for over fifty years, Alice and Phil remained devoted to one another, sharing breakfast and dinner when they were together, and phoning each other at least twice a day when they were apart. "They used to fight and love it, and nag at each other." Phyllis remembered. "They had their own way of communicating. And they did communicate. When I was a child at the Palm Springs house, my bedroom was next to theirs, and I could hear them in the middle of the night, at two or three in the morning. They'd wake up and have a glass of sherry and sit up in bed and talk, for maybe an hour. They did it every night, then they went back to sleep. I guess that was the time they did their communicating."

Ultimately, the secret formula for the longevity and apparent success of Alice and Phil's relationship rests with Alice and Phil. They must have encountered the usual number of rough patches in a marriage that spanned half a century; what the bad parts were and how they resolved them also rests with them. Viewed from the outside, Alice and Phil each possessed qualities that must have helped. Phil was unabashedly sentimental, and while he could direct his humor at all and sundry, he never took shots at Alice. To him, she was always "my girl." Alice, in turn, was very much a loner, as one daughter put it, and had no difficulty staying by herself while Phil traveled. Additionally, there remained the same commitment to making the marriage work that led her to cut back on films and travel with him during the radio years, even at the expense of spending time with her girls. Phyllis remembered watching her mother pack Phil's things for yet another of his trips. "She'd pack his clothes in the guest room and she wrapped everything in tissue paper," she remembered. "And she did it by day, you know, the underwear, the socks, the handkerchiefs, Monday, Tuesday, Wednesday." Phyllis asked Alice why she let him go all the time instead of telling him he couldn't. "Oh, no," she recalled Alice saying, "they're going to go anyway and you don't ever want them to leave home upset or angry. You want them to leave home happy, then they come home happy."

Finally, former child performer Jeanine Roose offered her own perspective on what may have made Alice and Phil's relationship work. "They obviously loved each other very much, but they were very different. He was very much the outgoing, impulsive, fun-loving person. She was much more the central, stabilizing influence," Roose said. Musing on why such opposites might attract, she continued, "In thinking about the kind of environment Hell's Kitchen represented when Alice was growing up, I can imagine that Phil's kind of masculine energy was present there. So it might not have been unfamiliar to her." Alice's sense of marital propriety, derived from her working-class, immigrant roots, might have revolved around a sort of blue-collar machismo where men gathered on street corners to shout about politics, laugh at risqué jokes, and rail against the economy, while their womenfolk occupied a separate sphere in which house and family were paramount.

If Alice ever questioned the direction her life had taken since she left the movies, she had occasional reminders of what she was and was not missing. In 1958, six years after the Harrises moved to Thunderbird, for example, Alice was stunned to learn that her friend and costar Tyrone Power had died of a heart attack at the age of forty-four. She and Ty had not kept in close contact in the years since she left Fox, but more often than not during that time a greeting of some sort commemorating their shared birthday would find its way to her. He had been in Spain filming a dueling scene with George Sanders for his production company's new movie *Solomon and Sheba* when he collapsed with a heart attack. He died en route to the hospital, leaving behind his new wife, Debbie, who was seven months pregnant with their first child.

To Alice, Tyrone Power was yet another casualty of the film industry. "Ty was the victim of the Hollywood system that grinds actors and actresses down, makes them give their blood and their souls (and, in Ty's case, his life) to making movies. There is never any respite for a movie star," Alice later wrote. She felt that he might have survived the attack had he been nearer to modern medical facilities. Moreover, she believed that he might not have suffered heart trouble at all had he gotten out like she did, although little chance of that existed. Power had loved acting and the adulation too much.

Alice knew that movie stardom remained a tough racket and acknowledged that it had become even tougher in the climate of free agency that had sprung up since her retirement. Only three years before, in1955, another of Alice's costars had died of a heart attack. Lovely Carmen Miranda had made a guest appearance on Jimmy Durante's television show, returned home late in the evening, and dropped dead as she crossed the floor of her bedroom. She was forty-two years old. Miranda underwent the same typecasting ordeal at the hands of Darryl Zanuck that Alice had experienced. "She was a big draw for Fox, so naturally they wouldn't let her do anything else but what she was doing," Alice stated in a 1994 interview. "She made a lot of money for them. *Of course* the deck was stacked against us." Frustrated at having to repeat her same old schtick in the changing postwar climate, Miranda bought out her Fox contract and struck out on her own. She made the moderately successful *Copacabana* with Groucho Marx, suffered from a long bout of ill health, and drifted into television.

As demanding as life could be for a studio player, it did not compare to the uncertainties of independence, as Miranda discovered. Throughout the 1950s, however, increasing numbers of contract actors would have to learn about life beyond the studio gates. In that sense, Alice's bid for personal independence in 1945 could be considered trendsetting. The big studio system that created and nurtured the stars was in massive decline and no longer able to afford to maintain a large stable of coddled performers. In the postwar years studios waged a multifront war against television, McCarthyism, and the enforced divestiture of their theater chains, a war they were losing.

From her haven in Palm Springs, Alice watched the foundations of the big studio system crumble and saw many of her friends and acquaintances claimed as its casualties. In September 1952 Twentieth Century-

Fox canceled Linda Darnell's contract. The same year M-G-M released Clark Gable. Betty Grable saw the handwriting on the wall and chose to leave Fox in 1953; that same year the studio fired Jeanne Crain, Anne Baxter, Gene Tierney, and Mitzi Gaynor. Film historian Ron Davis stated, "Most actors initially felt they had been pardoned from a prison sentence. Later they would look back on the ease and protection they had enjoyed under the big studios and regret the passing of a golden age." Most startling to Alice, perhaps, was the news that one of the authors of that golden age, the invincible Darryl Zanuck, had also been cut loose. In 1956 after a long-running feud with Spyros Skouras over television, Zanuck resigned as head of production at Twentieth Century-Fox and left Hollywood for several years of quasi-exile in Europe.

Alice witnessed the storms rocking the film industry from a safe distance. She could sympathize when they affected people she knew and cared for, and she could continue to count her blessings. "I believe I was very fortunate to get out when I did," she wrote. "If I hadn't, it would have eaten me up." Her new life, apart from keeping up with Phil, had evolved into a tranquil routine of exercise, housekeeping, lunches with friends, and travel. By choice, it involved few of the trappings of stardom. They would not have been necessary in the desert anyway. It seemed as if everybody was somebody in Palm Springs; that was its attraction. Out of the spotlight, behind the walls of the clubs and the gated communities, the well-known and well-heeled could relax among their peers.

Thunderbird provided a focal point for an increasing number of Alice's activities, especially after her mother's death in Los Angeles in 1959. Although she never seriously took up golf, she slipped into the suburban country-club lifestyle enjoyed by many prosperous Americans in the 1950s; only her friends' celebrated names distinguished her circle in any way. Alice began taking painting classes at Thunderbird with a group of ladies that included Mousie (Mrs. William) Powell and silent screen star Billie Dove. "I'm far from an expert painter, but I thoroughly enjoy it," Alice said. Clark Swanson, the frozen dinner magnate, bought a house across the street from the Harrises, and Alice and Florence Swanson became close. Another new neighbor was tennis champion Nancy Chaffe, who had just married baseball Hall-of-Famer Ralph Kiner. In the midst of moving in, Nancy was startled to find Alice on her doorstep with a bouquet of flowers to welcome her to Thunderbird. "There were only about four houses on the property at that point, this is in 1951, and there was a knock on my door and there she was," Nancy remembered. "I had played the Wimbeldon tournament in 1950 and had seen her at a dinner place called the Embassy Club in London. I went up to her and got her autograph and told her I was a real fan of hers and she was very sweet and nice. I just thought how funny it was that eighteen months later she'd be my neighbor."

Alice took advantage of her position to indulge in private benevolences and act as the genuinely nice human being she was. In 1953, for example, Nancy and Ralph Kiner learned they were expecting their first child while Ralph played for the Chicago Cubs. "I was away from home and nobody had given me a baby shower," Nancy remembered. "Alice and Phil were staying at the old Edgewater Beach Hotel and she called me to come over there. When I went to her suite, she had these two huge white boxes about the size that you'd put fur coats in. And she had gone to Marshall Fields and bought me the whole layette for the baby. I was just flabbergasted. I never saw such a fabulous thing. She must have hand-picked everything." When Bing Crosby and Kathryn Grant married in October 1957, after postponing the wedding five times, Alice fed them an impromptu wedding dinner of quail and macaroni and cheese.

On another occasion, Alice learned that doctors had diagnosed an old costar from *You're a Sweetheart*, William Gargan, with throat cancer while he was performing in San Francisco in *The Best Man*. The surgery that removed Gargan's esophagus and saved his life also ended his career. Alice, Nancy Kiner, and Florence Swanson decided to chair a benefit at Thunderbird to raise money for the William Gargan Fund he had started through the American Cancer Society. "We raised about $200,000 for him, and got him a new car from Bill Ford, at the Ford Motor Company, because we all knew him," Nancy said. "Bob Hope presented him with the keys, very exciting. Alice wasn't the kind of person who just used her name to get the door open, she completed the job as well."

Very occasionally during this time Alice would agree to guest appearances on various television programs involving her friends. She debuted in the medium in 1959 on a show hosted by Phil and costarring Dean Martin and Betty Hutton. Wearing a black strapless evening gown with her hair swept up she sang a medley of her movie hits with Betty Hutton. She also performed on *Hollywood Palace* and the *Perry Como Show*. The *Perry Como Show* also brought Jewel Baxter, her friend, assistant, and spokeswoman, into her life. Baxter had originally suggested Alice and Phil for the Como show and they became fast friends. "They became the shoulder I could lean on when I lost my twin sister," Baxter remembered. "Alice invited me to their home to stay afterwards, and I shall always love them for that."

Alice's life reflected an enviable balance of active leisure seasoned with just enough professional activity to make it interesting. Her accomplishments in the years since she walked out on Zanuck were many. She preserved her marriage, raised her daughters, traveled widely, enjoyed a long run on her own popular radio show, and never once regretted her decision to leave the studio. She learned and practiced everyday independence, and although she never excelled at driving, she did manage to get herself back and forth the few blocks or so between her house at Thunderbird and the clubhouse. Over the years her cooking improved—navy bean soup became one of her specialties—and she might have been confused with any other wife of a prosperous businessman had she not made occasional guest appearances on television. For the most part, Alice immersed herself in a quiet whirl of Palm Springs society, and proved that there was a happy and absorbing life to be found out there beyond the silver screen.

CHAPTER 12

Celebrity Fulfilled

In 1961, at Phil's suggestion, Alice decided to make another motion picture. Phil continued to pursue an intense travel schedule, Alice Jr. had just married New Orleans stockbroker Ted Alcus, and Phyllis was about to begin courses at the University of Arizona in the fall. Alice's family life was fairly settled. So when producer Charles Brackett began phoning Alice "out of the blue" urging her to accept the role of Melissa Frake in a new remake of Rogers and Hammerstein's *State Fair* for Twentieth Century-Fox, Alice actually gave it consideration. "He was so persistent, he called three or four times a day for four days," Alice said. "I looked at the script and told Phil and he said I'd be crazy not to take it. So I said yes, and the next morning I woke up screaming saying 'what have I done?'" But she admitted that she was flattered too. "I was just a mother and housewife," she insisted. "Occasionally I took on a TV show and sometimes I accompanied Phil on his golf tournament trips. But it's nice to be remembered by the fans and the money was nice too."

State Fair also represented the kind of material with which Alice felt comfortable. "It's the kind of clean, entertaining picture I'd want my daughters to see," she stated. This would be Fox's third version of *State Fair*; the second as a musical. The first version, a nonmusical version filmed in 1933 with Will Rogers, Louise Dresser, and Janet Gaynor, had been directed by Alice's favorite, Henry King. Had Alice wished, she could have played the

Vivian Blaine role in the second version, released in 1945 and also starring Dana Andrews, Jeanne Crain, and Dick Haymes. One of the attractions of the newest version was that Richard Rogers had agreed to write five additional songs for the film, acting as his own lyricist, including a special solo just for Alice called "Never Say No to a Man." Alice's old director Walter Lang, who guided her through *Tin Pan Alley* and *Weekend in Havana*, had already begun location work in Dallas, and she also had hopes that Don Ameche would be cast opposite her as hog farmer Abel Frake. Despite her anxiety over returning to movies, Alice had high hopes for the project and moved forward with cautious enthusiasm.

As soon as Alice committed to the film, the studio publicity machine kicked into high gear. Articles profiling her career, her life, her tastes, and so forth saturated publications nationwide. Columns ran with headlines like "The Queen Returns" and assured viewers that she appeared just as trim and attractive as she ever had. Alice took comfort in how little had changed in the studio's approach to publicity, and in many respects she found her return to the Twentieth Century lot reassuring as well. Not only was the dreaded Zanuck long gone but scores of technicians and crew members from her previous films welcomed her return with unconcealed delight. One columnist noted, "There was nostalgia in the air as waitresses, studio policemen, and executives came over to greet Alice at her lunch table in a remote corner of the Commissary." On the first day of filming, when Alice again went through her usual case of the jitters, she took comfort from old familiar faces. "What made it easy for me was that I was completely surrounded by friends," she said. "Most of the crew and technicians had worked with me on movies sixteen years ago. They all coddled me, kept telling me I was good—and soon I began to believe them a little bit." As for the jitters, she flatly stated, "I expected it. I had the jitters the first scene of every day I worked on every picture." On her first day she did get a good laugh from a telegram Bing Crosby sent to her from London, where he was filming *Road to Hong Kong*—"Welcome back to the taxpayers' list!"

The honeymoon period of Alice's comeback proved short-lived, however. Don Ameche did not get the role as Abel Frake. It went instead to Broadway actor Tom Ewell, best known to moviegoers as Marilyn Monroe's leading man in *The Seven Year Itch*. Illness forced Walter Lang to withdraw, and Fox assigned José Ferrer to direct the film. Ferrer, described by one critic as "the Puerto Rico-born, Princeton-trained scholar and all-purpose theater man," constituted an unlikely choice to direct an American heartland musical. His limited understanding of the charms of rural life seriously handicapped his direction. In contrast, the charms of Pamela Tiffin, who played Alice's daughter, did not escape him so easily, and a good portion of his time on the set was spent in aggressive pursuit of the young actress, again to the film's detriment. Ferrer's directorial style and extracurricular antics failed to ease Alice's anxieties, made worse by her unfamiliar and unfriendly leading man, and hampered her ability to turn in a performance that satisfied her.

In addition to personality conflicts on the set, Alice experienced difficulty in adjusting to some of the changes the preceding sixteen years had wrought in making movies. "They'd torn down the back lot to build Century City," Alice later remembered. "The dressing rooms were shot, and the sets had holes in them. All I could think of was, 'My God this is tacky! What am I doing here?'" Additionally, Alice had never experienced location work. Most of her previous films called for day trips to locales in and around southern California, if they required outdoor realism. The producers had decided that this version of *State Fair* would take place in Texas, at the spectacular deco fairgrounds built in Dallas in 1936 to celebrate the state's centennial. Because the real Texas state fair took place in September and October, the cast and crew had to work before it opened at the peak of the Texas summer. When Alice arrived, Hurricane Carla had just assaulted the Gulf coast, raising humidity throughout the state to unbearable levels. To add to the general level of discomfort, her first day of location work took place at the fairground's hog pavilion, among forty prize Hampshire and Duroc boars. One can only imagine Alice's state of mind as the heat, humidity, noise, and smell took their toll throughout the day.

The company shot the farm sequences at Cecile Wilkens's ranch outside of Kemp, Texas, about an eighty-mile drive from their hotel in Dallas. Carpenters erected a dummy silo, to lend a touch of midwestern authenticity to an area in which silos were uncommon. As Alice worked, Phil flew in and out of Dallas, playing in local golf tournaments, enjoying hunting trips to Mexico, and flying back and forth to New Orleans to visit with Alice Jr., who was expecting the Harrises' first grandbaby late in the fall. Alice caught a two-pound bass in the lake at the Wilkens ranch, but found it small compensation for the lack of air conditioning and bathrooms. "*State Fair* was very difficult," she recalled. "In my era most films were shot in the studio so there were creature comforts available that are not present on location. We were outside most of the time and, of course, we all were supposed to look fresh and beautiful, but in those 100-degree plus temperatures, looking fresh and beautiful is difficult. It was a grueling and uncomfortable few weeks for me."

On a more positive note, Alice was stunned to be met by numbers of fans almost everywhere she went in and around Dallas. A battery of photographers and newsreel cameramen greeted her plane when it arrived at Love Field, and bevies of autograph seekers, many of them young enough to have only seen her movies on television, flocked around her. She particularly enjoyed working with Pat Boone and Ann-Margret, who, in spite of the many obstacles in filming, managed to make the film their own. Another pleasant episode occurred shortly after the cast's arrival in Dallas, when the six stars of the picture, Alice, Pat Boone, Bobby Darin, Tom Ewell, Ann-Margret, and Pamela Tiffen, gave a benefit performance a the State Fair Music Hall on behalf of the victims of Hurricane Carla. On the whole, however, Alice did not enjoy the experience and subsequently referred to *State Fair* as a bad mistake and a bad picture. "I thought it was great for Ann-Margret," Alice said in a later interview. "It was her beginning and she was great in it; but it was a disaster for me. I really don't know why I did it, except that Phil thought it would be fun for me."

Critics tended to agree with Alice's assessment after the studio released the film in the spring of 1962. They received *State Fair* unkindly, placing most of the blame for its lack of "homespun charm, warmth, and verve," on José Ferrer, whom they rightly felt was out of his element. Critic John Rosenfield, who had a hometown stake in the movie's success, described Ferrer's direction as "competent but strange in its emphasis, and unstyled and sodden in spots." Regarding Alice's performance in the less-than-successful picture, *Time* magazine commented, "Alice Faye . . . looks refreshingly real; she is middle-aged now and she doesn't try to hide it," while another film critic quipped that "Alice Faye came out of retirement to play Melissa Frake and promptly went back in again."

Had Alice entertained notions of a more permanent return to films, her experience with *State Fair* quashed them. She returned to her haven at Thunderbird and continued in a state of semiretirement, focusing on her private life and occasionally doing guest spots on television. In 1963, her younger daughter, Phyllis, married an Arizona rancher, beginning a new chapter in their family life. Alice remembered that after her daughters were grown and gone, "I wasn't doing so much radio and television any more, and I had to sit myself down and have a long talk with myself about how I was going to fill up my days." Phyllis frankly stated that, during the 1960s, "I think she got bored. I hate to say that. Daddy went on and did his thing with his friends, hunting and fishing and stuff like that. She was not really into all that and she spent more time at home by herself." Not that Alice remained idle. She continued to take exceptionally good care of herself, exercising and keeping her figure. She also made a record album of her movie hits for Reprise, a company owned at the time by her neighbor Frank Sinatra.

Alice found painting particularly absorbing. "She had a little studio," Nancy Whitaker remembered. "When the kids grew up, she took their room, which was off the kitchen and turned it into a little art studio and she used to do a lot of palette painting. She was very good, but she never thought she was very good." Validation came her way when Frank Sinatra bought a painting of a little girl at the beach she had done for Barbara Sinatra's auction benefiting abused children. He gave it to his daughter Nancy, and his gesture thrilled Alice. She also found a niche for herself as a volunteer at the Eisenhower Medical Center, where she enjoyed distributing magazines and books and visiting with patients. It was the kind of low-key contact with people she could manage without succumbing to her usual stage fright. She had tried fundraising but almost predictably found herself uncomfortable in that kind of role. "It was certainly for a worthy cause, and I contributed myself, but I didn't have it in me to go up to somebody and ask for a contribution," she said.

Alice pursued these activities through the 1960s and early 1970s. She still enjoyed doing occasional television spots, but as the years progressed changes in show business reminded her that her kind of entertainment was slowly fading away. The big studios had given way to independent producers who filmed stories with more adult themes. Violence, sex, and social relevance, not fluffy escapism, marked the new Hollywood productions. In an interview with Rex Reed, Alice stated flatly, "I don't understand Jane Fonda or 'Deep Throat.' I went to see an X-rated film with a girlfriend once in San Francisco and we had three double martinis afterwards." Increasingly, television followed the lead of films. Newer, youth-based programs replaced the old variety formats, just as rock and roll superseded the cardigan-sweatered crooners of Alice's generation. "It's a whole new show business as far as I'm concerned," Phil said in a 1967 interview. "I want to stick to the happy shows like Dean [Martin's] and the *Hollywood Palace*." During this period, Phil, with his distinctive voice and brash personality, did find a niche for himself at the Disney Studios, providing voice characterizations for their animated features. Generations who know nothing of the *Jack Benny Show* or the big band era remember Phil Harris as the voice of Baloo the Bear from Disney's *Jungle Book* or

O'Malley the Alley Cat from *The Aristocats*. Other members of Alice and Phil's generation were not as fortunate and found themselves pursuing other avenues or going back on the road in summer stock or dinner theater. Many simply went into hibernation, pending the day that their kind of entertainment would meet with greater favor.

The obituary page also provided Alice with somber reminders of the changing times. In February 1967 Phil's band member and sidekick Frank Remley died of a heart attack at the age of sixty-five. Phil and Jack Benny acted as honorary pallbearers. The following year, producer George White succumbed to leukemia. Marilyn Maxwell, with whom Alice had entertained in Germany, died of heart complications at the age of forty-nine in 1972. But it was Betty Grable's death in July 1973 at the age of fifty-six that hit closest to home. Alice had kept in touch with Betty over the years, as they each raised their daughters and tried to keep up with their bandleader husbands. "We used to kid about doing a sister act together across the street from where Phil and Harry James had turned up to perform," Alice remembered in a 1973 interview. In an ironic twist, Grable had had to fight Darryl Zanuck *not* to take dramatic roles, continually refusing his requests to act in such strictly dramatic films as *The Razor's Edge*. Alice had been one of the first friends with whom Betty shared the news of her prognosis, and Alice visited Betty often at a Los Angeles hospital as she battled lung cancer. "Poor Betty, God bless her," Alice said, "she wouldn't quit smoking. I tried to talk to her, but she wouldn't, or couldn't listen. So she smoked until the end." Six hundred mourners attended Betty Grable's funeral at All Saints Episcopal Church in Beverly Hills, including Alice and Phil, and Fox alums Cesar Romero, June Haver, and Dan Dailey. It represented a milestone of sorts, indicating just how far removed they all were from the "golden days" of their youth, from the era of the big studio system, and from the epicenter of popular culture.

In a world dominated by the Rolling Stones, *The Godfather*, and an unpopular war in Vietnam, Alice and other entertainers of her generation might have quietly faded away had it not been for a peculiar blip on the cultural radar screens generally referred to as the Nostalgia Craze. A reaction to the grim and gritty entertainment fare of the late 1960s and early 1970s combined with a yearning for less complicated times, the nostalgia boom produced movies like Twiggy's *The Boyfriend,* and *The Sting,* with its enormously popular Scott Joplin soundtrack, and revived musicals like the 1920s success, *No, No, Nanette.* It was only a matter of time before the publicity people and public alike rediscovered a favorite like Alice. The first hint of interest in the early Alice Faye occurred in 1968 when the *San Francisco Chronicle* ran an article on "The Alice Faye Eyebrow." In it, Martine Compere-Mortel, the new beauty editor of *Elle,* touted a 1930s retro look for women, which included red lips and fingernails, and round thin eyebrows, which she called the Alice Faye eyebrow "in honor of the American actress whose eyebrows often appeared to be completely penciled half moons."

In 1971 people's interest in Alice grew more serious after a publisher named Leonard Mogel decided to revive *Liberty Magazine* as *Liberty: The Nostalgia Magazine,* publishing "great old stories from the past reprinted from photographic plates of the original magazine's pages." It would come out quarterly, cost seventy-five cents, and only the advertising would be new. *Liberty's* inaugural gala was held at the Rainbow Room in New York and managed by Jewel Baxter, Alice's friend from the *Perry Como Show.* "They gave me a bunch of old *Liberty* magazines to help with PR," Baxter remembered, "and I noticed that Alice was in almost every issue. I pointed it out and they asked if I could get her there as the main attraction." Baxter did, arranging for Alice to receive an award as "the star to remember" at the gala. The coverage was phenomenal. "I want to tell you that it was the biggest thing that ever happened in the Rainbow Room," Baxter said. "They had to take out the chairs and tables. It was wall-to-wall people. Every network showed up, and Debbie Reynolds, Benny Goodman, and Connee Boswell. It was unbelievable. And from that people knew that Alice Faye was moving around and doing things. It's just that no one ever thought of asking her."

A third of the *New York Times* review of the event profiled Alice, giving her equal coverage with the magazine itself. Rex Reed, a longtime Alice Faye fan, generated even greater interest by devoting an entire column to her, describing her "big navy blue moo-cow eyes and husky moon-struck voice" and declaring her the "same petite 120-pound dish she was when she walked off the 20th Century lot at the height of her fame and told Darryl F. Zanuck where to stuff it." Nostalgia maven Harry Rigby, who was reviving such musicals as *No, No, Nanette* with Ruby Keeler and *Irene* with Debbie Reynolds, took notice. "Alice got *Good News* as a result of that appearance at the Rainbow Room," Jewel Baxter said. Alice had gone to see Ruby Keeler and her old Fox costar Patsy Kelly in *No, No, Nanette*. "Afterward," Alice remembered, "they invited me out with Harry Rigby and, to my amazement, he said he'd love to get a show for me. I said, 'Oh, my god, I'd die!'" Nevertheless, the offer interested Alice. After a forty-year hiatus in Hollywood, she was finally being offered the chance to star in a Broadway show.

Mindful of Alice's mixed experiences and ultimate disappointment with *State Fair*, Phil did not encourage her to pursue *Good News*. One publicity piece for the play announced that Phil had told Alice he thought it was silly to return to show business when she did not need the money. Alice's childhood dream to star on Broadway may have carried enough weight that she was willing to endure the hardships of learning the techniques of the theater, the travel, the inevitable stage fright, and the tensions of backstage life in order to make it come true. She received a great deal of support from Ruby Keeler and Debbie Reynolds who, as stars of two other Rigby revivals, could pass along useful advice and insights. Although the whole project intimidated Alice, especially the "enormous script" sent to her by writer Abe Burrows, she dug in and pursued it. Her characteristic tenacity and determination apparently led her to overcome her innate insecurity to make a solid success out of her one and only starring theatrical role. "I thought that took a lot of courage," said Alice Jr. "It's such a hokey show, but it was good for her."

A pure nostalgia piece, *Good News* was not designed to win critical acclaim or Tony awards or to dazzle the leading lights of the serious stage. Like so many of Alice's vehicles, it boasted only the thinnest of plots on which to hang a selection of good-spirited production numbers. In its original version it told the story of a college football hero who had to pass a crucial examination in order to play in the upcoming championship game. M-G-M filmed the story in the 1940s with Peter Lawford as the quarterback and June Allyson as the student librarian who tutors him. Abe Burrows, who directed the piece, rewrote the book by Laurence Schwab and Buddy de Silva, casting the football coach and the astronomy professor as the romantic leads. Harry Rigby wanted Alice to play the astronomy professor.

One factor that led Alice to accept the offer was her costar, whom she handpicked. "I told Harry Rigby, the producer, I'd only do the show if I could have someone I knew—like John Payne—as my co-star," Alice told columnist Douglas Dean. "I hadn't seen him in seventeen years, but I knew we'd work well together. Harry contacted him and when he said yes—well, I was hooked. I knew I had to do the show then." Rigby also realized that reuniting the two popular costars could only enhance the show's box office appeal. The public would be as eager to see John Payne again as they were to see Alice Faye, and the combination would be dynamite. Payne's movie career had effectively ended in 1961, when he stepped out in front of a car in New York traffic. He sustained injuries to his face, which required 150 stitches, and his leg, which was broken in four places. Laid up for months, he gradually healed, but had to teach himself to walk again. Fortunately, his skill as a businessman and some astute real estate investments assured him of a livelihood after the loss of his acting career. "John was a very well-read person and a fine businessman," Alice once stated, the combination once leading him to buy the film rights to a little-known short story called "Miracle on 34th Street." He was, she said, "the least actorish of all the men I worked with."

Rigby planned for the play to open in Boston at the end of 1973, then tour the country for a year before it went to Broadway. As he always did when they were separated, Phil phoned Alice twice a day during rehearsals from wherever he happened to be. Usually he was off hunting or fishing with Bing Crosby, prompting Alice to say, "If I ever sue Phil for divorce, I'll name Bing co-respondent." Rehearsals did not go well, even allowing for the presence of two unseasoned theater performers like Alice Faye and John Payne. One article mentioned that December 17, opening night at Boston's Colonial Theatre, was not only the first time the cast had worn their costumes but was also the first time they ran through the entire show. Circumstances like these could only have inflamed Alice's chronic stage fright, and she ordered her family to keep away from the show for the time being.

Shortly before Alice opened in *Good News,* she had found herself at a dinner party with her old *Alexander's Ragtime Band* costar Ethel Merman. Alice asked Ethel for advice on coping with the jitters. Merman's answer was "just go out and do it." As this story made the rounds, it prompted one wag to state that Alice had "asked the one actress in the entire business who hasn't a single nerve in her body. Helen Hayes would have said to go to the loo, throw up, and you'll feel better." By opening night, Alice had probably figured out the Hayes technique for coping with nerves on her own. Clearly as she stepped out into the footlights she was "conspicuously nervous," which the critics noted. The audience did not. At the first sight of Alice, the crowd got to its feet and cheered in their delight at seeing her again. After such an enthusiastic reception, the hesitant quality of Alice's performance gradually gave way to assurance. "Faye's opening night was understandably a bit tentative," the reviewer for the *Monitor* wrote, "but one had no difficulty discerning the warmth and charm that will eventually come through with increased confidence."

Alice toured the country in *Good News* for more than a year, playing more than four hundred performances and gaining confidence in each one. "I really had to learn from scratch," she told one interviewer, "but now I feel secure." On the whole the critics were kind and the audiences enthusiastic, and she always played to full houses. Alice also took her share of knocks and, in the face of some harsh reactions, developed more resilience than she had previously possessed. At a performance in January 1974, as she launched into a solo number called "I Want to Be Bad," one patron in the gallery yelled, "You are!" William B. Collins, critic for the *Washington Review,* lacerated *Good News* by saying, "It's not humor, it's archaeology."

Nevertheless, Alice gained confidence as her life with the musical settled into something of a routine. "Thank God for needlepoint," she declared at one point, "It's saving my life." She enjoyed the company and her costars and even managed to overcome the panic induced by learning that such theatrical legends as Carol Channing and Ethel Merman were in the audience. "If I can survive that I can survive anything," she said.

Alice enjoyed the life on the national tour accompanied by Jewel Baxter and her white poodle, Cece. Outside of the show, Alice lived quietly, and as performing became more routine for her, Alice let Phil and her daughters see the show. "Phil was a cryer, and when she did *Good News* in Los Angeles, he took us to see it and cried the whole time," Judy McHarg remembered. "There was a pile of Kleenex under his chair. Finally, during a scene in which Alice had to toss something across the stage, she lobbed it right at Phil."

Unfortunately, the Los Angeles venue marked the beginning of the end for *Good News.* "I loved *Good News,*" Alice later said. "We did so well on the road and it was such fun. I mean, what more did they want? I wasn't trying for anything, but that horrible man with the *L.A. Times* killed the show. After his review they started trying to change everything." Everything in this case meant replacing several songs as well as the director, which delayed the show's New York opening for more than a month. When the company finally did open at the St. James Theatre in New York on December 23, 1974, they did it without John Payne, whose original contract had expired by that time. "His leg hurt a great deal," Alice remembered, "making it very difficult for him to sing and dance and finally just move around on the stage. It wasn't as much fun anymore."

Producer Harry Rigby considered both Van Johnson and Don Ameche as replacements for Payne but finally signed actor Gene Nelson. "At that point in my career *Good News* was a job, really," Nelson said. "I wanted to be in New York for other reasons and that afforded me the opportunity to do so." Nelson's attitude would have probably distressed Alice had she been aware of it. "I didn't like the show," he said. "I didn't like the character. I didn't have a hell of a lot to do." He placed the blame for the musical's Broadway failure squarely on Alice, which was unfair considering the introduction of some drastic changes, its prior success on the road, and the potential impact of his own dissatisfaction with the play. "I loved working with Alice Faye," Nelson said. "She's a divine lady, but a lousy stage actress. Just can't hear her that's all. And that's what killed the show. Two weeks and we were closed."

Due to an unfortunate combination of problems—Alice and her anxieties, major last-minute changes, and a leading man unhappy with his role, *Good News* clearly did not meet the standards of a discerning Broadway audience. Its failure to succeed on Broadway disappointed Alice tremendously. "*Good News* was great for Mother," Alice's daughter Phyllis stated. "It really pulled her out. I wish it had done better and gone on longer." For over a year, Alice had conquered her fears sufficiently to step out before a live audience on a nightly basis, something she had not done since her days as a band singer for Rudy Vallée. It was a completely different life from that which she had led in Palm Springs, and she discovered much in it she found attractive. And, although *Good News* had closed on Broadway, other American cities remained interested in seeing it. When producers introduced the idea of a brief summer tour the following year, Alice readily accepted.

Don Ameche signed on as her costar for the tour. "I think I was supposed to do seven weeks, and we wound up doing six," he said. "Alice is a lovely person, a lovely, lovely individual. But she was so nervous," he stated, noting that her anxiety had not abated in the least in the thirty years since they had last worked together. "She was just the same. Just as nervous as she ever was." Alice's preperformance jitters may have been just as severe as always, but her *Good News* experience seemed to render her more receptive to opportunities as they came up. When a friend mentioned that a few more screen appearances would make Alice eligible for some kind of retirement benefit from the Screen Actors Guild, she did a brief cameo in the 1976 movie *Won Ton Ton, the Dog Who Saved Hollywood.* In 1978, Alice met Bonita Granville Wrather, who was casting *The Magic of Lassie* with Jimmy Stewart and Mickey Rooney, at a party. Wrather mentioned she had a waitress role she was considering doing herself, and Alice said, "How about me? I'd love to do it, just for kicks." And she did. She traveled to San Francisco for a film retrospective of her career at the Warfield Theater in 1979, and, although she was irked at screen credits that mistakenly included *The Dolly Sisters* and *How to Marry a Millionaire,* she found the audience's standing ovation and shouts of "We love you, Alice" thoroughly gratifying.

Invitations here and there, large and small, found their way to Alice as the 1970s gave way to the 1980s. She derived more and more satisfaction in accepting them, and they kept her name alive and the public interested. She appeared twice on Mary Martin's *Over Easy* television show from San Francisco and once on the British nostalgia program *Looks Familiar.* She starred with Noah Beery Jr. on an episode of *Love Boat,* filmed at the Twentieth Century-Fox Studios. She admitted television filming moved too quickly for her and that she was still "not blasé" in front of a camera, but she did enjoy a brief reunion with Helen Parker, a *Love Boat* script supervisor with whom she had worked on *Weekend in Havana* and *Tin Pan Alley.* In 1981, Alice boarded a real cruise ship when Rotterdam World Cruises sponsored a shipboard Alice Faye Film Festival. "They said we could pick up any leg of an around-the-world cruise we wanted," remembered Jewel Baxter, who accompanied her. "So I said 'Alice, we've never been to Egypt and India, let's go someplace we haven't been.'"

One of the highlights of Alice's career was a televised actor's fund benefit called *The Night of 100 Stars,* which took place on Valentine's Day in 1982, and aired a few weeks later. Alice found it a thrilling evening both as a participant and as a film fan. She once said, "All the actors used to hang around in cliques according to studio. So everyone always looked at the other studios and thought 'Those are the real movie stars.'" During *The Night of 100 Stars* Alice finally had the opportunity to rub shoulders with the "real stars." "I was thrilled to death to bump into Paul Newman!" Alice said. "Lauren Bacall had an autograph book and was getting everyone to sign. Someone said Helen Hayes had one too, but I don't believe that. It was really a great night." Alice shared a dressing room with Lillian Gish, Jane Russell, and June Allyson, none of whom she had ever met before. She met Bette Davis and recalled the diva's remark when confronted with Joan Collins in a perilously low-cut gown: "You know, it takes a lot of . . . guts to wear a dress like that!" Alice, in contrast, wore a more modest gown, but her friend Kay Gregory remembered how dazzling Alice looked as she walked out on stage. "She was so gorgeous she could have stopped a clock," Gregory recalled. "She had on a black taffeta dress with a high neck and long sleeves and a big ruffle at the bottom. She came very nearly last and she made everybody else look awful."

Alice's fabulous appearance and well-known commitment to taking care of herself, combined with her occasional public appearances and continued popularity, resulted in an unusual offer in 1984. Over the course of the next several years, it would give her a renewed sense of purpose and achievement and help her to overcome a lifetime of self-consciousness. Pfizer Pharmaceuticals was looking for a spokesperson for an upcoming senior event and during a brainstorming session one manager suggested a golden age film star. In casting about for someone appropriate, one Pfizer employee remembered, they had to consider several factors. They wanted someone familiar to their target audience, someone who could handle the time commitments, someone Pfizer could afford, and, finally, someone whose appearance promoted the image of good health. Someone mentioned Alice Faye, and they decided to invite her to participate.

What Pfizer wanted specifically was a well-known personality to represent them at programs they presented to senior citizens and health care professionals around the country. At the public events for senior citizens, the spokesperson would give a brief talk on the importance of keeping physically fit and mentally active, answer general questions, and sign autographs afterwards. At the private programs for doctors and hospital administrators, the spokesperson would make some brief opening remarks, turn the program over to a gerontologist who would lecture, then attend a reception afterwards where a photographer would be on hand for members of the audience to have their pictures taken with the celebrity. Pfizer originally envisioned these events to take place two or three times a year, but as the program grew in popularity, they expanded it to one road trip a month for ten months each year.

Alice thought the offer sounded reasonably interesting but was concerned about the public speaking component of the program. Pfizer put together a training session to groom her for her new role, in somewhat the same way Fox had groomed Alice for stardom fifty years before. In front of a coach and a cameraman, Alice would rehearse her speech and field "impromptu" questions. Together they would review the film, with the coach pointing out small quirks, such as lip biting or stammering, and generally polishing her public speaking skills. "They put her through the paces and gave her enough to lead the question-and-answer sessions," Baxter remembered.

Alice's first year on the road with Pfizer was rough, but gradually she grew more composed in her role and began to relish it. Her job was to deliver a message of good health practices, referred to as the "Pfizer Five," to senior citizens, whom she called "young elders," around the nation. These health tips included staying active and involved, eliminating cigarettes, eating a balanced diet, exercising regularly, and communicating with their doctor, particularly about prescription drugs and their proper use. With modern medicine allowing more people than ever to grow older than had been possible in previous generations, Pfizer perceived the need for a role model to encourage people to take active steps to feel better. Alice radiated health and vitality and proved a smashing success in her new role. Paul Ritz, Pfizer's program coordinator, remembered, "It snowballed as she became comfortable with it and as we found other venues and health-care-focused programs to bring her to. It just blossomed. She was nervous at her public appearances, but it was an internal, behind-the-scenes nervousness. Once she got over that, I think she enjoyed the give-and-take with the audience." Audiences, in return, flocked to see Alice, bringing in old sheet music and photographs to show her and have her sign. "I went with her a couple of times here in New Orleans," Alice Jr. said, "and she'd fill a room. I mean there would be hundreds of these old folks in there and they'd be so excited to see her." The New Orleans newspaper interviewed some of the members of that audience: "As I was coming in, she was getting out of the limousine, and she shook hands and kissed me, and I almost fainted," gushed one fan. Another marveled, "Look how small she is! I thought she'd be a heavy woman, but she's a tiny thing. She looks great."

As the Pfizer program developed, Alice's work with it evolved into a routine. Jewel Baxter and Paul Ritz would go ahead to go over the local arrangements—hotel rooms, car service, program venues, and so forth—then she would join them. "Alice was sixty-seven or sixty-eight when she started, so she was seventy-four or seventy-five towards the end of the program," Ritz said. "She was a trouper. We'd do morning radio programs, afternoon TV, a senior event in the afternoon, and then a reception for physicians in the evening. That was a full day. And there were some times when we had to pace it and do the radio and TV at the same time." Pfizer selected cities geographically to follow the sun, landing Alice in the Sun Belt in the winter and bringing her to more northern cities as their weather warmed, which made it easier on both Alice and the elderly audience coming to see her. After the formal program, Pfizer provided Alice with stacks of photographs to autograph, and she never let the public down by cutting a session short. "She would sign, and sign, and the line would be at least one hundred people long," Ritz remembered. "The local Pfizer sales managers would be charmed. She was always so gracious." Wherever she went, Alice conveyed to everyone that she was happy to be there, made sure her healthy lifestyle message was delivered, and in all ways acted as a complete professional.

Alice considered her work for Pfizer a serious job, and she took it seriously. For the formal part of the program, Alice worked from a prepared text, mixing specific points with gentle humor. When she needed to use an example, she generally brought up her brother Sonny, who had suffered from arthritis for so many years, or Phil, whose popular image she played on: "He says if he'd know he was going to live this long, he'd have taken better care of himself." At the physician receptions, she made a point of finding out with whom it was most important for her to speak, and would pose for photographs with dozens of people. As the photographer snapped the shots, Paul Ritz made a note of their names. After each trip, he sent Alice the photographs and the list of names so she could inscribe each of the photographs personally. "It was close to fifty pictures each time," he said. "She'd send them back to me, I'd send them on to the local Pfizer representatives and they'd walk into peoples' offices and say 'Here is your picture with Alice Faye. It's autographed.' She was always more than happy to do it."

Alice maintained her professional demeanor, despite the repetitive nature of her fans' questions and expectations. People always wanted to know what it had been like to kiss Tyrone Power, or to work with Shirley Temple, and sometimes asked about her "feud" with Betty Grable. Occasionally, someone would forget that she had no medical background and ask her something technical, to everyone's amusement. Often, they simply forgot themselves and went on and on about what she had meant to them, how they had named their daughters for her, or how they'd always remember her personal appearance at the Paramount Theater in 1939, when she had worn a green dress. "Alice was always very gracious," Ritz said. "She always took it in stride, always spent time."

People frequently asked why Phil was not there with her, a question Alice would pass off by replying that someone had to look after the house. Paul Ritz noticed, however, that whenever it happened "you could see the hair on the back of her neck rise a little, because this was her time, this was Alice Faye in the spotlight. Not that she was selfish or begrudging," he continued. "But I think she needed to be seen as her own person and to have a role of her own." Alice's work with Pfizer was something in which she could take pride all on her own. It rested on her celebrity and hard work as a movie star. In fact her role as an "ambassador of good health" could not have been further removed from Phil's celebrated image as a world-class carouser. In reality, Phil's health was as robust as Alice's, thanks to the outdoor life he so enjoyed. He had given up smoking, and although he drank, it was not to the bacchanalian excess that the public expected from his days on the *Jack Benny Show.* Alice regarded the Pfizer job as her own personal platform through which she helped people improve the quality of their daily lives. The pride and self-esteem she derived from it were hers alone, and she preferred to keep it that way. "I want to be able to do things for myself," she wrote about independence in later life. She and Phil were just as happy together as they were apart. "Maybe that is a reaction to all those years when the studio overprotected me. I don't want anybody else doing it now. So Phil has his life and I have mine."

As one component of the program, Pfizer had produced a forty-minute film featuring Alice called *We Still Are,* which they made available to community groups free of charge. A longer version of Alice's standard speech, it combined health advice with personal reminiscences and clips from her films. Particularly useful in this context was *Wake Up and Live,* the 1937 movie in which Alice played the motivational broadcaster whose message was to get engaged with life. At the conclusion of the Pfizer film, Alice even launches into a chorus of "Wake Up and Live," in a huskier but still resonant voice and a mildly defiant smile, as if to say "I've still got it!" Made in 1985, thirteen years before her death, it is the last commercial film in which she sang.

Alice's Pfizer career inspired another project, a book published in 1990 that was a combination reminiscence and self-help book she wrote with journalist Dick Kleiner called *Growing Older, Staying Young.* Someone had suggested to Alice that she do a book about her Pfizer work, and she eventually contacted Kleiner, a book review editor for the *Desert Sun* who had ghosted Jackie Cooper's memoirs, *Please Don't Shoot My Dog.* Kleiner followed Alice through several of her Pfizer appearances, then sat down with her over the course of six months to create a unique memoir in which they laced Alice's gospel of good health with a smattering of anecdotes about her Hollywood heyday. In the first chapter, for example, Alice addressed the issue of America's preoccupation with youth. "Who could ever imagine an elderly Jean Harlow or a doddering Robert Taylor?" she asked, noting that studio bosses allowed none of the principals in *Alexander's Ragtime Band* to age a dot in the twenty years the movie covered. On the other hand, she noted that the rigors of performing forced her into a healthy lifestyle, in which she exercised, ate right, and went to bed early. *Publisher's Weekly* called the book "a bland recollection of her heyday in Hollywood" that offered "no magic formula for remaining young in body or mind." Yet Alice produced a Hollywood memoir with more purpose than those of many of her peers. That it contained "no magic formula" but an abundance of common sense and achievable recommendations suggests that Alice may have had a firmer grip on the realities of aging than many gimmick-based advice books.

The fundamental achievement of Alice's work as a Pfizer spokeswoman, however, was neither the film nor the book but something less tangible and far more personal. In the eight years Alice remained with the program, she grew in a way that she had never done as a film or radio star. She achieved a degree of self-assurance that had eluded her most of her life. She became comfortable with people, able to address huge crowds with humor and spontaneity, or chat one-on-one with total strangers. "I feel comfortable with most people now," she told a *Chicago Tribune* columnist in 1987. "Lots of times I didn't like walking into rooms with people, that's when I was young and I was in pictures. I wasn't comfortable . . . I think you're uptight when you're younger. There were times that I would absolutely die from nervousness. My legs were shaking and I was sick to my stomach. That happened to me many times." Yet Alice had outgrown those fears sufficiently to become a poised and gracious corporate representative, admitting that her favorite format was conventions "where Pfizer sets up a booth and I can just mingle with the people as they walk by." The nervousness "doesn't happen so much anymore, now that I'm a young elder. It doesn't shake me at all," she declared.

Alice's work for Pfizer represented an ideal relationship between a corporation and its spokesperson, for as much benefit as the company derived from her, she derived more from her experience with Pfizer. Paul Ritz remembered that over the years that Pfizer ran the program, the managers would often comment on their good fortune in selecting Alice Faye. Not only was she free of any hint of scandal or inappropriate behavior but she truly believed what she said. "We always felt proud that she was our spokesperson," he said. "There was never any doubt that she lived what she was saying. She still had a twenty-five-inch waist. When she was touring with us she would exercise, she'd walk. I think she was happy with the work she was doing for Pfizer because we were doing good work for advancing health and fitness for senior citizens." Alice's daughters are quick to point out how much their mother gained out of her job. "It's amazing what they did for her. Absolutely incredible," asserted Phyllis. "Before she went to work for them she couldn't speak. She could get up and do lines for a movie, but she couldn't get up in front of people and talk. She was always very uncomfortable, and I think Pfizer really pulled her out of her shell." Alice Jr. remembered that when her mother quit the movies she was "really very shy and didn't know how to do anything. Then all those years later when she got that Pfizer job, she traveled all over the United States. She could get up at a moment's notice and do a half an hour speech. It was unbelievable. I think it was great for her self-esteem. She was much stronger after that."

At a time of life when many of her show business associates were retiring for good, letting themselves go, or battling illness and boredom, Alice emerged out of her state of semiretirement to forge a whole new career. Through her role as "ambassador of good health," she gained not only a sense of achievement but a new interest in people and a renewed appreciation of her own celebrity. "I feel very glamorous now," she declared, in contrast to her movie star life, which she once described as "grungy." She traveled, enjoyed wearing beautiful clothes by Chanel, Adolfo, and Bill Blass, and worked very hard. Her reward was the realization of just how popular a star she had always been. Being remembered by so many people so many years later brought home to Alice a greater appreciation of the fame she had achieved at a time of life when she was better prepared to enjoy it. For Alice, the "golden years" were truly golden—a time of purpose, fulfillment, and joy.

Epilogue

Alice emerged from the limousine wearing an elegant black knit suit and full-length mink coat and looking less than thrilled. Due to appear on a new talk show being launched in England, she had grown increasingly anxious as the driver went on and on driving all over Los Angeles. "Are we still in California?" she asked her companion, Jewel Baxter, in irritation. Alice remained completely unaware that her chauffeur was delaying their arrival deliberately, while a last-minute hitch in a handsome surprise was ironed out. Wishing to arrive on time, Alice became cross, her confidence in their driver diminishing rapidly as the minutes ticked by. Now that they had finally arrived at the studio, Alice stood by the limo looking on in consternation as the British host of the purported new show approached her with a microphone and a cameraman. "Alice Faye?" he questioned, the tape already running, "This is your life." "Oh, no, you wouldn't," she exclaimed in return. "You wouldn't do this to me. I don't want it!"

What followed on that evening in 1985, once Alice got over her shock and began to enjoy herself, was a splendid celebration of family, friends, fans, and colleagues, produced by the BBC, and televised in Britain as an hour-long special. Included in the lineup were Phil, Alice Jr., Phyllis, Alice and Phil's grandchildren, Pat Boone, Flo Haley, June Haver, Bob and Dolores Hope, Ruby Keeler, Fred MacMurray, Mary Martin, Senator

George Murphy, Cesar Romero, Rudy Vallée, and Jane Withers, with filmed greetings by Don Ameche, John Payne, Anthony Quinn, and Ginger Rogers. It was a benchmark evening in the period of command performances, celebrations, and film festivals that characterized the last two decades of Alice's life. Events like these added sparkle and zest to Alice's later years and brought her back into contact with friends, fans, and coworkers collected from her long-ago movie days.

The continued popularity of her films thrilled Alice, and she was happy to appear at many of the retrospectives celebrating them. One evening while watching the CBS news with Dan Rather, she was stunned to hear South African leader Nelson Mandela mention her as one of the stars he had enjoyed in the movies he watched during his long imprisonment. She performed for Queen Elizabeth on three occasions, one of which was a 1986 "Hollywood Musical" charity event that reunited her with Don Ameche, who admitted that she had been his favorite leading lady. Wearing a black evening gown with one white sleeve embroidered in black and one black sleeve embroidered in white, Alice sang "You'll Never Know," to a rapt audience. "She always liked London," said Jewel Baxter. "At one royal performance I remember particularly she had the most wonderful straight-down black sequin dress, just elegant. I was backstage and I could see the dress shimmering—her knees were knocking. Well, she got out on the stage and I'll tell you for three minutes she couldn't open her mouth. People were screaming, yelling, applauding. They loved her."

Alice learned, to her chagrin, that not all events were managed with the smoothness of a royal command performance. An invitation from the Motion Picture Academy to sing "You'll Never Know" for the Oscars evolved into a less-than-flattering opportunity to sit onstage and listen while someone else sang her signature tune to millions of viewers around the world. Upset and insulted, she placed a hasty phone call to Phil in Palm Springs, who told her, "Come on home, honey," and out she walked. Her absence from that evening's broadcast was conspicuous and received a lot of play in the press. A similarly bungled situation occurred with the

Carnegie Hall tribute to Irving Berlin on his one hundredth birthday. Producers had cleared the date on Alice's calendar six months in advance but later neglected to issue an invitation, resulting in yet another noticeable absence. "I really feel strange about it. I had hoped to be there," Alice admitted to one reporter. "But you have to roll with the punches. I always send Mr. Berlin a card on his birthday. This year, I'm sending him an American Beauty rose."

Such callousness reflected the new Hollywood, to which the Hollywood of Alice's era was gradually succumbing. Although many members of the older generation of stars were slipping away, young filmmakers seemed to have little time to spare for their predecessors in the industry. Alice was fortunate that work and travel kept her engaged and unable to dwell too long on obituaries announcing the deaths of so many of her close colleagues. In the 1980s, she lost mentors Henry King and Rudy Vallée, as well as Harry Rigby, the producer of *Good News*. In December 1989 John Payne died of congestive heart failure in Malibu, and four years later prostate cancer claimed Don Ameche at the age of eighty-five. Alice, in the meantime, kept going strong, staying active, and continuing to look after herself. Her biggest indulgences during this time continued to be facials and massages, and in the late 1980s she visited a plastic surgeon to get her eyes done. "They were bagging and I was working in front of the public and doing cameos and things like that," she said. "It wasn't very attractive." While Alice was under the anesthetic, the surgeon also treated a crease between her eyes with acid, which created a conspicuous sore. When her friend Judy McHarg inquired about where the crease had come from, Alice snorted, "Why wouldn't I have a crease? I cried in every movie I ever made."

Milestones seemed to come with greater frequency in the 1980s and 1990s. In 1981, Alice and Phil's daughters threw them a surprise party to celebrate their fortieth anniversary. It represented a remarkable achievement for a couple that Hollywood observers had dubbed the most likely to divorce. "We went up to visit Phyllis in Tucson," Alice said. "The night of our anniversary we were supposed to go to a local restaurant. Then about nine o'clock the door bell rang and these people started coming in from all over. It was the biggest kick I'd ever had!" The Harrises eventually celebrated not only their fiftieth wedding anniversary but several more beyond that, one of which Phil commemorated by presenting Alice with a stunning emerald ring. In 1990, Phil threw Alice a seventy-fifth birthday party at Chasen's in Los Angeles. Their friend and neighbor at Thunderbird, Virginia Zamboni, handled all the arrangements, for the small party of friends and family. She decorated the room in lavender, Alice's favorite color, and heaped it with Alice's adored lilacs, even though they were out of season and hard to come by. On July 2, 1991, the Harrises' first greatgrandchild was born, and three years later, to celebrate Phil's ninetieth birthday, the city of Palm Springs gave Alice and Phil their own stars in the city's star walk.

As Alice and Phil became more settled in their later years, they found more things to do together. For many years they sponsored an annual fall luncheon and golf tournament to benefit the Arthritis Foundation. Alice, who had long supported the charity because of its debilitating effects on her brother Sonny, had begun to suffer from the disease as well. Sonny, who died in 1977, had had little more than aspirin with which to combat the pain throughout his life. "He was terribly crippled," Alice Jr. remembered. "The worst arthritis I've ever seen in my life. His elbows and knees looked like bowling balls, and he couldn't get going until the middle of the afternoon." Though she suffered nowhere to the extent her brother had, Alice nevertheless contended with painfully gnarled hands, and eventually developed leg trouble as well. Her friends Virginia Zamboni and Gabé Farrell surmised that it may have been one of the reasons Alice eventually gave up painting. She remained an advocate for the foundation for the rest of her life, and when she passed away in 1998, her daughters asked that donations be sent there. "Mother did the tournament for years and kept it going even after Daddy died," said Alice Jr. "Arthritis remained her big charity."

Another common interest began in the early 1980s, when Phil's hometown of Linton, Indiana, invited him to perform on behalf of a local scholarship program. Together he and Alice headlined the show, which included a local Dixieland band and other minor celebrities. During rehearsals, the benefit's organizer, Don Steward, remembered driving with Phil past a flower shop. "He said 'Stop. Do they have lilacs in here?'" and jumped out of the car to have the shop send Alice some lilacs at the hall where she was rehearsing. The show proved a popular attraction for the small community. So did the collection of materials Alice and Phil decided to place in the community's library, a large amalgamation of scripts, scrapbooks, photographs, correspondence, and recordings of their radio show. The Linton golf tournament and show developed into an annual event. Over the years it has raised over $400,000 to help send five to seven local students to college each year.

Alice attended the Linton celebration almost every year and usually performed. Alice Jr., Phyllis, and their children would often show up as well. "Alice would go up because her family would be there and Phil wanted her to be there," said Gabé Farrell. The Harris family and other visiting celebrities took over the local motel for several days each year and indulged themselves in small-town entertainment in between appearances at the various events. One of the organizers of the program, realizing that Alice painted, arranged for her to visit the famous art colony in Brown County nearby. They cooked out on the parking lot at the motel or shopped or dropped by the diner downtown. "The girls would come home with some cute clothes," said Farrell. "Somebody up there had a dress shop they enjoyed. And they had a photographer who took a marvelous family portrait." The only drawback to that corner of Indiana was its lack of libation. "You couldn't get a drink in that town," said Alice Jr. "So I'd send a case of liquor every year from New Orleans. I'd send it to the funeral home in case it leaked, because you're not supposed to send liquor through the mail. I figured if it leaked they'd think it was formaldehyde or something. But my family had to have something to drink."

Both Alice and Phil had grown closer to their daughters as the years progressed. "I know that when Alice and I were younger we weren't really an integral part of their lives," Phyllis said. "We were always away at school or college or married. But when we got older, then Alice and I took turns staying at home for long periods of time, because they kind of needed some help. Daddy and Alice were very close and they could always laugh and have a good time. And I used to go home and take mother shopping or chum around and have lunch at the club." Alice loved being with her daughters after they were grown and once said to Don Steward in Linton that the thing she regretted most was not spending all of her time with them when they were small. When Alice Jr. or Phyllis came to visit, Alice was conspicuous in her desire to keep them all to herself. Her friend Kay Gregory remembered, "She didn't want to share the two of them with anybody. I might call and suggest lunch, but she would turn me down, saying, 'Alice is going to be here today.' She didn't want to see anybody else when they were in." Alice Jr. recalled one occasion when her mother's possessiveness proved frustrating. "I remember one time Mr. Sinatra called up and said, 'Why don't you come over and watch a movie?' They used to have groups in. And Mom said, 'I can't. My daughter's here from New Orleans.' He told her to bring my husband and me along, but she told him she couldn't possibly. My husband was in awe, saying 'Frank Sinatra!' and I was saying, 'But *Mom*, I wanted to go!'"

When Alice was home between trips, and later when she traveled less, she continued to live a normal, subdued life. She loved to cook and shop at the grocery store, where the clerks all knew her. She watched old movies on television and read a great deal. She would buy bestsellers, preferably biographies and autobiographies, then loan them out to friends once she had finished them. Two or three times a week, she and friends would catch the 4:30 matinee at the movie theater, after which they would go out for a quiet dinner. Jewel Baxter would visit and said she most enjoyed the days they spent quietly together in or around Alice's home. Baxter had loved the informality and peace of the Harris home at Thunderbird since the days when Bing Crosby would walk in the back door and lift up the lids of the pots on the stove. "The housekeeper would set the table and leave, and Alice and Phil would cook, then I insisted that they watch TV while I cleared off the table. It was just that kind of atmosphere. When Alice and I were there alone, we'd have dinner and watch television. We just sat and talked and laughed, just had a beautiful relationship," Baxter said.

Alice's public performance schedule diminished over the years, but she loved to sing and continued to do it informally among friends. She had a handful of favorite restaurants where she and friends would often go to dinner. Kay Gregory said, "At one place she always sat in the bar. It was a lovely bar where all our friends sat. There was a pianist there and she would sing all through the evening. She did that often. She loved to sing. That I think was her favorite thing to do. She was timid with strangers. She'd sing at the club when people insisted, but what she liked to do was just sing in a small group." Gabé Farrell marveled at Alice's shyness in the face of her talent as a singer. "You really had to push her to sing in front of large groups. But in people's homes, someone would start and she would join in. And she would sing in the car. When we'd drive with her to La Costa, we put tapes on and sing the whole way. And we'd always stop in at the In and Out in Hemmet. Alice loved their hamburgers."

By the early 1990s Alice and Phil had slowed down considerably. Their health had begun to deteriorate, and their daughters began spending even more time with them in Palm Springs. Alice and Phil's odd-couple relationship continued along in the same pattern it always had—Alice the elegant introvert and Phil the sentimental extrovert. Linton, Indiana, barber Jack Shelton remembered Phil tearing up over something and Alice remarking off to the side, "Oh, don't mind him. He cried when Hitler died." The rose growers of San Mateo, California, experienced Alice's wry take on her relationship with Phil at the dedication of the Alice Faye Rose in 1992. Alice's friend and fan, Roy Bishop remembered her off-the-cuff remarks that day and how she startled the audience by saying, "You know

I'm very pleased that you asked me to come up here and name a rose after me. But I just want to know one thing. Are you going to name a rose after Phil? Because if you are, you can have mine back." The audience roared.

Bishop noted the other side of Alice, however, the one upon which so many other friends and acquaintances commented. Whenever she and Bishop were out, she always phoned so she and Phil could check in with one another. Paul Ritz noticed the same thing when he and Alice were on the road. Answering Alice's phone in New Orleans one night, Ritz found himself talking to Phil, who was concerned about news of a hurricane due to hit the city. Paul and Alice were meeting Alice Jr. for dinner and he remembered Phil saying, "Now, Paul, I hope you're going to take care of my girls." Gabé Farrell said, "They were always fine when they were apart, but they talked every single day no matter where they were. It was a long-enduring love affair."

The Harrises' dedication to one another seemed to grow stronger as they grew older. Alice would phone the club to tell him dinner was ready, then worry about him driving even the short distance between the clubhouse and their home. She fussed about Phil's health, keeping track of his medicine and encouraging him get out and do things. "Phil was sick about a year before he died," Farrell said, "and she kept pushing him. She wouldn't let him stay in bed. She'd get him up and try to get him to swim. She had the handrail installed so he could get in and out of the pool more easily. She was really the strong one during the time before his death." Toward the end, when Phil experienced difficulty in walking, Alice continued to urge him to get out for a change of scene. He would put on a fresh pair of pajamas and a robe and drive his golf cart across the street to visit their neighbors Gabé Farrell and Virginia Zamboni. "He'd always have a couple of jokes when he came in," they remembered, confessing that they always called another friend to feed them jokes to give back to him.

In May 1995 Phil made what would be his last trip to perform in Linton, Indiana. He was ninety years old and on dialysis but did not want to disappoint event organizers by not appearing. He emceed the show from a chair, but still managed to convey much of the familiar Harris vinegar. As his finale, Phil sang "What a Wonderful World" and "Younger than Spring," then retired from the stage to return home to California. He died a few months later on August 11 at the age of ninety-one. Those who knew him, even if only slightly, felt his loss keenly. Alice's spokeswoman, Jewel Baxter, called him funny and beautiful and wondered at his remarkable energy. "Phil was never without something to do. He had a million friends, he did the golf, he did the Crosby thing. He had people around him all the time," she said. Alice's collaborator, Dick Kleiner, remembered that Phil would always have a joke on his answering machine. "I tried to make it my business when I knew he wasn't there to call him so I could hear his joke," he said. Perhaps columnist Steven Mikulan presented the best eulogy in his article "Death of a Leisurecrat," which appeared in the September 1995 *L.A. Weekly:* "He had it all: the canals of booze Harris reputedly drained apparently bypassed his liver completely, his retreat to the desert while still in his mid-40s and his bent for doing only easy television spots had absolutely no impact on his standard of living. And none of the familial holocausts experienced by a Crosby or Sinatra ever troubled Harris, who remained married to Alice Faye for 54 years."

Phil's death marked the beginning of a long physical decline for Alice. It was as if, having kept old age at bay for so long, she underwent an accelerated aging process. During the fifty-four years of their marriage, Alice had built her life around Phil. Whether she accompanied him, accommodated him, or reacted to him, he constituted the center of her world. She may have spent much of her time by herself, or pursuing independent projects, but Phil was always in the background. He walked through the door in the evenings or rang her up at the hotels where she stayed. Alice found the task of coping without him daunting. "She didn't like being alone," said Virginia Zamboni. "She liked being alone during the day, but she wanted someone to come home at night." Roy Bishop remembered her telling him that she had lost her best friend when Phil died. "I thought Alice was going to go on forever," he said. "She seemed like she was in such good health and she looked so good, but after Phil died her health went downhill."

Precipitating a chain reaction of ongoing bad health was an ankle Alice broke soon after she lost Phil. Regina Kramer, one of the members of the party from Linton, remembered her shock at seeing Alice at the memorial service, held later that fall, in a wheelchair. "She was at a party and jumped up and said she wanted to go home," Alice Jr. said. "Instead of waiting for someone to walk her out, she went ahead and broke her ankle." While she wore the cast Alice kept accidentally hitting her other foot, resulting in an open wound that would not heal. She eventually went to UCLA for a consultation and learned that her arteries were clogged. The loss of circulation was what had prevented her wound from healing properly. Alice's condition posed an immediate risk of stroke, and the next day doctors performed vascular surgery, first to clear the arteries, then later in the week to open up her veins. Sometime after that, she fell at home while changing her clothes after a party and broke her wrist. Her neighbors ran her up to Eisenhower Hospital, where two pins had to be inserted in her arm.

As Alice Jr. and Phyllis shuttled back and forth between their homes and hers to look after Alice, they grew more and more concerned. Alice's physical problems distressed them but more disquieting was her attitude. "It was funny," said Alice, Jr., "after all those years of tromping around the country telling senior citizens to keep moving and exercise and do stuff, she kind of just sat down and quit." Phyllis remembered trying to get her mother involved in something to take her mind of her troubles, suggesting that they might do some painting together. "I used to worry a lot after Dad passed on," Phyllis said. "She died of a broken heart because she didn't have Daddy to pick on anymore. When he died, she just shut down. She didn't want to go anywhere. She used to love to go out to dinner. She didn't want to get dressed. I don't think Mother needed to die. She just didn't have the will to live. I think she just missed Daddy." Gabé

Farrell noted, "She just got miserable with the whole thing. She missed Phil and her health just began to wear on her."

The second year after Phil died, Alice tried to get away for a change of scene and took a two-month lease on a house in Carmel. "She liked it up there and I think would liked to have had a home there," said Phyllis. "We used to stay at the Crosbys' house when we were younger. Then she rented a house a couple of times. Daddy didn't care for it. He'd go, stay a little while, then he'd take off." Gabé Farrell said, "It was her favorite place and always her dream to have a summer home up there." Alice rented the house with high hopes. She wanted her daughters to visit and had also invited Farrell and Virginia Zamboni to come up. She stayed there a month but found that she did not enjoy it. It was not the same. "You know the saying that you can't go home again," said Farrell. "It was like that. She called and told us not to come up. She had rented it for two months and didn't make it but one. She came home and didn't finish out her lease."

Sometime after the disappointment of Carmel, Alice underwent surgery to remove her spleen. The doctors performing the operation noticed a growth, which proved to be a malignant tumor. True to form, Alice did not say anything about it to her friends. "She told everybody she was fine and in good health," Roy Bishop said. "I'm sure Alice did this because she wanted people to react to her the same way they always had. And if you know somebody has cancer, it's going to affect your behavior towards them. I don't know that as a fact, I just have the feeling that that's why she didn't tell anybody." People in closer proximity to Alice knew that she was ill but had no idea of the seriousness of the situation. Alice apparently had difficulty facing up to the situation herself. "She never wanted to know," said Farrell. "They kept telling her she had to go to the oncologist and she kept putting it off. She'd make an appointment and cancel." The difficulties of the preceding two years, complications with her arthritis medication, and genuine loneliness took their toll on Alice. "I think she just got to the point where she couldn't bear it any more," Farrell said. "Her world got very narrow. She didn't want to see too many people and she didn't want to go out much." She finally underwent surgery in April 1998 but did not improve. After a brief illness, Alice died at her home on May 9, four days after her eighty-third birthday, with Alice Jr. and Phyllis at her side.

Not many of Alice Faye's peers from Hollywood were on hand to bid her farewell at the memorial service that occurred in Palm Desert the week after her death. Jane Withers, Jane Wyman, and Loretta Young possessed some of the few famous faces in a church packed with friends and family. That occurrence seemed to illustrate how remote in time Alice's movie career had been. Most of the famous contemporaries from her heyday, between 1934 and 1945, were significantly older than she. Many had either passed away long before 1998 or had grown so fragile they could not to attend. Furthermore, the absence of a swarm of celebrities seemed to represent the relative importance, or lack thereof, of her movie career to Alice's subsequent life. She enjoyed many of the consequences of her profession: the financial independence, the pride she could take in her work, and the appreciation of her devoted fans. But to Alice stardom was a means to an end, not the end itself. "I'd say she was Miss Average," said Dick Kleiner. "She started out as a chorus girl and singer to make some money, and I think she would have married and had kids, but the thing got away from her and she had a career. She took it very well and didn't let it go to her head. I think she would have been just as happy as a housewife in the Bronx."

Yet, as so many members of the public realized, Alice was never average. "Living in the Madonna era would be unbearable if I didn't remember Alice Faye," wrote columnist and author Florence King. "She had a tangible effect on movie audiences. I remember the shuffling vibration as patrons tapped their feet in a carpeted version of the old soft-shoe when she sang 'On Moonlight Bay' in *Tin Pan Alley* . . . and the moment Faye started belting out "America, I Love You" a palpable electricity filled the theater and exploded in applause when the last note ended." Recalling Alice's appearance on an American Movie Classics interview in 1992, King noted that "in contrast to other aged actresses . . . her hair was frankly white and her face frankly unlifted. She had come to what Marilyn Monroe and other sex symbols dread so much that they die young rather than face it, yet as the interview progressed it was clear that Alice Faye had chosen the better part. This was a woman who knew exactly who she was and where she stood, too secure for publicized nervous breakdowns, battles with booze and pills, and maudlin announcements of 'At last I've found true love.' Hail and farewell, dear Miss Faye. There'll never be another like you."

Alice Faye possessed the gift of alchemy, transforming the banal, mass-market productions of Twentieth Century-Fox into the cherished favorites of an entire generation. "She could spin magic with her songs," as one writer put it, neglecting to mention such additional transforming powers as the wry smile, the arched eyebrow, or the blue velvet eyes. Certainly the studio never found another like her. Subsequent Fox blondes, including Betty Grable and Marilyn Monroe, each held measures of honesty, vulnerability, and sex appeal, but never in the same captivating combination as Alice. Nor did they serve their owners as well. Alice's fortune rested in her face and figure, her voice, and the quiet determination of her character. She worked hard and played straight, with her audience and with herself, conveying an enchanting ordinariness that proved extraordinary. There will most certainly never be another like her.

FILMOGRAPHY

George White's Scandals. Distributed by Fox Film Corp., released March 16, 1934, executive producer Robert T. Kane, director Thornton Freeland, starring Rudy Vallée (Jimmy Martin), Jimmy Durante (Happy McGillicuddy), Alice Faye (Kitty Donnelly), Adrienne Ames (Barbara Loraine), Gregory Ratoff (Nicholas Mitwoch), George White (himself). 80 minutes.
SONGS: "Nasty Man," "So Nice," "Hold My Hand," "Following in Mother's Footsteps," "My Dog Loves Your Dog," "Six Women," "Sweet and Simple," and "Every Day Is Father's Day with Baby," music by Ray Henderson, lyrics by Jack Yellen and Irving Caesar; "Cabin in the Cotton and the Cotton in the Cabin," music and lyrics by Irving Caesar; "The Flying Trapeze," original melody by George Leybourne, lyricist unknown.

Now I'll Tell. Distributed by Fox Film Corp., released May 11, 1934, producer Winfield Sheehan, director Edwin Burke, starring Spencer Tracy (Murray Golden), Helen Twelvetrees (Virginia), Alice Faye (Peggy Warren), Robert Gleckler (Al Mositer), Henry O'Neill (Tommy Doran), Shirley Temple (Mary Doran). 87 minutes.
SONGS: "Fooling with the Other Woman's Man," music and lyrics by Lew Brown and Harry Akst.

She Learned About Sailors. Distributed by Fox Film Corp., released June 29, 1934, producer John Stone, director George Marshall, starring Lew Ayres (Larry Wilson), Alice Faye (Jean Legai), Frank Mitchell

(Peanuts), Jack Durant (Eddie), Harry Green (Jose Lopez Ruben-stein). 76 minutes.

SONGS: "She Learned About Sailors" and "Here's the Key to My Heart," music by Richard Whiting, lyrics by Sidney Clare.

365 Nights in Hollywood. Distributed by Fox Film Corp., released October 12, 1934, producer Sol M. Wurtzel, director George Marshall, star-ring James Dunn (Jimmie Dale), Alice Faye (Alice Perkins), Frank Mitchell (Percy), Jack Durant (Clarence), John Bradford (Adrian Al-mont), Grant Mitchell (J. Walter Delmar). 74 minutes.

SONGS: "Yes to You" and "My Future Star," music and lyrics by Richard Whiting and Sidney Clare.

George White's 1935 Scandals. Distributed by Fox Film Corp., released March 29, 1935, producer Winfield R. Sheehan, director James Tin-ling, starring Alice Faye (Honey Walters), James Dunn (Eddie Taylor), Ned Sparks (Elmer), Lyda Roberti (Manya), Eleanor Powell (Mari-lyn Collins), George White (himself). 83 minutes.

SONGS: "I Got Shoes, You Got Shoesies," "Oh, I Didn't Know You'd Get That Way," "Hunkadola," and "It's Time to Say Goodnight," lyrics by Jack Yellen and Cliff Friend, music by Joseph Meyer; "I Was Born Too Late" and "It's an Old Southern Custom," lyrics by Jack Yellen, music by Joseph Meyer; "According to the Moonlight," lyrics by Jack Yellen and Herb Magidson, music by Joseph Meyer; "You Belong to Me," lyrics by Jack Yellen, music by Cliff Friend.

Every Night at Eight. Distributed by Paramount Productions, released Au-gust 2, 1935, producer Walter Wanger, director Raoul Walsh, starring George Raft (Tops Cardona), Alice Faye (Dixie), Frances Langford (Susan Moore), Patsy Kelly (Daphne O'Connor). 80 minutes.

SONGS: "Take It Easy," "I Feel a Song Comin' On," "Every Night at Eight," and "I'm in the Mood for Love," music and lyrics by Dorothy

Fields and James McHugh; "Then You've Never Been Blue," music by Ted Fio Rito, lyrics by Joe Young and Frances Langford.

Music Is Magic. Distributed by Twentieth Century-Fox Film Corp., released November 1, 1935, associate producer John Stone, director George Marshall, starring Alice Faye (Peggy Harper), Ray Walker (Jack Lambert), Bebe Daniels (Diane De Valle), Frank Mitchell (Peanuts Harper), Jack Durant (Eddie Harper), Hattie McDaniel (Amanda). 66 minutes. SONGS: "Music Is Magic," words by Sidney Clare, music by Arthur Johnston; "Love Is Smiling at Me" and "Honey Chile," lyrics by Sidney Clare, music by Oscar Levant; "La Locumba," original music and lyrics by Raul Roulien, English lyrics by Sidney Clare.

King of Burlesque. Distributed by Twentieth Century-Fox Film Corp., released January 3, 1936, associate producer Kenneth MacGowan, director Sidney Lanfield, starring Warner Baxter (Kerry Bolton), Alice Faye (Pat Doran), Jack Oakie (Joe Cooney), Mona Barrie (Rosalind Cleve), Gregory Ratoff (Kolpolpeck), Fats Waller (Ben). 88 minutes. SONGS: "(I'm) Shooting High," "Lovely Lady," "Spreading Rhythm Around," "Too Good to Be True (I've Got My Fingers Crossed)," and "Whose Big Baby Are You?" music and lyrics by Jimmy McHugh and Ted Koehler; "I Love to Ride the Horses on a Merry-Go-Round," music by Lew Pollack, lyrics by Jack Yellen.

Poor Little Rich Girl. Distributed by Twentieth Century-Fox Film Corp., released July 24, 1936, associate producer B. G. DeSylva, director Irving Cummings, starring Shirley Temple (Barbara Barry), Alice Faye (Jerry Dolan), Gloria Stuart (Margaret Allen), Jack Haley (Jimmy Dolan), Michael Whalen (Richard Barry), Jane Darwell (Woodward). 72 minutes. SONGS: "But Definitely," "When I'm with You," "Oh, My Goodness," "You've Gotta Eat Your Spinach, Baby," "I Like a Military Man," and "Buy a Bar of Barry's," music and lyrics by Mack Gordon and Harry Revel.

Sing, Baby, Sing. Distributed by Twentieth Century-Fox Film Corp., released August 21, 1936, associate producer B. G. DeSylva, director Sidney Lanfield, starring Alice Faye (Joan Warren), Adolphe Menjou (Bruce Farraday), Gregory Ratoff (Nicky Alexander), Ted Healy (Al Craven), Patsy Kelly (Fitz), Tony Martin (Tony Renaldo). 90 minutes.

SONGS: "Love Will Tell" and "Sing, Baby, Sing," music and lyrics by Lew Pollack and Jack Yellen; "You Turned the Tables on Me," music and lyrics by Louis Alter and Sidney D. Mitchell; "When Did You Leave Heaven," music and lyrics by Richard A. Whiting and Walter Bullock.

Stowaway. Distributed by Twentieth Century-Fox Film Corp., released December 25, 1936, producer B. G. DeSylva, director William A. Seiter, starring Shirley Temple (Ching-Ching/Barbara Stewart), Robert Young (Tommy Randall), Alice Faye (Susan Parker), Eugene Pallette (The Colonel), Helen Westley (Mrs. Hope), Arthur Treacher (Atkins). 87 minutes.

SONGS: "Goodnight My Love," "You've Gotta S-M-I-L-E to Be H-A-double-P-Y," and "One Never Knows, Does One?" music and lyrics by Mack Gordon and Harry Revel; "That's What I Want for Christmas," music and lyrics by Irving Caesar and Gerald Marks.

On the Avenue. Distributed by Twentieth Century-Fox Film Corp., release February 12, 1937, associate producer Gene Markey, director Roy Del Ruth, starring Dick Powell (Gary Blake), Madeleine Carroll (Mimi Caraway), Alice Faye (Mona Merrick), Ritz Brothers (themselves), George Barbier (Commodore Caraway), Alan Mowbray (Frederick Sims), Cora Witherspoon (Aunt Fritz). 90 minutes.

SONGS: "The Girl on the Police Gazette," "He Ain't Got Rhythm,"

"I've Got My Love to Keep Me Warm," "Slumming on Park Avenue," "This Year's Kisses," and "You're Laughing at Me," music and lyrics by Irving Berlin.

Wake Up and Live. Distributed by Twentieth Century-Fox Film Corp., released April 23, 1937, associate producer Kenneth Macgowan, director Sidney Lanfield, starring Walter Winchell (himself), Ben Bernie and Orchestra (themselves), Alice Faye (Alice Huntley), Patsy Kelly (Patsy Kane), Ned Sparks (Steve Cluskey), Jack Haley (Eddie Kane). 91 minutes.
SONGS: "There's a Lull in My Life," "It's Swell of You," "Wake Up and Live," "Never in a Million Years," "I'm Bubbling Over," "I Love You Much Too Much, Muchacha," and "Ooh, But I'm Happy," music and lyrics by Mack Gordon and Harry Revel.

You Can't Have Everything. Distributed by Twentieth Century-Fox Film Corp., released August 3, 1937, associate producer Laurence Schwab, director Norman Taurog, starring Alice Faye (Judith Poe Wells), Ritz Brothers (themselves), Don Ameche (George Macrae), Louise Hovick (Lulu Riley), Rubinoff (himself), Tony Martin (Bobby Walker). 100 minutes.
SONGS: "Afraid to Dream," "You Can't Have Everything," "The Loveliness of You," "Please Pardon Us—We're in Love," "Danger—Love at Work," music and lyrics by Mack Gordon and Harry Revel.

You're a Sweetheart. Distributed by Universal Pictures Co., released December 26, 1937, producer B. G. DeSylva, director David Butler, starring Alice Faye (Betty Bradley), George Murphy (Hal Adams), Ken Murray (Don King), Charles Winninger (Cherokee Charlie), Andy Devine (Daisy Day), William Gargan (Fred Edwards). 96 minutes.
SONGS: "My Fine Feathered Friend," "You're a Sweetheart," "Who Killed Maggie?" "Broadway Jamboree," and "Oh, Oh, Oklahoma,"

music and lyrics by Jimmy McHugh and Harold Adamson; "Scraping the Toast," music and lyrics by Charles Tobias and Murray Mencher; "So It's Love," music and lyrics by Lou Bring, Mickey Bloom, and Arthur Quenzer.

Sally, Irene, and Mary. Distributed by Twentieth Century-Fox Film Corp., released March 4, 1938, associate producer Gene Markey, director William A. Seiter, starring Alice Faye (Sally Day), Tony Martin (Tommy Reynolds), Fred Allen (Gabriel Green), Jimmy Durante (Jefferson Twitchell), Gregory Ratoff (Baron Zorka), Joan Davis (Irene Keene). 86 minutes.

SONGS: "Half Moon on the Hudson," "I Could Use a Dream," "This Is Where I Came In," "Help Wanted—Male," and "Who Stole the Jam?" music and lyrics by Walter Bullock and Harold Spina; "Got My Mind on Music" and "Sweet as a Song," music and lyrics by Mack Gordon and Harry Revel; "Minuet in Jazz," music and lyrics by Raymond Scott.

In Old Chicago. Distributed by Twentieth Century-Fox Film Corp., released April 15, 1938, associate producer Kenneth Macgowan, director Henry King, starring Tyrone Power (Dion O'Leary), Alice Faye (Belle Fawcett), Don Ameche (Jack O'Leary), Alice Brady (Molly O'Leary), Andy Devine (Pickle Bixby), Brian Donlevy (Gil Warren). 115 minutes.

SONGS: "In Old Chicago," music and lyrics by Mack Gordon and Harry Revel; "I'll Never Let You Cry," "I've Taken a Fancy to You," and "Take a Dip in the Sea," music and lyrics by Lew Pollack and Sidney D. Mitchell; "Carry Me Back to Old Virginny," music and lyrics by James Bland.

Alexander's Ragtime Band. Distributed by Twentieth Century-Fox Film Corp., released August 19, 1938, associate producer Harry Joe Brown, director Henry King, starring Tyrone Power (Alexander, Roger Grant), Alice Faye (Stella Kirby), Don Ameche (Charlie Dwyer), Ethel Merman (Jerry Allen), Jack Haley (Davey Lane). 105 minutes.

SONGS: "Alexander's Ragtime Band," "Ragtime Violin," "That International Rag," "Everybody's Doin' It Now," "Now It Can Be Told," "This Is the Life," "When the Midnight Choo-Choo Leaves for Alabam'," "For Your Country and My Country," "I Can Always Find a Little Sunshine in the Y.M.C.A.," "Oh! How I Hate to Get Up in the Morning," "We're on Our Way to France," "In My Harem," "When I Lost You," "Say It with Music," "A Pretty Girl Is Like a Melody," "Some Sunny Day," "Blue Skies," "Everybody Step," "What'll I Do," "Remember," "Pack Up Your Sins and Go to the Devil," "My Walking Stick," "All Alone," "Heat Wave," "Easter Parade," "Cheek to Cheek," "Lazy," "Marie," and "Marching Along with Time," music and lyrics by Irving Berlin.

Tail Spin. Distributed by Twentieth Century-Fox Film Corp., released January 27, 1939, associate producer Harry Joe Brown, director Roy Del Ruth, starring Alice Faye (Trixie Lee), Constance Bennett (Gerry Lester), Nancy Kelly (Lois Allen), Joan Davis (Babe Dugan), Charles Farrell (Bud), Jane Wyman (Alabama). 84 minutes.

SONGS: "Are You in the Mood for Mischief," music and lyrics by Mack Gordon and Harry Revel.

Rose of Washington Square. Distributed by Twentieth Century-Fox Film Corp., released May 12, 1939, associate producer Nunnally Johnson, director Gregory Ratoff, starring Tyrone Power (Bart Clinton), Alice Faye (Rose Sargent), Al Jolson (Ted Cotter), William Frawley (Harry Long), Joyce Compton (Peggy). 86 minutes.

SONGS: "Rose of Washington Square," music and lyrics by James F. Hanley and Ballard MacDonald; "I Never Knew Heaven Could Speak," music and lyrics by Mack Gordon and Harry Revel; "I'm Always

Chasing Rainbows," music and lyrics by Harry Carroll and Joe Mc-
Carthy; "My Man" music and lyrics by Maurice Yvain, Al. Willemetz,
and Jacques Charles, English lyrics by Channing Polack; "Toot, Toot,
Tootsie (Goodbye)," music and lyrics by Gus Kahn and Ernie Erd-
man; "The Curse of an Aching Heart," music and lyrics by Al Pi-
antadosi and Henry Fink, "I'm Sorry I Made You Cry," music and
lyrics by N. J. Clesi; "The Vamp," music and lyrics by Byron Gay;
"California, Here I Come," music and lyrics by B. G. DeSylva, Joseph
Meyer, and Al Jolson; "My Mammy," music and lyrics by Joe Young,
Sam Lewis, and Walter Donaldson; "Pretty Baby," music and lyrics
by Tony Jackson and Egbert Van Alstyne; "Ja-Da," music and lyrics
by Bob Carleton; "Rock-a-bye Your Baby with a Dixie Melody," music and lyrics by Jean Schwartz, Sam M. Lewis, and Joe Young; "I'm
Just Wild about Harry," music and lyrics by Noble Sissle and Eubie
Blake.

Hollywood Cavalcade. Distributed by Twentieth Century-Fox Film Corp.,
released October 13, 1939, associate producer Harry Joe Brown, director Irving Cummings, starring Alice Faye (Molly Adair), Don
Ameche (Michael Linnett Connors), J. Edward Bromberg (Dave Sp-
ingold), Alan Curtis (Nicky Hayden), Stuart Erwin (Pete Tinney),
Buster Keaton (himself). 96 minutes.

Barricade. Distributed by Twentieth Century-Fox Film Corp., released December 8, 1939, associate producer Edward Kaufman, director Gregory Ratoff, starring Alice Faye (Emmy Jordan), Warner Baxter (Hank
Topping), Charles Winninger (Samuel J. Cady), Arthur Treacher (Up-
ton Ward), Keye Luke (Ling). 71 minutes.

Little Old New York. Distributed by Twentieth Century-Fox Film Corp., released February 9, 1940, associate producer Raymond Griffith, director Henry King, starring Alice Faye (Pat O'Day), Fred MacMurray

(Charles Browne), Richard Greene (Robert Fulton), Brenda Joyce (Harriet Livingstone), Andy Devine (Commodore), Henry Stephenson (Robert R. Livingstone), Ward Bond (Regan). 100 minutes.
SONGS: "Who Is the Beau of the Belle of New York?" music and lyrics by Mack Gordon.

Lillian Russell. Distributed by Twentieth Century-Fox Film Corp., released May 24, 1940, associate producer Gene Markey, director Irving Cummings, starring Alice Faye (Lillian Russell), Don Ameche (Edward Solomon), Henry Fonda (Alexander Moore), Edward Arnold (Diamond Jim Brady), Leo Carrillo (Tony Pastor). 127 minutes.
SONGS: "Adored One," music and lyrics by Alfred Newman and Mack Gordon; "Blue Love Bird," music and lyrics by Gus Kahn and Bronislau Kaper; "Waltz Is King," music and lyrics by Mack Gordon and Charles Henderson; "Back in the Days of Old Broadway," music and lyrics by Charles Henderson and Alfred Newman.

Tin Pan Alley. Distributed by Twentieth Century-Fox Film Corp., released November 29, 1940, associate producer Kenneth Macgowan, director Walter Lang, starring Alice Faye (Katie Blane), Betty Grable (Lily Blane), Jack Oakie (Harry Calhoun), John Payne (Skeets Harrigan), Allen Jenkins (Casey), Esther Ralston (Nora Bayes). 92 minutes.
SONGS: "America I Love You," music and lyrics by Edgar Leslie and Archie Gottler; "Goodbye Broadway, Hello France," music and lyrics by C. Francis Reisner, Benny Davis and Billy Baskette; "K-K-K-Katy," music and lyrics by Geoffrey O'Hara; "Moonlight Bay," music and lyrics by Edward Madden and Percy Wenrich; "Honeysuckle Rose," music and lyrics by Thomas "Fats" Waller; "You Say the Sweetest Things (Baby)," music and lyrics by Mack Gordon and Harry Warren; "The Sheik of Araby," music and lyrics by Harry B. Smith, Francis Wheeler, and Ted Snyder; "When You Wore a Tulip and I Wore a Big Red Rose," music and lyrics by Jack Mahoney and Percy Wenrich.

That Night in Rio. Distributed by Twentieth Century-Fox Film Corp., re-
leased April 11, 1941, associate producer Fred Kohlmar, director Irv-
ing Cummings, starring Alice Faye (Baroness Duarte), Don Ameche
(Larry Martin/Baron Manuel Duarte), Carmen Miranda (Carmen),
S. Z. Sakall (Arthur Penna), J. Carrol Naish (Machado), Leonid
Kinskey (Pierre Dufond). 90 minutes.

SONGS: "I, Yi, Yi, Yi, Yi (I Like You Very Much)," "Chica, Chica,
Boom, Chic," "Boa Noite (Good Night)," "They Met in Rio," and
"The Baron Is in Conference," music and lyrics by Mack Gordon
and Harry Warren.

The Great American Broadcast. Distributed by Twentieth Century-Fox Film
Corp., released May 9, 1941, associate producer Kenneth Macgowan,
director Archie Mayo, starring Alice Faye (Vicki Adams), Jack Oakie
(Chuck Hadley), John Payne (Rix Martin), Cesar Romero (Bruce
Chadwick), James Newill (Singer), The Four Ink Spots, Nicholas
Brothers. 90 minutes.

SONGS: "The Great American Broadcast," "It's All in a Lifetime," "I
Take to You," "Where You Are," "Chapman's Cheerful Cheese," "Long
Ago Last Night," and "I've Got a Bone to Pick with You," music and
lyrics by Mack Gordon and Harry Warren; "Give My Regards to
Broadway," music and lyrics by George M. Cohan; "Alabamy Bound,"
music and lyrics by Ray Henderson, B. G. DeSylva, and Bud Green.

Week-End in Havana. Distributed by Twentieth Century-Fox Film Corp.,
released October 17, 1941, producer William LeBaron, director Walter
Lang, starring Alice Faye (Nan Spencer), Carmen Miranda (Rosita
Rivas), John Payne (Jay Williams), Cesar Romero (Monte Blanca),
Cobina Wright Jr. (Terry McCracken), Sheldon Leonard (Boris). 80
minutes.

SONGS: "A Week-End in Havana," "When I Love, I Love," "The
Man with the Lollypop Song," and "The Nango," music and lyrics

by Mack Gordon and Harry Warren; "Tropical Magic," music and lyrics by Mack Gordon and Harry Warren, Spanish lyrics by Ernesto Piedra; "Romance and Rhumba," music by James V. Monaco, lyrics by Mack Gordon.

Hello, Frisco, Hello. Distributed by Twentieth Century-Fox Film Corp., released March 26, 1943, producer Milton Sperling, director Bruce Humberstone, starring Alice Faye (Trudy Evans), John Payne (Johnny Cornell), Jack Oakie (Dan Daley), Lynn Bari (Bernice Croft), Laird Cregar (Sam Weaver), June Havoc (Beulah Clancy). 98 minutes.

SONGS: "You'll Never Know," music and lyrics by Mack Gordon and Harry Warren; "Hello, Frisco, Hello," music by Louis A. Hirsch, lyrics by Gene Buck; "Gee, But It's Great to Meet a Friend from Your Old Home Town," music by James McGavisk, lyrics by William Tracey; "Grizzly Bear," music by George Botsford, lyrics by Irving Berlin; "Ragtime Cowboy Joe," music by Maurice Abrahams and Lewis F. Muir, lyrics by Grant Clarke; "Sweet Cider Time, When You Were Mine," music by Percy Wenrich, lyrics by Joseph McCarthy; "Has Anybody Here Seen Kelly?" music and lyrics by C. W. Murphy and Will Letters, American version by William C. McKenna; "They Always Pick on Me," music by Harry von Tilzer, lyrics by Stanley Murphy; "It's Tulip Time in Holland," music by Richard A. Whiting, lyrics by Dave Radford; "By the Light of the Silvery Moon," music by Gus Edwards, lyrics by Edward Madden, "Bedelia," music and lyrics by Jean Schwartz and William Jerome.

The Gang's All Here. Distributed by Twentieth Century-Fox Film Corp., released December 24, 1943, producer William LeBaron, director Busby Berkeley, starring Alice Faye (Eadie Allen), Carmen Miranda (Dorita), Phil Baker (himself), Benny Goodman (himself) and His Orchestra, Eugene Pallette (Andrew J. Mason Sr.), Charlotte Greenwood (Blossom Potter), Edward Everett Horton (Peyton Potter). 103 minutes.

SONGS: "No Love, No Nothing," "A Journey to a Star," "The Lady in the Tutti Frutti Hat," "The Polka Dot Polka," "You Discover You're in New York," "Paducah," and "Minnie's in the Money," music and lyrics by Leo Robin and Harry Warren; "Brazil," music by Ary Barroso, English lyrics by S. K. Russell.

Four Jills in a Jeep. Distributed by Twentieth Century-Fox Film Corp., released March 17, 1944, producer Irving Starr, director William A. Seiter, starring Kay Francis (herself), Carole Landis (herself), Martha Raye (herself), Mitzi Mayfair (herself), Jimmy Dorsey and His Orchestra, John Harvey (Capt. Ted Warren), Phil Silvers (Sgt. Eddie Hart), Dick Haymes (Lt. Dick Ryan), Alice Faye (herself), Betty Grable (herself), Carmen Miranda (herself), George Jessel (Master of Ceremonies). 89 minutes.

SONGS: "You're in the Army Now," music by Isham Jones; "No Love, No Nothing," music by Harry Warren. "How Blue the Night," "You Send Me," "How Many Times Do I Have to Tell You," and "Crazy Me," music and lyrics by Jimmy McHugh and Harold Adamson; "Cuddle Up a Little Closer, Lovey Mine," music by Karl Hoschna, lyrics by Otto Harbach; "Over There," music and lyrics by George M. Cohan; "If You Can't Sing It You'll Have to Swing It," music and lyrics by Sam Coslow; "You'll Never Know" and "I, Yi, Yi, Yi, Yi (I Like You Very Much)," music by Harry Warren, lyrics by Mack Gordon; "The U.S. Field Artillery March," music and lyrics by Edmund L. Gruber.

Fallen Angel. Distributed by Twentieth Century-Fox Film Corp., released October 26, 1945, producer Otto Preminger, director Otto Preminger, starring Alice Faye (June Mills), Dana Andrews (Eric Stanton), Linda Darnell (Stella), Charles Bickford (Mark Judd), Anne Revere (Clara Mills), Bruce Cabot (Dave Atkins). 98 minutes.

SONGS: "Slowly," music and lyrics by David Raksin and Kermit Goell.

State Fair. Distributed by Twentieth Century-Fox Film Corp., released March 9, 1962, producer Charles Brackett, director Jose Ferrer, starring Pat Boone (Wayne Frake), Bobby Darin (Jerry Dundee), Pamela Tiffin (Margie Frake), Ann-Margret (Emily Porter), Tom Ewell (Abel Frake), Alice Faye (Melissa Frake). 118 minutes.

SONGS: "Isn't It Kinda Fun?," "It Might as Well Be Spring," "Its a Grand Night for Singing," "Our State Fair," and "That's for Me," music by Richard Rodgers, lyrics by Oscar Hammerstein II; "It's the Little Things in Texas," "More Than Just a Friend," "Never Say No," "This Isn't Heaven," and "Willing and Eager," music and lyrics by Richard Rodgers.

Won Ton Ton, the Dog Who Saved Hollywood. Distributed by Paramount Pictures (USA), released 1976, producer Michael Winner, director Michael Winner, starring Bruce Dern (Grayson Potchuck), Madeline Kahn (Estie Del Ruth), Art Carney (J. J. Fromberg), Ron Leibman (Rudy Montague), Teri Garr (Fluffy Peters), Alice Faye (secretary at gate).

The Magic of Lassie. Distributed by International Picture Show (USA), released 1978, produced by Jack Wrather, directed by William Beaudine, starring Mickey Rooney (Gus), Mike Mazurki (Apollo), Pernell Roberts (Jamison), James Stewart (Clovis Mitchell), Alice Faye (waitress).

SONGS: "A Rose Is Not a Rose."

BIBLIOGRAPHICAL ESSAY

The following abbreviations are used in the notes:

AF AMPAS   The Alice Faye clipping files at the Margaret Herrick Library, Academy of Motion Picture Arts and Sciences

AMPAS   The Margaret Herrick Library, Academy of Motion Picture Arts and Sciences

CUOHP   Columbia University Oral History Project

JRC DPL   John Rosenfield Collection, Dallas Public Library.

NYPL   Alice Faye clipping files in the Billy Rose Theatre Collection at the New York Public Library, Lincoln Center

PHAFC   Phil Harris-Alice Faye Collection, Linton, Indiana

PPC   Pfizer Pharmaceutical Collection

RBC   Roy Bishop Collection

RVC   Rudy Vallée Collection, Thousand Oaks Public Library, Thousand Oaks, California

SMU   Ronald L. Davis Oral History Collection on the Performing Arts, Southern Methodist University

TCF USC   Twentieth Century-Fox Collection, Doheny Library, University of Southern California

UC USC   Universal Collection, Doheny Library, University of Southern California

Introduction

No single repository, collection, or book provides a comprehensive, chronologically complete account of Alice Faye's personal and professional lives.

Evidence is scattered throughout the nation in printed works, manuscript collections, and other media. Three books provide biographical information about her, although none is a full-scale biography. Moshier, *The Alice Faye Movie Book,* is the best and most correct overview of her film career and includes a biographical sketch; Faye, *Growing Older Staying Young,* contains a disparate collection of reminiscences in her own voice; and Rivadue, *Alice Faye, a Bio-Bibliography,* provides a brief biographical sketch to accompany a bibliography of printed and recorded works by and about her. This latter has been criticized by fans for a number of errors, particularly in the section dealing with Faye's recording career. An hourlong episode of *Biography,* produced by A&E and entitled *Alice Faye: The Star Next Door,* is perhaps the best general introduction to her life.

Clipping files on Alice Faye have been maintained at NYPL shedding light primarily on her work and appearances on the East Coast. AMPAS has maintained clipping files on Alice, each of her movie productions, and gives a more comprehensive picture of her public life from the mid 1930s until her death. AMPAS has also maintained files on Faye's husbands: singer Tony Martin, to whom she was married between 1938 and 1940, and bandleader/comedian Phil Harris, whom she married in 1941 and to whom she stayed married until his death in 1995. The most comprehensive archive is the privately held RBC, which consists of clippings as well as photographs, memorabilia, copies of scripts, voice and video recordings, etc. Specific information about each of Faye's movie productions (annotated scripts, memos, conference minutes, etc.) can be found in the individual production files of TCF USC; UC USC's contains detailed production notes from one of the few films Alice did on loan, *You're a Sweetheart.*

CUOHP contains interviews with Faye's *Fallen Angel* (1945) costar Dana Andrews and Fox screenwriter Nunnally Johnson. SMU contains a wealth of interviews with performers and other employees who shed light not only on Alice Faye but the workings of Twentieth Century-Fox and its studio head Darryl F. Zanuck. These include Don Ameche, Lynn Bari, Pat Boone, Dan Dailey, Ann Doran, Gene Fowler Jr., Marjorie Fowler,

Otto Lang, David Raskin, Cesar Romero, and Harry Warren. Broad assessments of Alice Faye's appeal and her place in the Hollywood pantheon came from Cesar Romero and Michael Feinstein's liner notes to her album compilations *Outtakes and Alternates, vol. 2, 1988,* and *More Gems, vol. 3, 1992,* respectively; director Henry King's foreword to Moshier, *The Alice Faye Movie Book,* obituaries written by Kelly Leiter and Florence King; Mordden, *Hollywood Musicals;* Smulyn, *Selling Radio,* and finally author interviews with Faye's longtime fan and collector Roy Bishop (who has compiled statistics on her effectiveness as a song plugger). Her spokeswoman Jewel Baxter, book collaborator Dick Kleiner, childhood friend Betty Scharf, and daughters Phyllis Middleton and Alice Regan (author interviews) address the issue of Faye's lack of confidence, her deep reserve, and her reluctance to talk about herself or her past history.

4	"infinitely compelling": Feinstein, *More Gems.*
5	"The cold facts are": Faye, 225.
5	"Alice never had a music lesson": Romero, *Outakes.*
5	"In my late teens": Leiter, "Alice Faye's."
6	"I missed my mother a lot": Bishop, author interview.
6	"In her performances": Dean 16.
7	"Expressing the human appetite": Mordden 144.
7	"Her spirit was very late thirties": Mordden 144.
7	"I moved forward": Faye 68.
7	"There were a couple of guys": Bishop, author interview.
8	"Everything I wrote": Kleiner, author interview.
8–9	"Alice kept a lot inside": Baxter, author interview.
9	"She never discussed": Scharf, author interview.
9	"Mother wasn't real chummy": Middleton, author interview.
9	"I remember": Gregory and Regan, author interview.
9	"I probably know less": Middleton, author interview.
9	"My mother was crazy about": Regan, author interview.
10	"It's not that": Kleiner, author interview.

Chapter 1. Broadway Baby

Much talk has centered on whether the year of Alice Faye's birth was 1912 or 1915. The *New York City Index of Births Reported in Manhattan* shows no one named Leppert born in 1912, but shows a "Celia" J. Leppert born May 5. If this is indeed Alice, apparently some kind of mistake occurred, for she was named after her mother, Alice, just as her brother Charles was named for their father. The 1920 U.S. Census for Manhattan (New York 1920 T-625 Roll 1194, New York, Manhattan Borough, ED 441, sheet 1, line 23, records Alice (as Alice) as a four-year-and-seven-month-old girl. Since even the most obtuse census taker could probably distinguish between a four-year-old and a seven-year-old, this seems to indicate that 1915 is the correct date.

Alice Faye was not one to reminisce, therefore direct information about her childhood is sparse. It consists of a few anecdotes found in *Growing Older, Staying Young* and in published interviews in the clipping files. Author interviews with Alice Faye's childhood friend Betty Scharf and her Rancho Mirage neighbor Gabé Farrell contain additional information about the circumstances in which she grew up in Hell's Kitchen. Published works that provide background for Hell's Kitchen include the WPA's *Comprehensive Guide to the Five Boroughs . . .*; Kisseloff, *You Must Remember This;* O'Connor, *Hell's Kitchen;* and Taylor, *Inventing Times Square.* Those that illustrate her father's predicament as an underpaid beat cop in Manhattan in the 1910s and 1920s include *Duties and Compensation of the Uniformed Patrolmen . . .* and Hickey, *Our Police Guardians.* Dan Dailey in SMU describes life as a dancer in a Manhattan movie palace during this era. The city's nightlife and the world of a teenaged chorus girl are vividly brought to life in Durante and Kofoed, *Night Clubs,* and Erenberg, *Steppin' Out;* while Granlund, *Blondes, Brunettes, and Bullets,* provides a fresh and detailed account of Alice Faye's discovery unavailable in any other source.

12   "a very ordinary slum": Dreiser 197.

12   "always sounds": Faye 19.

12	"had to scratch": Faye 20.
12	"It wasn't until": Faye 22.
12–13	"I was always very comfortable": *Chicago Tribune,* Dec. 20, 1987, PPC.
13	"I remember equating": Faye 20, 21.
13	"My grandmother Moffitt": *Chicago Tribune,* Dec. 20, 1987, PPC.
14	"clubbing, shooting": WPA Guide 156.
16	"This is in no way": *Duties* 50–51.
17	"With my grandmother": Faye 124.
17	"was great for us kids": Faye 124.
17	"doctors and hospitals": Faye 130.
18	"was such an experience": Farrell, author interview.
18	"used to see Alice around": NYPL.
19	"Well, what did you get": Farrell, author interview.
19	"Here was too much toil": Dreiser 196–97.
20	"If you were pretty": Rivadue 2.
20	"The trees were all": Faye 21–22.
21	"On payday": NYPL.
21	"I worshipped her for years": Hartley, 20, 22.
22	"My mother said": *Chicago Tribune,* Dec. 20, 1987, PPC.
22–23	"The hard work knocked": NYPL.
23	"just get up there": Dailey, SMU.
23	"It is a weird": "Behind the Scenes" *NYT.*
23	"I liked the name": Moshier 7.
24	"many really close": Faye 219.
24	"I grew up": Scharf, author interview.
24	"I could pay": Scharf, author interview.
24	"The truth is": Scrapbook Vol. 118, Jan.–Feb. 1937, RVC.
24–25	"Girls in show business": Granlund 162–63.
25	"If you were in show business": Granlund 139.
25–26	"I envisioned": Granlund 139.

26	"picks out the best": Durante 222.
26	"It put on the same": Durante 235.
26	"Opening night featured": Granlund 212–13.
26	"NTG was great at": Bruce, author interview.
27	"Look, you're pretty cute": Granlund 212–13.
27	"in the [Texas] Guinan manner": Durante 222.
27	"Alice Faye was a girl": Granlund 212–13.
28	"For $1,000": Burke n.p.
28	"When we closed shop": Granlund 212–13.
28	"I was too poor": *Modern Screen,* Nov. 1934, RVC.
28	"I was a show girl": *Modern Screen,* Nov. 1934, RVC.
28	"There was no monkey business": *Modern Screen,* Nov. 1934, RVC.

Chapter 2. Vallée's Satin Doll

Primary source material on *George White's Scandals* comes from SMU's Oral History with *Scandals* star Ray Bolger, while Scharf, *Composed and Directed,* describes Faye's growing success as a singer in and around Manhattan. McCarthy, *Big Band Jazz;* Nachman, *Raised on Radio;* Payne, *The Swing Era;* Rust, *The Dance Bands;* Smulyn, *Selling Radio;* Walker, *Great Dance Bands* contain background on popular music and broadcasting in the early 1930s, when Faye worked as Rudy Vallée's vocalist for live performances and then later on the *Fleischmann Hour* radio show, Vallée's hourlong muscial variety show broadcast on NBC.

Information on Rudy Vallée is derived from his three autobiographies, *My Time, Let the Chips Fall,* and *Vagabond Dreams Come True,* as well as a fourth memoir completed by his wife Eleanor after his death, *My Vagabond Lover.* Numerous scrapbooks held in the RVC contain news items delineating Alice Faye's activities with his orchestra as they toured and broadcasted throughout 1931 and 1932, including extensive coverage of their near-fatal car accident. The everyday life of a band singer was vividly described by stage and television star Carol Bruce, who led just such a life at the beginning of her career, although several years later.

30	"He did not try": Bolger, SMU.
31	"There was no competition": Bolger, SMU.
31	"first-rate show": *NYT* review, Sept. 15, 1931.
31	"They dance, they sing": *NYT* review, Sept. 15, 1931.
31	"She used to spend hours": Reed, "Look Out Harlow" RVC.
32	"She was the most beautiful": Bolger, SMU.
32	"Rudy Vallée was the Elvis": Scharf 25.
33	"Little that developed": Walker 32.
33	"Heigh-ho everybody": E. Vallée 3.
33	"somewhat self-important": Nachman 158.
34	"the apotheosis": Erenberg 245.
34	"A top producer": E. Vallée 78.
35	"He and his orchestra": Granlund 212–13.
36	"I am motivated": Boston ad, Mar. 7, 1931, scrapbook vol. 56, RVC.
37	"Miss Alice Fay [sic]": Tour of 1933, scrapbook vol. 76, RVC.
38	"mostly in some greasy spoon": Faye 94–95.
38	"there is added interest": Tour of 1933, scrapbook vol. 76, RVC.
39	"He wanted his people": Moshier, liner notes, *On the Air,* vol. 2.
38	"the radio was bigger": Scharf 27.
41	"liked girls in satin": McClelland, "Forties," 36–37.
42	"a girl of the proletariat": Mordden 172.
42	"the first to create": Parsons, "You Wouldn't," n.p.
43	"Rudy apparently fell asleep": Faye 29.
43	"will operate in an effort": *NY Journal,* Aug. 21, 1933, Scrapbook 77, RVC.
43	"left scars": Faye 29.

45	"She couldn't smile": "The Girl I Married Twice," PHAFC.
45	"Incidentally, tell Alice": Irving Caesar to RV, Oct. 12, 1933, RVC.
45	"Rudy Vallée is denying": *NY Mirror,* Oct. 13, 1933, RVC.
46	"kidding the proprietors": Scharf 18–19.
46	"were the highest in high society": Scharf 18–19.
46	"I can't do it": Scharf 22.
47	"with that deep voice": Scharf 22.

Chapter 3. Scandals

Articles contained in the clipping files and scrapbooks of the NYPL, AMPAS, and RVC give ample coverage of Alice Faye's emergence as a Hollywood sensation, as well as blow-by-blow descriptions of her alleged affair with Vallée and its impact on Vallée's notorious divorce from his wife, Faye Webb. Insight into Alice's personal life during this difficult transition are available in Scharf, *Composed and Directed,* the author's interview with Betty Scharf, and Faye, *Growing Older.* Moshier, *The Movies of Alice Faye,* gives summaries and background on each of her films, beginning with *George White's Scandals* (released in 1934) and including the little-known B pictures shot at Fox's old Western Avenue lot. Published works covering Fox, its merger with Twentieth-Century, Darryl F. Zanuck, and the studio's corporate culture include Custen, *Twentieth-Century's Fox;* Gomery, *Hollywood Studio System;* Gussow, *Darryl F. Zanuck;* Puttman, *Movies and Money;* Solomon, *Twentieth-Century Fox;* Stanley, *Celluloid Empire.* Descriptions of the studio's two lots and life on them come from Jane Withers (author interview) and Don Ameche, Lynn Bari, Dan Dailey, Otto Lang, and Cesar Romero at SMU.

48	"My brother isn't making": Scharf, author interview.
49	"Rudy, he's the best pianist," Scharf, author interview.
49	"We were good company": Scharf, author interview.

50   "I went along": *Chicago Tribune,* Dec. 20, 1987, PPC.

50   "She said 'You have to'": Scharf, author interview.

50   "It was clean": Ameche, SMU.

51   "Alice Faye denies romance": AF AMPAS.

51   "But the truth was": Faye 26.

51   "I went to a dinner": Buckley, "Alice Faye," 26.

51   "We want this girl": R. Vallée 117.

52   "Had I been an extra": Jones, 55.

52   "If you want to get into motion pictures": Jones, 85, 90.

52   "You can't say": Ameche, SMU.

52   "I could never watch myself": *Chicago Tribune,* Dec. 20, 1987, PPC.

53   "I never thought": *Chicago Tribune,* Dec. 20, 1987, PPC.

53   "one vast graduate school": Faye 22.

53   "I was so unsure of myself": Faye 189–90.

53   "intimate on numerous occasions": *NYT,* Jan. 9. 1934, 19.

54   "On the road in strange cities": "The Secret Life of Rudy Vallée," n.d. RVC.

54   "ridiculous": *Los Angeles Examiner,* Jan. 9, 1934, AF AMPAS.

54   "I just loved Alice so much": Scharf, author interview.

55   "Time and again": *Los Angeles Examiner,* Jan. 18 and Jan. 25, 1934, AF AMPAS.

55   "I owe my radio career": *Radioland,* July 1934, RVC.

55   "Alice Faye was lucky": *Modern Screen,* Aug. 1934, RVC.

56   "will always be near": Faye 236.

57   "That was certainly not": Scharf 29–30.

57   "to express my hope": RV to Sheehan, Feb. 6, 1934, RVC.

57   "I was very young": *Parade,* Oct. 1987, PPC.

57   "I guess I'll always sing": Reed "Look Out Harlow," RVC.

58   "frequently empty": *Picture Play,* June 1934, RVC.

58   "high amid its faults": *Hollywood Reporter,* Mar. 23, 1934.

58   "flashy blonde newcomer": *NYT,* RVC.

58   "Miss Faye, who figured": JRC DPL.

58   "The studio makeup department": Faye 168–69.

59   "I really wanted": McClelland, "Forties," 36–37.

59   "And it was so wonderful": Burke, "Alice Faye Blonde."

60   "Miss Faye may be": "Foran to Punish Son If He Weds," NYPL.

60   "Oh, I loved her": Scharf, author interview.

60–61   "And not only that": Scharf, author interview.

61   "very intimate": Withers, author interview.

61   "They didn't want": Scharf, author interview.

62   "There was so much studio space": Lang, SMU.

62   "always competent": Stanley 82.

63   "Not only did they cut corners": Faye 6.

64   "Miss Faye lusciously": Moshier 46–47.

66   "He was smart as hell": Bari, SMU.

66   "Writers did not write": Puttman 136–37.

Chapter 4. New Studio, New Star

Events leading to Faye's development as an A-list star are covered in the clipping files, Behlmer, *Memo from Darryl F. Zanuck;* Faye, *Growing Older;* Temple, *Child Star;* and production files from FC USC. Details of the Scharfs' marriage are from author's interview with Betty Scharf. Information regarding the death of Alice's father are from the Rudy Vallée Collection.

68   "I'd read stories": Faye 8–9.

69   "Alice Faye declared": AF AMPAS.

69   "There I would be": Faye 8–9.

70   "Rudy got so mad": Scharf, author interview.

71   "She was a wonderful": Scharf, author interview.

71–72   "he had not been able": *New York Mirror,* Dec. 1 and 2, 1935, RVC.

72   "a kindly, grizzled": *Movie Mirror,* Mar. 1936, RVC.

72   "has now become indispensable": *NYT,* Dec. 8, 1935

72	"Alice Faye buries her father": *New York Evening Post,* Dec. 7, 1935, RVC.
73	"The studios protected": Faye 8.
73	"did everything": Dailey, SMU.
73	"Our names and faces": Faye 8.
74	"I liked the studio system": Faye 8.
74	"Every studio had its drama coach": Romero, SMU.
74	"The studio told you": Faye 198.
74–75	"Most Hollywood stars": Faye 186.
75	"You had no choice": Faye 26–27.
75	"But more often": Faye 26–27.
76	"all it takes": Faye 58.
76	"We were all aware": Faye 15.
77	"Our job as a trio": Temple 129–30.
77	"Alice Faye demonstrates": Moshier 62.
78	"Stay more to real story": *Sing, Baby, Sing,* TCF USC.
78	"I have never seen her look so gorgeous": Behlmer 5–6.
79	"None of these were exactly movie star material": Gussow 71,
79	"had something that": Custen 208.
79	"It was my first real movie": Martin 61.
80	"Most of the time": Martin 63.
80	"was the first picture": Ed Sullivan article, NYPL.
80	"The costumes I was squeezed into": Faye 193.
81	"He said I had better do something": Faye 93, 102.
81	"this is by far the most serious set-up": *Stowaway,* TCF USC.
82	"Tony Martin is a daily visitor": NYPL.
82	"I seethed in secret": Temple 151.

Chapter 5. Breakthrough

Tony Martin's account of his courtship and marriage to Alice Faye, its eventual disintegration, and the increasingly heavy responsibilities of her career can be found in Martin, *Two of Us;* and Buckley, "Alice Faye." The various clipping file collections document the public aspects of Faye and Martin's troubled relationship as well as their careers.

Behind-the-scenes information on the development and filming of Zanuck's formulaic approach to creating the would-be blockbuster *On the Avenue* come from Barrett, *Irving Berlin;* Belmer, *Memo;* Bergreen, *As Thousands Cheer;* Buckley, "Alice Faye;" Custen, *Twentieth Century's Fox.* Gabler, *Winchell;* Hemming, *Movie Musicals;* and Mordden, *Hollywood Musicals;* give insight into *Wake Up And Live* (1936), a movie acclaimed at the time as one of the best film musicals ever made.

Previously mentioned works by Buckley and Custen, as well as Denton, "Henry King," Faye, *Growing Older;* Gussow, *Darryl F. Zanuck;* Moshier, *The Alice Faye Movie Book;* Shepard and Perry, *Henry King Director;* SMU's Oral Histories with Don Ameche, Gene Fowler, and Cesar Romero, and the Fox production files at USC provide many details about the impact of Jean Harlow's death on the filming of *In Old Chicago,* the studio's reluctance to choose Faye as her replacement, the challenges of filming the disaster epic, and the emergence of Don Ameche, Alice Faye, and Tyrone Power as the studio's successful triple threat at the box office.

83	"one of the queens": Martin 64.
84–85	"She was a real girl": Martin 64.
85	"She liked a few luxurious things": Martin 68.
85	"She was a sex symbol": Martin 64.
85	"climbing to stardom so rapidly": Behlmer 5–6.
86	"Everything about *On the Avenue*": Bergreen 358.
86	"an ambitious misfire": Bergreen 358.
87	"these stockings with jewels:" Faye 200–201.
87	"the tolerant thing to do": Bergreen 359.
88	"the absolute tops": JRC DPL.
88	"fast-stepping, sparkling": Gabler 226.
88	"Back then we used to make movies": *Chicago Tribune,* Dec. 20, 1987, PPC.

, Dec. 20,

89 "There was the wardrobe woman": *Chicago Tribune,* Dec. 20, 1987, PPC.

89 "She was so nervous": Ameche, SMU.

89 "I was kind of shy": *Chicago Tribune,* Dec. 20, 1987, PPC.

89 "But that was the way I was": Faye 24–25.

89 "I think Ty Power fell in love": Martin 63–64.

90 "maybe chased Alice Faye": *Life,* 12 (Spring 1989): 8.

90 "I have faith in my singing": Gladys Hall Collection, AMPAS.

90 "but she never complained": Scharf, liner notes, *Music from Hollywood.*

90 "was geared to a certain style": Scharf, liner notes, *Music from Hollywood.*

90 "was a very good singer": Clooney, liner notes, *Music from Hollywood II.*

91 "Pretty soon": Martin 65–66.

91 "become an Episcopalian": Martin 65.

92 "The question of the relative status": Martin 65–66.

92 "I wanted to marry this girl": Martin 65–66.

93 "a character like Frances Farmer": *In Old Chicago* TCF USC.

93 "Actually all those films": *Variety,* Alice Faye obit, May 11, 1998.

94 "You are to get out": *In Old Chicago,* TCF USC.

94 "I felt he [Gable] was too old": King foreword to Moshier.

95 "I took him": Kendall 11.

95 "We're trying to finish": Shepard and Perry 111.

95 "I felt a strong empathy": Faye 214–15.

95 "Jean's tragic death": King foreword in Moshier.

95 "It had to be someone": King foreword in Moshier.

96 "the shortest test": Shepard and Perry 112.

96 "During the past year": AF AMPAS.

96 "I knew I could inspire": King, foreword in Moshier.

97 "There was a lot of fun": Ameche, SMU.

97	"Ours was always": Faye 13.
97	"This poor gal": Shepard and Perry 112.
97	"I worked with her": Shepard and Perry 112.
97	"It came out perfectly": King, foreword in Moshier.
98	"We had, I think": Ameche 23.
98	"When I was doing": *Chicago Tribune,* Dec. 20,1987, PPC.

Chapter 6. Treadmill

Atkins, *David Butler,* gives insight into the production of *You're a Sweetheart.* Its production file in the Universal Collection at USC includes weekly status reports, which detail the inequities of the deal Fox cut with Universal for their loan of Alice Faye, and the exorbitant late fees extracted by Fox under the terms of the contract, which forced Faye and her costars to work an especially grueling schedule. Faye's description of the studio as a "luxurious prison" and her reaction to the restricted lifestyle it fostered come from Faye, *Growing Older.*

Details of the making of *Alexander's Ragtime Band,* its popular reception, and its significance to the fortunes of both the studio and Alice Faye are found in Barrett, *Irving Berlin;* Behlmer, *Memo from Darryl F. Zanuck;* Bergreen, *As Thousands Cheer;* Custen, *Darryl F. Zanuck;* Faye, *Growing Older;* Scharf, *Composed and Directed;* Shepard and Perry, *Henry King;* and Don Ameche at SMU, as well as the clipping files and TCF USC.

99	"Now I was in command": Martin 67.
99	"climaxed a romance": *Citizen News* Sept. 6, 1937, AF AMPAS.
99	"lilies of the valley": AF AMPAS.
100	"He tried to talk me": Buckley 517.
100	"superb baritone voice": Scharf 217.
101	"Don't say I told": AF AMPAS.
102	"It is absolutely impossible": *You're a Sweetheart* UC USC.
102	"really saved the place": Atkins 156.

102	"working last Sunday": *You're a Sweetheart* UC USC.
103	"the most beautiful filly": Atkins 159.
103	"Zanuck, Bill Goetz": Atkins 159–60.
103	"Miss Faye has added": Moshier 90.
104	"She can look": JRC DPL.
104	"You can't imagine": Hayes, "Give It Another Chance."
104	"It's too bad": Martin 68.
104	"it felt good realizing": Martin 68.
105	"She was a big star": Martin 71.
105	"Once on the set": McClelland 40.
105	"Faye sings and romances": Mordden 107.
105	"a forthright exploitation": Moshier 86.
106	"Our fans were so anxious": Moshier 94.
106	"Things usually work out": Hartley, "Play."
106	"In solemn conference": Hayes, "Give It Another Chance."
106	"Some people may": AF AMPAS.
107	"For a while it worked": Martin 69–71.
107	"a good seat": Martin 71–72.
107	"I think if she could have": Martin 72.
108	"The other night": Ed Sullivan, NYPL.
108	"I was thinking about my father": Ed Sullivan, NYPL.
108	"Alice Faye looks ravishing": Rivadue 54.
109	"what Darryl Zanuck": Barrett 159–60.
109	"Alice Faye and Ethel Merman": Barrett 159.
109	"more sophisticated adaptations": Furia 195.
109	"When the camera": Scharf 77.
109	"something exciting": Barrett 153.
110	"Never before had my father": Barrett 153.
110	"Sometimes he'd just sit": "The Role I Liked Best," AF AMPAS.
110	"lack of genuine honesty": Bergreen 362.
110	"In *Alexander's Ragtime Band*": Faye 11.

110   "Zanuck's complicated nostalgia": Custen 203–4.

110   "lightweight escapist confection": Custen 203–4.

111   "He was a superb director": Lang, SMU.

111   "Like most sensitive": King, foreword in Moshier.

111   "I would say 'Like you'd died": *Chicago Tribune,* Dec. 20, 1987, PPC.

111–12 "By 1938 the recovery": Faye 6–7.

112   "the greatest number": Shepard and Perry 114.

113   "Alice Faye is homesick": AF AMPAS.

113   "a honeymoon to remember": Martin 67–68.

113   "make it on my own": Martin 72.

114   "The film is a triumph": Moshier 103.

114   "Alice Faye hits the high spot": Rivadue 57.

114   "I made both of them": Shepard and Perry 114.

115   "Every girl in the world": Faye 17–18.

116   "It is constructed": Moshier 107.

116   *"Tail Spin . . . does an inglorious nosedive":* Rivadue 58.

116   "Alice Faye has a poor role": Moshier 107.

116   "Miss Faye and Miss Bennett": Rivadue 59.

Chapter 7. Queen of the Lot

Articles in the clipping files contain Fanny Brice's reaction to *Rose of Washington Square,* a thinly disguised account of her marriage to gambler Nick Arnstein, and her subsequent lawsuit, as does Goldman, *The Original Funny Girl;* Grossman, *Funny Woman.* Louella Parsons, whose columns are included in the Faye and Martin clipping files at AMPAS, provides day-to-day coverage of Faye's divorce action against Martin, while Betty Scharf and Judy McHarg (author's interviews) attest to Faye's distress over her divorce as well as her almost complete silence on the subject.

McClelland, *Forties Film Talk,* supplements Moshier, *The Alice Faye Movie Book,* with Faye's own thoughts regarding her films made from 1940

(*Lillian Russell*) until 1945, when she retired after *Fallen Angel*. Henry Fonda's frustration over his assignment in *Lillian Russell* after his triumph in *The Grapes of Wrath* is contained in *Fonda, My Life*.

Carmen Miranda's life and struggles with the big studio system and Twentieth-Century Fox are outlined in her biography Gil-Montero, *Brazilian Bombshell*, and also in a particularly fine video documentary (in which Faye appears) called *Bananas Is My Business*.

118	"Alice Faye visibly": AF AMPAS.
119	"Well, then get me": AF AMPAS.
119	"Alice Faye Orders": AF AMPAS.
119	"Alice says it won't do": AF AMPAS.
119	"Talk around town": AF AMPAS.
119	"That was another wedge": Martin 72.
120	"This is a story": *Rose of Washington Square*, TCF USC.
120	"We knew we were in trouble": Scharf 63.
120	"I was told not to show": NYPL.
120	"defamation of character": Grossman 231–32.
121	"who excels in representing": Rivadue 61.
121	"Miss Faye doesn't resemble": Grossman 231–32.
121	"The most awful man": Moshier scrapbook, AMPAS.
121	"I felt badly all through": AF AMPAS.
121–22	"If I didn't show up": Faye 6–7.
122	"I have been out": AF AMPAS.
122	"launched a publicity campaign": Barnous 105.
123	"was tough": Faye 7–8.
123	"a great strapping hulk": Faye 61.
123	"slept like a baby": Faye 61.
124	"Mr. Z. feels": *Hollywood Cavalcade*, TCF USC.
124	"several elements": *Hollywood Cavalcade*, TCF USC.
124	"one of the least memorable": Scharf 43.
125	"I never had so much fun": Faye 17.

125	"I started out looking": Scharf 43–44.
125	"a quiet, reserved gentleman": Faye 17.
125	"I was never too outgoing": Faye 17.
126	"suddenly had to become": Faye 197.
127	"piece of liverwurst": Faye 58.
127	"They changed the story": Faye 58.
127	"She begins to realize": Moshier 128.
127	"As it was, since I had already": AF AMPAS.
128	"Tony and I have celebrated": AF AMPAS.
129	"darkest left field": Martin 76.
129	"Tony is a grand person": AF AMPAS.
129	"I am convinced": Martin 72.
130	"I saw very little of him": AF AMPAS.
130	"if it's necessary": Hartley, "Play Truth."
130	"the marriage simply": Faye 33.
131	"Playing Lillian Russell": McClelland 57.
131	"convey to modern-day audiences": *Lillian Russell,* TCF USC.
131	"When it came to what memory": Custen 202.
131	"a big picture": *Lillian Russell,* TCF USC.
131	"glamorous, romantic": *Lillian Russell,* TCF USC.
131	"It was my fifth film": McClelland 57.
131–32	"Well the first film": Fonda 134.
132	"Everything was handmade": Faye 202.
133	"The way it went": Buckley 517.
133	"Our idea is to make": *Down Argentine Way,* TFC USC.
133	"almost an exact science": Gussow 100.
134	"I was on the lot": Scharf 45.
134	"a major abdominal operation": *NYT,* June 8, 1940: 18.
134	"It has been written": McClelland 58.
135	"His [Zanuck's] number one girl": Scharf 45.
135	"I used to have temper": Faye 35.
135	"was the talk of the lot": Scharf 45.

136   "this oddest of all": AF AMPAS.

136   "The banks owned the company": Ameche, SMU.

Chapter 8. So This Is Harris

The advent of Betty Grable and Zanuck's attempts to develop her as a Faye replacement are discussed in Davis, *The Glamour Factory;* and Warren, *Betty Grable.* Production files from any of the Fox musicals developed between 1940 and 1945 further reflect Zanuck's attitude that all musical actresses were interchangeable. Alice Faye's negative body image is described by Loretta Young in Kobal, *People Will Talk,* and by Faye herself in *Growing Older.* Woll, *The Hollywood Musical Goes to War;* and Gil-Montero, *Brazilian Bombshell,* discuss the advent of war in Europe and its impact on foreign markets for American films. Gil-Montero in particular analyzes the success, or lack thereof, of Zanuck's approach to Latin America as he designed musicals with that audience in mind.

Biographical information on Phil Harris comes from a series of newspaper articles published by Regina Kramer, the curator of PHAFC. This collection consists of scrapbooks, memorabilia, photographs, scripts, sound recordings of the Phil Harris-Alice Faye radio show, and a small collection of personal papers. Published sources containing information about Harris's career include Benny, *Sunday Nights at Seven;* Fein, *Jack Benny;* Walker, *Great Dance Bands.* Information about the complications ensuing from Harris and Faye's first wedding in Mexico and their subsequent remarriage four months later in Galveston come from the Gladys Hall and Hedda Hopper Collections at the Margaret Herrick Library.

138   "Zanuck always ran the studio": Custen 9.

138–39   "There was no guarantee": Jones 88–89.

139   "a once-in-a-lifetime": Jones 90.

140   "a dangerous piece of casting": Warren 119.

140   "a flighty girl": *Tin Pan Alley,* TCF USC.

140	"Make her conservative": *Tin Pan Alley*, TCF USC.
140	"they were total opposites": Gregory-Regan, author interview.
140–41	"was just something": Faye 23.
141	"Alice, you've got eyes": Warren 119.
141	"The truth was": Faye 23.
141	"She was a hell of a good performer": Romero SMU.
142	"feels that no matter": *Tin Pan Alley*, TCF USC.
142	"Who can forget the pantalooned pair": McClelland, "Good News," 38.
142	"*Tin Pan Alley* was famous": Faye 193.
142	"I begged Fox executives": Faye 23.
143	"Alice Faye is in here": Kobal 398.
143	"She could wear dresses": Faye 23.
143–44	"theatremen operating showhouses": "Showmen Select," RBC.
145	"no longer light-hearted": JRC DPL.
145	"a scandalous dress": JRC DPL.
146	"a lovely figure": *That Night in Rio*, AMPAS.
146	"pretty young thing": Faye 49.
146	"The boys are laying": AF AMPAS.
147	"There never has been": AF AMPAS.
147	"One night while I": Faye 217.
147	"It was quite a lovely argument": Faye 217–18.
147	"one mad round": *Linton Daily Citizen*, May 30, 1991, PHAFC.
147	"Theirs was one of the most": AF AMPAS.
148	"I think mother will stay on": AF to PH, n.d., PHAFC.
148	"I wanted to go": AF to PH, n.d., PHAFC.
148	"Nobody remembered": Faye 33.
150	"broad-shouldered Max Baer": PHAFC.
150	"the kind of a guy": recording of *Jack Benny Show*, Oct. 4, 1936.
150	"romantic tripe": recording of *Jack Benny Show*, Oct. 4, 1936.

151   "Among our mainstays": Benny 118.

151   "Phil Harris in his personal life": Benny 118.

152   "Phil is not a kid": Gladys Hall, AMPAS.

152   "Alice and Phil say": AF AMPAS.

153   "Alice Faye Writes Husband Daily": AF AMPAS.

153   "in two more months": AF AMPAS.

153   "I wondered if you really know": Hedda Hopper Collection, AMPAS.

154   "We thought [Phil] would breeze": Coslow 226.

155   "This outdoor business": AF AMPAS.

155   "I sleep at night": AF AMPAS.

155   "If he also can play": AF AMPAS.

155   "I think it is bad": AF AMPAS.

Chapter 9. Movies and Motherhood

Cartwright, *Galveston,* provides supplemental details of the Harris remarriage in Galveston, while tapes of the *Jack Benny Show* from the late spring and early fall of 1941 illustrate the fun that the show's writers had with the Harris marriage and the announcement of Faye's pregnancy. Information about the birth of Alice Jr. and of Phyllis two years later comes from both the clipping files and PHAFC, which contains files with the cards and telegrams sent to Faye during her two hospital stays, as well as from Alice Regan (author's interview).

Zanuck's leave from Fox to serve in the war and his replacement by Bill Goetz is discussed in Custen, *Twentieth Century's Fox;* Gussow, *Darryl F. Zanuck;* and SMU's Oral Histories with Gene and Marjorie Fowler. Background on Alice's signature song "You'll Never Know" comes from SMU's Oral History with Harry Warren, while Rubin, *Showstoppers,* covers Busby Berkley's first foray into Technicolor on *The Gang's All Here,* with supplemental information from Davis, *Hollywood Beauty,* McClelland, *Forties Film Talk;* and Moshier, *The Movies of Alice Faye.* The Twentieth-Century Fox

Collection at USC includes production files on vehicles designed for Faye that went to other actresses when she began her period of semi-retirement.

157	"It gave me another comedy role": McClelland 58.
157	"we want to get all": *Weekend in Havana*, TCF USC.
158	"Some people have said": Faye 218.
158–59	"I have always felt": NYPL.
159	"Definitely and absolutely": NYPL.
159	"I felt if anything happened": AF AMPAS.
160	"I have never been": AF AMPAS.
161	"Many of the soldiers": AF AMPAS.
162	"Everybody seems": AF AMPAS.
163	"I was beautifully": McClelland 58.
163	"Jack Oakie was a riot": McClellan 40.
163	"important that we": *Hello, Frisco, Hello*, TCF USC.
164	"quieter, more composed": Moshier 162.
165	"essentially it is not": Moshier 166.
166	"one of Berkeley's furthest": Rubin 167–68.
166	"spectacular patriotic number": *The Gang's All Here*, TCF USC.
167	"I wasn't as close to him": Moshier 166.
167	"Mr. Berkeley has some": Moshier 166.
167	"as big as canoes": McClelland 59.
168–69	"Heavens, no": NYPL.
169	"I was getting more mature": PPC.
169	"It's time now": Buckley 517.
170	"To the sweetest": PHAFC.
170	"There'll be another": AF AMPAS.
170	"We can now begin": PHAFC.
171	"one or the other": *The Dolly Sisters*, TCF USC.
171	"Somehow there's": AF AMPAS.
171	"There is one thing": Parsons, "You Wouldn't."
171	"I wanted to do more": *Chicago Tribune*, Dec. 20, 1987, PPC.

171	"turned her down": Faye 36–37.
172	"After all those years": Faye 36–37.
172	"The catastrophe": Hopper 324.
172	"stars were asked": Hopper 324.
172	"You'll be seeing": Parsons, "You Wouldn't."
173	"I know now": Parsons, "You Wouldn't."
173	"I had a nice satisfying talk": Parsons, USC.
173	"I read every one": AF AMPAS.

Chapter 10. Goodbye Fox

The final shooting script of *Fallen Angel* containing scenes cut from the final release of the movie came from the private collection of George Ulrich. Speculation regarding Faye's retirement from the screen after she walked out on the studio in 1945 generated a wealth of material in the press, which is documented in the clipping files, but Faye never discussed it herself. This is borne out by author interviews with her friends Judy McHarg, Betty Scharf, and Nancy Whitaker, as well as her many other friends who also provided insights into her personal life during this period.

The Harrises' 1948 trip to Europe with Jack Benny's troupe is outlined in a scrapbook in PHAFC and is also discussed in Benny, *Sunday Nights at Seven,* and Fein, *Jack Benny.* Phyllis Middleton and Alice Regan provided descriptions of the Encino estate and their family relationships, as does Remley, "The Happy Harrises," from an outsider's perspective.

175	*"Fallen Angel* was just": Buckley 517.
176	"She had seen *Laura*": Andrews, CUOHP.
176	"to justify Alice Faye": *Fallen Angel,* TCF USC.
176	"a somber murder story": *Los Angeles Times,* Dec. 15, 1945.
178	"When the script": Andrews, CUOHP.
178	"My agent said": Andrews, CUOHP.
178	"stubborn, humorless": Davis 89.

178–79	"Freedom of choice": Preminger 99–100.
179	"a certain practical adjustment": Preminger 99–100.
179	"no empathy for women": Preminger 99–100.
179	"just to get the feel": *Fallen Angel,* AMPAS.
179	"Preminger was very tough": McClelland 59.
179	"Oh, you wait and see": Andrews, CUOHP.
181	"I couldn't see myself": PPC.
181	"when she saw the picture": Andrews, CUOHP.
181	"That goes with me": *American Movie Classics.*
181	"even today": Moshier scrapbook, AMPAS.
181	"I was terribly upset": Moshier 174.
181–82	"I drove right out": Moshier 174.
182	"It wasn't hard at all": NYPL.
182	"We were protected": Faye 116–17.
182–83	"So the end of Alice Faye": Faye 37.
183	"struggled with": Faye 37.
183	"I just couldn't see": NYPL.
183	"It's probably hard": Faye 56.
183	"I once heard Bette Davis": NYPL.
183–84	"I never realized": NYPL.
184	"Watch and see": McHarg, author interview.
184	"Once I learned to drive": NYPL.
184	"People at the market": *Chicago Tribune,* Dec. 20, 1987, PPC.
184	"rich with promise": *Fallen Angel,* AMPAS.
184	"Alice does not sing": *Fallen Angel,* AMPAS.
185	"what is it with our musical": *Fallen Angel,* AMPAS.
185	"A fling is all right": Parsons, USC.
185	"It wasn't that my career": Faye 36.
185–86	"I was never really wild": NYPL.
186	"this dumb broad": PPC.
186	"I drove right through": PPC.
186	"There weren't big markets": *Chicago Tribune,* Dec. 20, 1987, PPC.

187	"I used to say": Middleton, author interview.
187	"For seventeen years": PHAFC.
187	"It liked men": Middleton, author interview.
187	"Where the octopus lived": Middleton, author interview.
187–88	"I used to sit in her dressing room": Middleton, author interview.
188	"It was neat when I think": Middleton, author interview.
188	"When I walked off": Faye 182.
188	"We'd go shopping": Scharf, author interview.
189	"I got a kick": McHarg, author interview.
189	"They would call each other": McHarg, author interview.
190	"Two or three times a year": Benny 74.
190	"After throwing confetti": Benny 191.
191	"They were crazy about her": Gregory-Regan, author interview.
191	"On this trip": Fein 95.
191	"temporary duty": PHAFC.

Chapter 11. Mrs. Harris

Alice's work on the Harris-Faye radio show is thoroughly documented by the PHAFC; additional insights come from child performer Jeanine Roose, who played one of the Harris daughters on the show (author interview). The state of radio in the late 1940s is discussed in Barnouw, *The Golden Web;* Dunning, *On the Air;* Nachman, *Raised on Radio;* and Smith, *Pharmacy and Medicine On the Air.*

The circumstances of the Harrises' eventual move to Palm Springs and descriptions of their house and lives there come from Kay Gregory, Phyllis Middleton, Alice Regan, and Nancy Whitaker.

194	"Remley became so famous": Fein 203.
194	"as a settled-down": Nachman 82.
194	"was the backbone": Nachman 82.

194	"Elliott and I": Nachman 81.
194	"totally extroverted": Roose, author interview.
197	"As a kid, I remember": Middleton, author interview.
197	"I am crazy about radio": AF AMPAS.
198	"just a genuinely nice": Roose, author interview.
198	"She would make no bones": Roose, author interview.
199	"Probably no show": PHAFC.
199	"It must be said that": PHAFC.
200	"never knock": Smith 74.
200	"About midway into that year": Roose, author interview.
201	"somewhat like": PHAFC.
201–2	"Did you detect": PHAFC.
202	"For a goodly portion": *New York News,* Sept. 19, 1949.
203	"Television is not for me": PHAFC.
203	"We were the first golf course": *Vanity Fair,* June 1999: 208.
203	"Every night after": Gregory-Regan, author interview.
204	"It's a three-bedroom house": AF AMPAS.
204	"While many of": Phil Harris, AMPAS.
204	"She liked to be at home": Middleton, author interview.
205	"Phil is nervous": Faye 215.
205	"Alice and Phil argued": McHarg, author interview.
205	"a funny kind of relationship": Whitaker, author interview.
205	"I know they loved": Middleton, author interview.
205	"I always thought Alice": Gregory-Regan, author interview.
205	"They didn't entertain": Middleton, author interview.
206	"We had had a huge place": Middleton, author interview.
206	"Daddy got up": Middleton, author interview.
206	"Alice and Phil": McHarg, author interview.
206–7	"I think that's probably": Gregory-Regan, author interview.
207	"They used to fight": Middleton, author interview.
207	"She'd pack his clothes": Middleton, author interview.
208	"They obviously loved": Roose, author interview.

208 "Ty was the victim": Faye 57.
209 "She was a big draw": *Bananas Is My Business*.
210 "Most actors initially": Davis 129–30.
210 "I believe I was": Faye 59.
210 "I'm far from an expert": NYPL.
211 "There were only": Whitaker, author interview.
211 "I was away from home": Whitaker, author interview.
211–12 "We raised about $200,000": Whitaker, author interview.
212 "They became the shoulder": Baxter, author interview.

Chapter 12. Celebrity Fulfilled

After the cancellation of the Phil Harris-Alice Faye radio show (1954), Faye spent the remainder of her life in semiretirement, periodically venturing back into the spotlight but never staying too long. Insight into her personal life throughout this period comes from her friends and her daughters (author interviews). Information about her work on *State Fair* (1962) comes predominantly from the clipping files, as well as Buckley, "Alice Faye"; Faye, *Growing Older*; Hemming, *Movie Musicals*; and Moshier, *The Alice Faye Movie Book*. Events leading up to and including her 1973–74 national tour in Harry Rigby's theatrical revival of *Good News* are also included in the clipping files and Dean, "It Had to Be Alice Faye," to which the reminiscences of her personal assistant and spokeswoman, Jewel Baxter (author interview), are added. W. Franklyn Moshier's scrapbooks, on deposit at the Margaret Herrick Library, are also invaluable.

Her work as a spokeswoman for Pfizer Pharmaceuticals in the 1980s and 1990 is documented in a series of scrapbooks the company kept that reflect the program, its goals, and its success. Paul Ritz at Pfizer provided access to this collection, as well as descriptions of the many years during which he and Faye were on the road with the program. Her daughters, Phyllis Middleton and Alice Regan (author interviews), freely described the ways in which they thought the Pfizer program improved their mother's confidence and self-esteem, something the studio had never accomplished.

213	"He was so persistent": NYPL.
213	"It's the kind of clean": NYPL.
214	"There was nostalgia": NYPL.
214	"What made it easy": AF AMPAS.
214	"I expected it": NYPL.
214	"Welcome back": NYPL.
215	"the Puerto Rico-born": JRC DPL.
215	"They'd torn down": PPC.
216	"*State Fair* was very": Faye 5–6.
216–17	"I thought it": Buckley 519.
217	"homespun charm": Hemming 37.
217	"competent but strange": JRC DPL.
217	"Alice Faye": Hemming 38.
217	"Alice Faye came out": Hemming 38.
217	"I wasn't doing so much": Faye 117.
217	"I think she got bored": Middleton, author interview.
217–18	"She had a little studio": Whitaker, author interview.
218	"It was certainly": Faye 119–20.
218	"I don't understand": Moshier scrapbook, AMPAS.
218	"It's a whole new show": Phil Harris, AMPAS.
219	"We used to kid": Moshier scrapbook, AMPAS.
219	"Poor Betty": Faye 113.
220	"in honor of": AF AMPAS.
220	"great old stories": *NYT,* April 21, 1971: 43.
220	"They gave me": Baxter, author interview.
220	"I want to tell you": Baxter, author interview.
221	"big navy blue": AF AMPAS.
221	"Alice got *Good News*": Baxter, author interview.
221	"Afterward they invited": McClelland, "Good News."

221   "I thought that": Regan, author interview.

222   "I told Harry Rigby": Dean 15.

222   "John was a very": McClelland 58.

223   "If I ever sue Phil": Moshier scrapbook, AMPAS.

223   "just go out": Moshier scrapbook, AMPAS.

223   "conspicuously nervous": Moshier scrapbook, AMPAS.

223   "Faye's opening night": Moshier scrapbook, AMPAS.

224   "I really had": NYPL.

224   "You are": Moshier scrapbook, AMPAS.

224   "It's not humor": Moshier scrapbook, AMPAS.

224   "Thank God for needlepoint": Moshier scrapbook, AMPAS.

224   "If I can survive": Dean 15.

224   "Phil was a cryer": McHarg, author interview.

224   "I loved *Good News*": Buckley 519.

225   "His leg hurt": McClelland 58.

225   "At that point": Nelson, SMU.

225   "I loved working": Nelson, SMU.

225   "*Good News* was great": Middleton, author interview.

226   "I think I was": Ameche, SMU.

226   "How about me": Buckley 519.

226   "We love you": NYPL.

226   "They said we could": Baxter, author interview.

227   "All the actors": Moshier scrapbook, AMPAS.

227   "I was thrilled": Buckley 516.

227   "You know": Buckley 516.

227   "She was so gorgeous": Gregory-Regan, author interview.

228   "They put her through": Baxter, author interview.

229   "It snowballed": Ritz, author interview.

229   "I went with her": Regan, author interview.

229   "As I was coming in": PPC.

229   "Alice was sixty-seven or sixty-eight": Ritz, author interview.

230   "She would sign": Ritz, author interview.

230   "He says if": PPC.

230   "It was close": Ritz, author interview.

231   "Alice was always": Ritz, author interview.

231   "You could see the hair": Ritz, author interview.

231   "I want to be able": Faye 53.

232   "Who could ever": Faye 11.

232   "a bland recollection": *Publisher's Weekly,* Feb. 23, 1990: 211.

233   "I feel comfortable": *Chicago Tribune,* Dec. 20, 1987, PPC.

233   "where Pfizer": Faye 240–41.

233   "We always felt proud": Ritz, author interview.

233   "It's amazing": Middleton, author interview.

234   "really very shy": Regan, author interview.

234   "I feel very glamorous": *Chicago Tribune,* Dec. 20, 1987, PPC.

Epilogue

Buckley, "Alice Faye," presents a nice retrospective of her career, as do the number of obituaries run in the national press at the time of her death in 1998. Neighbors Gabé Farrell and Virginia Zamboni (author interview) presented an intimate view of Phil Harris's last illness, Faye's vigilance in protecting his health, and her rapid decline following his death in 1995. Roy Bishop and George Ulrich (author interviews) described Alice Faye's memorial service, while Gabé Farrell provided a tape recording of the service and eulogy.

235   "Are we still": Baxter, author interview.

235   "Oh, no, you wouldn't": Bishop, author interview.

236   "She always liked London": Baxter, author interview.

237   "I really feel strange": NYPL.

237   "They were bagging": *Chicago Tribune,* Dec. 20, 1987, PPC.

237   "Why wouldn't I": McHarg, author interview.

237–38   "We went up to visit": Buckley 519.

238	"He was terribly crippled": Regan, author interview.
238	"Mother did the tournament": Regan, author interview.
239	"He said 'Stop": Steward, author interview.
239	"Alice would go up": Farrell-Zamboni, author interview.
239	"The girls would come home": Farrell-Zamboni, author interview.
239	"You couldn't get a drink": Regan, author interview.
240	"I know that": Middleton, author interview.
240	"She didn't want": Gregory-Regan, author interview.
240	"I remember one time": Regan, author interview.
241	"The housekeeper": Baxter, author interview.
241	"At one place": Gregory-Regan, author interview.
241	"You really had to push": Farrell-Zamboni, author interview.
241	"Oh, don't mind him": Shelton, author interview.
241–42	"You know I'm": Bishop, author interview.
242	"Now, Paul": Ritz, author interview.
242	"They were always fine": Farrell-Zamboni, author interview.
242	"Phil was sick": Farrell-Zamboni, author interview.
242	"He'd always have": Farrell-Zamboni, author interview.
243	"Phil was never": Baxter, author interview.
243	"I tried to make it": Kleiner, author interview.
243	"He had it all": Phil Harris, AMPAS.
243	"She didn't like": Farrell-Zamboni, author interview.
243–44	"I thought Alice": Bishop, author interview.
244	"She was at a party": Regan, author interview.
244	"It was funny": Middleton, author interview.
244	"I used to worry": Middleton, author interview.
245	"she just got miserable": Farrell-Zamboni, author interview.
245	"She liked it up there": Middleton, author interview.
245	"It was her favorite ": Farrell-Zamboni, author interview.
245	"She told everybody": Bishop, author interview.
245	"She never wanted": Farrell-Zamboni, author interview.

245–46   "I think she": Farrell-Zamboni, author interview.

246   "I'd say she was Miss Average": Kleiner, author interview.

246   "Living in the Madonna era": King 68.

247   "in contrast to other": King 68.

247   "She could spin": Leiter, *LaFolleette Press,* May 14, 1998.

BIBLIOGRAPHY

Manuscript Collections

Roy Bishop Collection

Columbia University Oral History Project

Phil Harris-Alice Faye Collection, Linton, Indiana

The Margaret Herrick Library, Academy of Motion Picture Arts & Sciences

Pfizer Pharmaceuticals, Inc., campaign scrapbook and photographs

Billy Rose Theatre Collection, New York Public Library

John Rosenfield Collection, Dallas Public Library

Twentieth Century-Fox Collection, Doheny Library, University of Southern California

Universal Collection, Doheny Library, University of Southern California

Rudy Vallée Collection, Thousand Oaks Public Library, Thousand Oaks, California

Films

A&E Biography. *Alice Faye, the Star Next Door.*

Denver Public Library. *Between the Lines,* ca. 1989/1990.

International Cinema, Inc. *Carmen Miranda: Bananas Is My Business,* 1994.

Pfizer Pharmaceuticals. *We Still Are.*

Recordings

Alice Faye. *On The Air, vol. 2, 1979.* Liner notes by W. Franklyn Moshier.

Alice Faye. *Outtakes and Alternates, vol. 2, 1988.* Liner notes by Cesar Romero.

Alice Faye. *More Gems, vol. 3, 1992.* Liner notes by Michael Feinstein.

Alice Faye. *Music from Hollywood,* vol. 1, 1993. Liner notes by Walter Scharf.

Alice Faye. *Music from Hollywood,* vol. 2, 1998. Liner notes by George Ulrich.

Gabé Farrell. Recording of eulogy at Alice Faye memorial service, May 1998.

Newspapers and Magazines

Dallas Morning News

Dallas Times Herald

[Feldene] *Sales Pacer* (pharmaceutical sales magazine)

Linton Daily Citizen

New York Times

Publisher's Weekly

Variety

Oral Histories and Interviews

Ameche, Don. Interview by Ronald L. Davis, Mar. 1, 1977. Southern Methodist University Oral History Project, Number 113, Dallas.

Andrews, Carver Dana. Oral Reminiscences of, Popular Arts Series, from the Oral History Collection of Columbia University, New York.

Bari, Lynn. Interview by Ronald L. Davis, Aug. 18, 1986. Southern Methodist University Oral History Project, Number 372, Dallas.

Baxter, Jewel. Telephone interview by author, Jan. 18, 1999.

Bishop, Roy. Interview by author, North Hollywood, Calif., June 6, 1999.

Boone, Pat. Interview by Ronald L. Davis, July 26, 1990. Southern Methodist University Oral History Project, Number 476, Dallas.

Bruce, Carol. Interview by author, Los Angeles, Calif., June 11, 1999.

Dailey, Dan. Interview by Sally Cullum, July 13, 1974. Southern Methodist University Oral History Project, Number 4, Dallas.

Doran, Ann. Interview by Ronald L. Davis, Los Angeles, Calif., Aug. 10, 15, 1983.

Farrell, Gabé, and Virginia Zamboni. Interview by author, Rancho Mirage, Calif., June 15, 1999.

Fowler, Gene, Jr. Interview by Ronald L. Davis, July 20, 1985. Southern Methodist University Oral History Project, Number 362, Dallas.

Fowler, Marjorie Johnson. Interview by Ronald L. Davis, Aug. 14, 1986. Southern Methodist University Oral History Project, Number 365, Dallas.

Gregory, Kay, and Alice Harris Regan. Interview by author, Rancho Mirage, Calif., June 14, 1999.

Johnson, Nunally, Oral Reminiscences of, Popular Arts Series, Oral History Collection of Columbia University, New York.

Kleiner, Dick. Telephone interview by author, Apr. 30, 1999.

Lang, Otto. Interview by Ronald L. Davis, Aug. 7, 1981. Southern Methodist University Oral History Project, Number 222, Dallas.

McHarg, Judy. Telephone interview by author, Aug. 24, 2000.

Middleton, Phyllis Harris. Telephone interview by author, Oct. 30, 2000.

Raskin, David. Interviews by Ronald L. Davis, Aug. 20, 1980; July 16, 17, 27, 1982. Contained in Hollywood Reflections on Linda Darnell. Southern Methodist University Oral History Project, Number 239, Dallas.

Regan, Alice Harris. Telephone interview by author, Mar. 26, 2000.

Ritz, Paul. Interview by author, Dallas, Jan. 28, 1999.

Romero, Cesar. Interview by Ronald L. Davis, Feb. 26, 1979. Southern Methodist University Oral History Project, Number 158, Dallas.

Roose, Jeanine. Interview by author, Sherman Oaks, Calif., June 7, 1999.

Scharf, Betty (Mrs. Walter). Telephone interview by author, July 12, 1999.

Steward, Don. Interview by author, Linton, Ind., Oct. 15, 1998.

Ulrich, George. Telephone interview by author, Apr. 22, 1999.

Warren, Harry. Interview by Ronald L. Davis, Aug. 23, 1977. Southern Methodist University Oral History Project, Number 117, Dallas.

Whitaker, Nancy. Telephone interview by author, Apr. 10, 1999.

Withers, Jane. Interview by author, Sherman Oaks, Calif., June 10, 1999.

Articles

"Alice Faye and the Fox Blondes." *Hollywood Studio Magazine* 21 (Jan. 1988).

"Alice Faye May Be Coming Your Way." *Hollywood Studio Magazine* 21 (Sept. 1988).

"Behind the Scenes: The Color and Bustle of the Stage Shows Before the Picture Comes On." *New York Times,* May 17, 1931.

Blackmar, Betsy. "Uptown Real Estate and the Creation of Times Square." In

William R. Taylor, ed., *Inventing Times Square: Commerce and Culture at the Crossroads of the World.* New York: Russell Sage Foundation, 1991.

Buckley, Michael. "Alice Faye, an Interview." *Films in Review,* Nov. 1982.

Burke, Marcella. "Alice Faye Blonde But Not Dizzy," *Screen Play,* Mar. 1935.

Chauncey, George, Jr. "The Policed: Gay Men's Strategies of Everyday Resistance." In William R. Taylor, ed., *Inventing Times Square: Commerce and Culture at the Crossroads of the World.* New York: Russell Sage Foundation, 1991.

Corbet, John. "Rise and Fall of the Golden Era: Fanfare for the Working Band (part 3)." *Down Beat* 64 (July 1997).

Corey, Herbert. "The Fight You Never See." *Collier's, The National Weekly* 65 (June 12, 1920).

Cuthbert, David. "Alice Faye Today: 20th Century's Fox." *Living, Times-Picayune,* Oct. 23, 1996.

Dean, Douglas. "It Had to Be Alice Faye." [From clipping files at Billy Rose Theatre Collection of New York Public Library.]

Denton, Clive. "Henry King." In *The Hollywood Professionals.* Vol. 2. New York: A. S. Barnes & Co., 1974.

Dudley, Fredda. "The Happy Harris Family," *Movieland* 3 (Oct. 1945).

Erenberg, Lewis. "Impresarios of Broadway Nightlife." In William R. Taylor, ed., *Inventing Times Square: Commerce and ulture at the Crossroads of the World.* New York: Russell Sage Foundation, 1991.

Furia, Philip. "Irving Berlin: Troubadour of Tin Pan Alley." In William R. Taylor, ed., *Inventing Times Square: Commerce and Culture at the Crossroads of the World.* New York: Russell Sage Foundation, 1991.

Hammack, David C. "Developing for Commercial Culture." In William R. Taylor, ed., *Inventing Times Square: Commerce and Culture at the Crossroads of the World.* New York: Russell Sage Foundation, 1991.

Hartley, Katharine. "Play Truth and Consequences with Alice Faye." *Photoplay* Apr. 1939.

Hayes, Barbara. "Give It Another Chance!" *Photoplay,* Nov. 1938.

Kendall, Robert. "Aiice Faye May Be Coming Your Way." *Hollywood Studio Magazine,* Sept. 1988.

———. "Sweetheart of the Musical Cinema." *American Classic Screen* (Nov.–Dec. 1976).

King, Florence. "Alice Faye Obituary," *National Review* 50 (June 22, 1998): 68.

Leiter, Kelly. "Alice Faye's Magical Songs Touched Hearts around the World," *LaFollette Press,* May 14, 1998.

McClelland, Doug. "Good News from Alice Faye." *After Dark,* Dec. 1973.

McNamara, Brooks. "The Entertainment District at the End of the 1930s." In William R. Taylor, ed., *Inventing Times Square: Commerce and Culture at the Crossroads of the World.* New York: Russell Sage Foundation, 1991.

Madden, James C. "Don Ameche." *Films in Review,* Jan. 1972, 8–22.

Moshier, W. Franklyn. "Alice Faye Had An Extroverted Blonde Beauty and a Natural Singing Voice." *Films in Review,* Oct. 1961.

Nicholson, Arthur. "Alice Faye Today," *Hollywood Studio Magazine* 19 (Mar. 1986).

Parsons, Louella. "You Wouldn't Know Alice Faye." *Photoplay,* Sept. 1944.

Remley, Frank. "The Happy Harrises: Closeup of a Perfect Marriage." *Radio and Television Mirror,* Feb. 1949.

Schallert, Elza. "Reconversion Alice," *Photoplay,* Dec. 1945.

Senelick, Laurence. "Private Parts in Public Places." In William R. Taylor, ed., *Inventing Times Square: Commerce and Culture at the Crossroads of the World.* New York: Russell Sage Foundation, 1991.

Taylor, William R. "Broadway: The Place that Words Built." In William R. Taylor, ed., *Inventing Times Square: Commerce and Culture at the Crossroads of the World.* New York: Russell Sage Foundation, 1991.

"This Is Your Life, Alice Faye," *Hollywood Studio Magazine* 18 (Apr. 1985).

Books

Atkins, Irene Kahn. *David Butler.* Metuchen, N.J.: Directors Guild of America and Scarecrow Press, 1993.

Baral, Robert. *Revue: A Nostalgic Reprise of the Great Broadway Period.* New York: Fleet Publishing Corporation, 1962.

Barnouw, Erik. *A Tower in Babel: A History of Broadcasting in the United States. Volume I—to 1933.* New York: Oxford University Press, 1966.

———. *The Golden Web: A History of Brodcasting in the United States. Volume II—1933 to 1953.* New York: Oxford University Press, 1968.

Barrett, Mary Ellin. *Irving Berlin: A Daughter's Memoir.* New York: Simon & Schuster, 1994.

Behlmer, Rudy, ed. *Memo from Darryl F. Zanuck: The Golden Years at Twentieth Century-Fox.* New York: Grove Press, 1993.

Benny, Jack, and Joan Benny. *Sunday Nights at Seven: The Jack Benny Story.* New York: Warner Books, Inc., 1990.

Bergreen, Laurence. *As Thousands Cheer: The Life of Irving Berlin.* New York: Viking, 1990.

Billips, Connie, and Arthur Pierce. *Lux Presents Hollywood: A Show-by-Show History of the Lux Radio Theatre and the Lux Video Theatre, 1934–1957.* Jefferson, N.C.: McFarland & Comany, 1995.

Briggs, Asa. *The Golden Age of Wireless.* London: Oxford University Press, 1965.

Burke, Billie, with Cameron Shipp. *With a Feather on My Nose.* New York: Appleton-Century-Crofts, 1949.

Cartwright, Gary. *Galveston: A History of the Island.* New York: Maxwell Macmillan, 1991.

Coslow, Sam. *Cocktails for Two: The Many Lives of Giant Songwriter Sam Coslow.* New Rochelle, N.Y.: Arlington House, 1977.

Crosby, Kathryn. *Bing and Other Things.* New York: Meredith Press, 1967.

Custen, George F. *Twentieth Century's Fox: Darryl F. Zanuck and the Culture of Hollywood.* New York: BasicBooks, 1997.

Davidson, Bill. *Spencer Tracy, Tragic Idol.* London: Sidgwick & Jackson, 1987.

Davis, Ronald L. *Hollywood Beauty: Linda Darnell and the American Dream.* Norman: University of Oklahoma Press, 1991.

Dreiser, Theodore. *The Color of a Great City.* New York: Boni and Liveright, 1923.

Dunning, John. *On the Air: The Encyclopedia of Old-Time Radio.* New York: Oxford University Press, 1998.

Durante, Jimmy, and Jack Kofoed. *Night Clubs.* New York: Alfred A. Knopf, 1931.

Duties and Compensation of the Uniformed Patrolmen of New York City, January 1922. New York: Report Prepared for the Patrolmen's Benevolent Association by the Labor Bureau, Inc., 1922.

Erenberg, Lewis A. *Steppin' Out: New York Nightlife and the Transformation of American Culture, 1890–1930*. Westport, Conn.: Greenwood Press, 1981.

Faye, Alice, with Dick Kleiner. *Growing Older, Staying Young*. New York: Dutton, 1990.

Fein, Irving A. *Jack Benny: An Intimate Biography*. New York: G. P. Putnam's Sons, 1976.

Fonda, Henry. *Fonda, My Life. As Told to Howard Teichmann*. New York: New American Library, 1981.

Gabler, Neal. *Winchell: Gossip, Power, and the Culture of Celebrity*. New York: Alfred A. Knopf, 1995.

Gil-Montero, Martha. *Brazilian Bombshell: The Biography of Carmen Miranda*. New York: Donald I. Fine, 1989.

Gish, Lillian, with Ann Pinchot. *The Movies, Mr. Griffith, and Me*. Englewood Cliffs, N.J.: Prentice-Hall, Inc., 1969.

Goldman, Herbert G. *Fanny Brice: The Original Funny Girl*. New York: Oxford University Press, 1992.

Gomery, Douglas. *The Hollywood Studio System*. New York: St. Martin's Press, 1986.

Granlund, Nils Thor, with Sid Feder and Ralph Hancock. *Blondes, Brunettes, and Bullets*. New York: David McKay Company, 1957.

Grossman, Barbara W., *Funny Woman: The Life and Times of Fanny Brice*. Bloomington: Indiana University Press, 1991.

Gussow, Mel. *Darryl F. Zanuck: "Don't Say Yes Until I Finish Talking."* New York: A Ca Capo Paperback, 1971.

Hickey, John J. *Our Police Guardians . . .* New York: John J. Hickey, 1925.

Hemming, Roy. *The Melody Lingers On: The Great Songwriters and Their Movie Musicals*. New York: Newmarket Press, 1986.

Hopper, Hedda, with James Brough. *The Whole Truth and Nothing But*. Garden City, N.Y.: Doubleday, 1963.

Jones, Charles Reed. *Your Career in Motion Pictures, Radio, Television*. New York: Sheridan House, 1949.

Kisseloff, Jeff. *You Must Remember This: An Oral History of Manhattan from the 1890s to World War II*. New York: Harcourt Brace Jovanovich, 1989.

Kobal, John. *People Will Talk*. New York: Alfred A. Knopf, 1985.

McCarthy, Albert. *Big Band Jazz*. New York: G. P. Putnam's Sons, 1974.

McClelland, Doug. *Forties Film Talk: Oral Histories of Hollywood, with 120 Lobby Posters*. Jefferson, N.C.: McFarland & Company, 1992.

Mordden, Ethan. *The Hollywood Musical*. New York: St. Martin's Press, 1981.

———. *Movie Star: A Look at the Women Who Made Hollywood*. New York: St. Martin's Press, 1983.

Moshier, W. Franklyn. *The Alice Faye Movie Book*. Harrisburg, Pa.: A&W Visual Library, [1974].

Nachman, Gerald. *Raised on Radio . . .* New York: Pantheon Books, 1998.

New York City Guide: *A Comprehensive Guide to the Five Boroughs of the Metropolis . . . Prepared by the Federal Wrters' Project of the Works Progress Administration*. New York: Random House Publishers, 1939.

O'Connor, Richard. *Hell's Kitchen: The Roaring Days of New York's Wild West Side*. Philadelphia and New York: J. B. Lippincott Company, 1958.

Ostransky, Leroy. *Jazz City: The Impact of Our Cities on the Development of Jazz.* Englewod Cliffs, N.J.: Prentice-Hall, 1978.

Payne, Philip W., ed. *The Swing Era. The Movies: Between Vitaphone and Video, 1936–1937.* New York: Time-Life Records, 1972.

Payne, Philip W., ed. *The Swing Era. Where Swing Came From, 1938–1939.* New York: Time-Life Records, 1970.

Pratley, Gerald. *The Cinema of Otto Preminger.* New York: Castle Books, 1971.

Preminger, Otto. *Preminger: An Autobiography.* Garden City, N.Y.: Doubleday & Company, 1977.

Puttnam, David, with Neil Watson. *Movies and Money.* New York: Alfred A. Knopf, 1998.

Reston, James, Jr. *The Lone Star: The Life of John Connally.* New York: Harper & Row, Publishers, 1989.

Rivadue, Barry. *Alice Faye: A Bio-Bibliography.* New York: Greenwood Press, 1990.

Rubin, Martin. *Showstoppers: Busby Berkeley and the Tradition of Spectacle.* New York: Columbia University Press, 1993.

Rust, Brian. *The Dance Bands.* New Rochelle, N.Y.: Arlington House Publishers, 1974.

Scharf, Walter. *Composed and Conducted by Walter Scharf.* Accompanied by Michael Freedland. Totowa, N.J.: Vallentine, Mitchell & Co. Ltd., 1988.

Schlesinger, Arthur M., Jr. *The Crisis of the Old Order, 1919–1933.* Boston: Houghton Mifflin Company, 1957.

Shepard, David, and Ted Perry. *Henry King Director: From Silents to 'Scope.* Ed. Frank Thompson. Los Angeles Directors Guild of America, 1995.

Shepherd, Donald, and Robert F. Slatzer. *Bing Crosby: The Hollow Man.* New York: St. Martin's Press, 1981.

Smith, Mickey. *Pharmacy and Medicine on the Air.* Metuchen, N.J.: Scarecrow Press, 1989.

Smulyan, Susan. *Selling Radio: The Commercialization of American Broadcasting, 1920–1934.* Washington and London: Smithsonian Institution Press, 1994.

Solomon, Aubrey. *Twentieth Century-Fox: A Corporate and Financial History.* Metuchen, N.J.: Scarecrow Press, 1988.

Stanley, Robert H. *The Celluloid Empire: A History of the American Movie Industry.* New York: Hastings House, Publishers, 1978.

Taylor, William R., ed. *Inventing Times Square: Commerce and Culture at the Crossroads of the World.* New York: Russell Sage Foundation, 1991.

Vallee, Eleanor, with Jill Amadio. *My Vagabond Lover: An Intmate Biography of Rudy Vallee.* Dallas: Taylor Publishing Company, 1996.

Walker, Leo. *The Wonderful Era of the Great Dance Bands.* Berkeley, Calif.: Howell-North Books, 1964.

Warren, Doug. *Betty Grable: The Reluctant Movie Queen.* New York: St. Martin's Press, 1981.

Warren, Doug, with James Cagney. *James Cagney: The Authorized Biography.* New York: St. Martin's Press, 1983.

Woll, Allen L. *The Hollywood Musical Goes to War.* Chicago: Nelson-Hall, 1983.

INDEX

Abbott and Costello, 197–98
Adventures of Sam Spade, The, 201
"Afraid to Dream," 91
Alcus, Ted, 213
Alexander's Ragtime Band, 108, 109–12, 113–14, 116, 124, 126, 133, 142, 148, 171, 192, 223, 232
"Alexander's Ragtime Band" (song), 191
Alice Faye (racehorse), 102–03
All Saints Episcopal Church (Beverly Hills), 219
Allen, Fred, 87, 105
Allen, Gracie, 85, 91, 194
Allyson, June, 222, 227
Ambassador Hotel (Los Angeles), 149
Ameche, Don, 50, 52, 79, 80, 89–90, 93, 96, 98, 108, 109, 110, 114, 131, 132, 136, 139, 144, 145, 146, 157, 214, 215, 226, 236, 237
"America, I Love You," 246
American Cancer Society, 211
American Movie Classics, 181, 247
American Red Cross, 197
American Sportsman, 205
Amos & Andy, 201, 202
Andrews, Dana, 52, 175, 176, 178, 179, 181, 214
Ann-Margret, 216
Apollo Theatre, 30
Arbuckle, Fatty, 55
Arden, Eve, 116
"Are You in the Mood for Mischief," 118
Aristocats, The, 219

Arnold, Edward, 132
Arnstein, Nick, 120
Arthritis Foundation, 238
Association of Motion Picture Exhibitors, 122
Astaire, Fred, 86, 87, 102, 150
Atkinson, Brooks, 31
Atlantic City, N.J., 32, 43

"Baby, It's Cold Outside," 195
Bacall, Lauren, 227
Ball, Lucille, 116, 196
Baltimore, Md., 36
Banjo on My Knee, 80
Bannon, Bonnie, 70
Banton, Travis, 132, 145
Bari, Lynn, 61, 66
Barnes, Howard, 64
Barrett, Mary Ellin, 109–10
Barricade, 127
Barroso, Ary, 134
Barry, Elaine, 77
Barrymore, Ethel, 28–29
Barrymore, John, 77
"Basin Street Blues," 91
Baxter, Anne, 175, 210
Baxter, Jewel, 8–9, 212, 220–21, 224, 227, 228, 229, 235, 236, 240–41, 243
Baxter, Warner, 66
Beardsley, Judge John, 158
Beery, Noah, Jr., 226
Bellevue Hospital, 71
Bennett, Constance, 116, 118

Benny, Jack, 87, 105, 150–51, 153, 158, 160, 170, 173, 187, 189, 190–92, 194, 195, 198, 199, 201–02, 219
Benny, Joan, 187, 190
Bergen, Edgar, 40, 198, 201
Bergman, Ingrid, 190
Berkeley, Busby, 165–68
Berle, Milton, 40
Berlin, Irving, 6, 70, 85, 86–87, 108–12, 114, 133, 237
Bernie, Ben, 87
Best Man, The, 211
Best Years of Our Lives, The, 177, 178
Beverly Hills, Calif., 7
Beverly Hills Hotel, 128
Bickford, Charles, 175
Biltmore Hotel (Los Angeles), 161
Bishop, Roy, 6, 7, 10, 241, 243, 244
Bistrain, Mr. and Mrs. George, 118
Blaine, Vivian, 214
Blake, Judge Samuel R., 130
Blanc, Mel, 199
Blondell, Joan, 170
Blue Skies, 109
"Blue Skies," 133
Bogert, Frank, 203
Bolger, Ray, 28, 30, 31, 32, 34
Bond, Ward, 127
Boone, Pat, 216, 235
Borge, Victor, 40
Boston, Mass., 36
Boswell, Connee, 220
Box Office Review, 6
Boyfriend, The, 220
Boys Town, 197
Brackett, Charles, 213
Brady, Alice, 94, 96, 97, 114
Brand, Harry, 68, 73–74, 78, 83–84, 96, 99, 112, 114, 118, 170
Brent, George, 92
Brice, Fanny, 41, 120–21, 151
Bridgeville, Del., 42, 43
Bronx, N.Y., 43, 72
Brooklyn Daily Eagle, 114

Brown County, Ind., 239
Brown, Richard, 181
Brown, Tom, 97
Bruce, Nigel, 132
Brunswick (record label), 84
Buenos Aires, Argentina, 133, 139–40
Bullock, Walter, 80
Burns and Allen (radio show), 40, 84, 92, 144, 201
Burns, George, 85, 91
Burrows, Abe, 221, 222
Bushell, Hyman, 34, 35, 50, 72, 83
Butler, David, 102–03
"Buttons and Bows," 195

Cabbot, Bruce, 175
Caesar, Irving, 45
Cagney, James, 143, 160
"California, Here I Come," 121
Cantor, Eddie, 40
Capitol Theatre, 22, 23
Carrillo, Leo, 132
Carmel, Calif., 245
Carnegie Hall, 237
Carradine, John, 112, 175
Carroll, Earl, *Vanities*, 22
Carroll, Madeleine, 86
Cashion, Bonnie, 175
Catalina Island, 160
Cavalier Hotel, 43, 44
Cedars of Lebanon Hospital, 82, 134, 161
Centennial Summer, 179
Century City, Calif., 215
Channing, Carol, 224
Charlie Chan series, 62
Charlie Foy's Supper Club, 147
Charlie's Aunt, 153
Chase National Bank, 63, 70
Chasen's (restaurant), 238
Chester Hale dance unit, 22–23, 24, 25, 36
Chesterfield Cigarettes, 90
Chevalier, Maurice, 34, 144
Chevillat, Dick, 192, 194, 200
Chicago, Ill., 189

Chicago *News,* 38
Chicago Tribune, 233
Chin Restaurant, 37
Christian Science Monitor, 223
Cincinnati, Ohio, 36, 118
Clarke, Charles, 163
Cleveland Air Races, 115
Cleveland, Ohio, 46
Clooney, Rosemary, 90
Coast Guard, 160, 162
Coconut Grove (nightclub), 149
Cohn, Harry, 89
Collector of the Port of New York, 60
Collins, William B., 224
Colonial Theater (Boston), 223
Columbia Broadcasting System (CBS), 90, 200, 202, 236
Come and Get It, 93
Connecticut Yankees, 33, 37, 45, 46, 49
Conte, John, 144, 151
Copacabana, 209
Coslow, Sam, 154
Cotton, Joseph, 190
Coty Perfume, 17
Coward, Noel, 40
Crain, Jeanne, 175, 210, 214
Crawford, Joan, 85
Crosby, Bing, 70, 149, 155, 189, 200, 203, 205, 211, 214, 223, 241, 245
Crosby, John, 199
Cummings, Irving, 131, 132, 167
Custin, George F., 110
Cutex Nail Polish, 150

Dailey, Dan, 23, 61, 73, 133, 141, 219
Dallas Morning News, 58, 88, 104
Dallas, Tex., 214, 215, 216
Dante, *Inferno,* 68
Dark Victory, 126
Darnell, Linda, 3, 166, 175, 177, 178, 180, 210
Darrin, Bobby, 216
Davey, Allen, 163
Davis, Bette, 143, 172, 183, 227

Davis, Joan, 86, 105, 116
Day, Dennis, 199
Day, Doris, 6
Dean, Douglas, 6, 222
Decca (record label), 84
DeHavilland, Olivia, 175
DeMille, Cecil B., 133
Desert Sun, 232
DeSilva, Buddy, 222
Detroit, Mich., 118
Devine, Andy, 97, 127
Disney Studios, 218–19
Dixie Syncopaters, 149
Dolly Sisters, The, 170–72, 226
Dove, Billie, 210
Down Argentine Way, 132, 133, 134, 135, 138–40, 144, 145, 159
Dresser, Louise, 213
DuBarry Was a Lady, 52, 136, 138
Dudley, Tom, 175
Dunne, Philip, 66
Durante, Jimmy, 58, 105, 209
Durbin, Deanna, 185

Eddy, Nelson, 69
Edgewater Beach Hotel, 211
Eisenhower Medical Center, 218, 244
Elizabeth Arden Spa, 155, 205
Elizabeth II, Queen of England, 236
Elle, 220
Embassy Club (London), 211
Embassy Club (New York), 45–47, 48, 49
Encino, Calif., 128, 134, 147, 172, 173, 185, 186, 187, 192, 203–04
English, Richard, 72
Ensenada, Mexico, 148, 152, 188
Every Night at Eight, 64, 68
Ewell, Tom, 215, 216

Fallen Angel, 3, 175–80, 183, 184
Farmer, Frances, 93
Farrell, Gabé, 238, 242, 245
Fay, Frank, 23

Faye, Alice: and alleged affair with Vallée, 43–45, 51, 53–55, 56; attitude toward her father, 8, 9, 14, 71–73, 108; birth of, 11; car accident, 42–45; childhood, 12–13, 17–19; in chorus, 22–23, 24, 31–32, 36–37; conflict with Zanuck, 3, 134–37, 159, 171–73, 175, 179–82, 184–85, 192, 209; daughters, 155–56, 158–59, 161–62, 168–69, 182, 186, 188, 204, 206, 224, 233, 239, 240, 241–42, 244–45; decline and death of, 243–46; discovery of, by Rudy Vallée, 32, 34–35; grandchildren, 235, 239; great-grandchild, 238; health, 82, 98, 106, 112, 115, 118, 121, 123, 125–26, 132, 134, 135, 146, 161–62, 233, 243–44; homes, 186–89, 203–04, 206, 240–41; image, 37, 41, 58–59, 60, 68–69, 74–75, 76, 78–79, 80–81, 95, 105–06, 110, 151, 195–96, 198, 202, 205, 214, 227, 228, 233, 237, 247; insecurity of, 7, 27, 46–47, 52, 69, 89, 90, 96, 97, 115, 142–43, 184, 186, 202, 223, 225, 226, 232–33, 234, 236, 241; interest in show business, 19–22; movie career, 50–51, 52, 53–56, 70–71, 75, 76, 78, 83–84, 85–86, 95–96, 98, 112, 114, 127, 129, 136, 143, 144, 146, 156, 159–60, 169, 179–80, 182–83, 197, 246; name change, 23, 72–73; personality, 4–8, 9, 27, 60, 71, 73, 85, 106–07, 111, 125, 143, 188, 198, 205, 206, 217–18, 232–33, 234, 238, 245, 247; radio work, 4, 39, 90–91, 101, 106, 114, 122–23, 160, 161, 164, 190, 193–97, 198–203, 204, 212; relationship with Phil Harris, 146–48, 154–56, 157, 158–59, 185–86, 187–92, 198–99, 204–07, 217, 223, 224, 231, 237–38, 239, 241–42, 243–45; relationship with Tony Martin, 8, 9, 80, 83–85, 91–92, 99–101, 102, 104–08, 112–15, 128–30; retirement, 119, 159, 168, 172–73, 180–83, 188, 192, 196, 208–10, 212; reviews, 58, 64, 65, 77, 80, 87, 88, 103–04, 105, 108, 114, 116, 121, 127, 184–85, 217, 232; solos, 27–29, 45–47; travel, 190–92, 212, 213, 226–27; as Vallée's band singer, 37–39, 41–42, 48–50; voice of, 4–5, 87, 90–91, 121, 164, 241, 247; and work for Pfizer, 227–34

Faye, Alice Leppert (mother), 12, 17, 20, 22, 59, 60–61, 69, 72, 73, 106, 107, 114, 130, 146, 148, 160, 161, 184, 210

Faye, Bill (brother), 12, 17, 60, 69–70, 71, 72, 73, 75, 99, 170, 193

Faye, Charles "Sonny" (brother), 12, 17, 48–49, 50, 60, 69–70, 71, 72, 73, 99, 230, 238

Fein, Irving, 191, 194

Feinstein, Michael, 4

Ferrer, José, 215, 217

Fibber McGee and Molly, 194

Fidler, Jimmy, 146, 152

Fields, W. C., 87

Film Weekly, 80, 88, 114

Firestone, Leonard, 203

Fitch Bandwagon, 4, 193

Fitch Shampoo, 193, 199

Fleischmann Hour, 4, 34, 39, 40–42, 44–45, 49, 68

Fleischmann's Yeast, 33, 40

Flemington, N.J., 60

Flynn, Errol, 85

Folies Bergere, 144

Fonda, Henry, 131–32, 157

"Foolin' with the Other Woman's Man," 56

Foran, Nick, 59–60, 69

Ford, Bill, 211–12

Ford, John, 92, 131

42nd Street, 86

Four Jills in a Jeep, 164

Fox Film Corporation, 62–63, 162

Fox Studios, 49, 51, 55, 59, 61, 62–63, 65, 66

Fox Theatre Corporation, 62–63, 162
Fox, William, 57, 62–63
Foy, Eddie, Jr., 132
Fuller, Lee, 175
Fulton, Robert, 127
Funny Girl, 120

Gable, Clark, 92, 94, 126, 143, 155, 163, 203, 210
Galveston, Tex., 149, 158
Gang's All Here, The, 165–68, 169
Garbo, Greta, 3, 126
Gardner, Mrs. George (aunt), 72
Gargan, William, 101, 102, 211–12
Garland, Judy, 6, 185
Gaynor, Janet, 66, 213
Gaynor, Mitzi, 210
George White's 1935 Scandals, 63–64, 68
George White's Scandals (film), 50, 51, 52–53, 55, 56, 57, 70
German tour, 191–92, 194, 219
Gershwin, George, 6, 28, 109
Gershwin, Ira, 109
Gilbert, Billy, 142
"Girl in the Police Gazette, The," 86–87
Gish, Lillian, 227
Goebel, George, 203
Goell, Kermit, 176
Goetz, William, 65, 103, 152, 162, 163, 165
Golden State Limited, 50
Goldstone, Nat, 99, 113
Goldwyn, Sam, 92
Gone with the Wind, 126, 158
Good News, 10, 221–26, 237
Goodbye Mr. Chips, 126
Goodman, Benny, 220
"Goodnight My Love," 81
Gordon, Gale, 200
Gordon, Mack, 88, 164
Grable, Betty, 6, 52, 93, 134, 138–39, 140, 141–42, 143, 157, 168, 171, 172, 173, 204, 210, 219, 230, 247

Granlund, Nils T. (NTG), 4, 25–28, 35, 37, 49
Grant, Kathryn, 211
Grapes of Wrath, The, 131
Grauman's Chinese Theater, 112
Great American Broadcast, The, 88, 148
Great Depression, 5, 7, 25, 30, 34, 36, 63, 162
Great Gildersleeve, The, 193
Green, Johnny, 150, 151
Greene, Richard, 127
Greenwood, Charlotte, 139
Greenwood, Del., 43
Gregory, Kay, 203, 227, 240, 241
"Grizzly Bear," 163
Gross, Nate, 147, 148
Growing Older, Staying Young, 7, 182, 232

Haley, Flo, 235
Haley, Jack, 77, 87, 112, 128, 138
Hampton, Lionel, 198
Harlow, Jean, 58, 64, 76, 94, 95, 232
Harris, Alice Faye, Jr. *See* Regan, Alice Harris
Harris, Harry (Phil's father), 148
Harris, Phil, 4, 10, 45, 146–53, 154–56, 157, 158–59, 160, 161, 162, 168, 169, 173, 182, 184, 185–86, 187–92, 193–97, 198–203, 204–08, 213, 216, 218–19, 221, 223, 224, 230, 231, 235, 236, 237–38, 239, 240, 241–43, 244–45
Harris, Phyllis. *See* Middleton, Phyllis Harris
Hart, Lorenz, 109
Hartley, Katharine, 130
Haver, June, 219, 235
Harvey, Lillian, 51, 52
Havana, Cuba, 157
Hawaii, 113, 149
"Hawaii," 6
Hayes, Helen, 223, 227
Hayes Office, 105, 167
Haymes, Dick, 198, 214
Hayworth, Rita, 159

"He Ain't Got Rhythm," 86
Hefner, Hugh, 6
Hello, Frisco, Hello, 5, 76, 93, 161, 162–64, 165
Hell's Kitchen, 7, 10, 11, 12, 13–14, 15, 18, 19–20, 208
Hemmet, Calif., 241
Hemming, Roy, 159
Henie, Sonja, 79, 143
Hepburn, Katharine, 115
Hersholt, Jean, 112
High and the Mighty, The, 204
High Window, The, 185
Hollywood, Calif., 3–4, 49, 50, 52, 55, 56, 60, 65, 72, 79, 92, 95, 100, 109, 119, 128, 138, 141, 144, 145, 152, 160, 169, 178, 185, 204, 208, 210, 218, 232, 237, 246
Hollywood Cavalcade (film), 122, 123–26
Hollywood Cavalcade (radio show), 201, 202
Hollywood Gardens (nightclub), 25, 26, 35
Hollywood Palace, 212, 218
Hollywood Reporter, 58, 146, 177
Hollywood Restaurant, 25, 26, 28, 29, 35, 37, 45, 49, 59
Holme, Celeste, 138
Holmes, Helene, 99
Holy Terror, The, 84
"Honeymoon Hotel," 39
Hope, Bob, 41, 203, 212, 235
Hope, Dolores, 235
Hopper, Hedda, 153–54, 170, 172
Horne, Lena, 198
Hotel Galvez, 158
Hour of Charm All-Girl Orchestra, 198
Hovick, Louise. *See* Lee, Gypsy Rose
How to Marry a Millionaire, 226
How to Succeed in Business without Really Trying, 33
Howard, Al, 46
Howard, Willie, 31
Hudson River Ferry, 78

Hughes, Howard, 100
Hughes, Olli, 74
Hume-Fogg High School (Nashville), 149
Hurricane, 92
Hurricane Carla, 215, 216
Hutton, Betty, 212

"I Feel a Song Coming On," 64
"I Love a Military Man," 77
I Love Lucy, 196
"I Want to Be Bad," 224
"I'll Build a Stairway to Paradise," 28
"I'll See You in My Dreams," 121
"I'm Always Chasing Rainbows," 121
"I'm Marching Along with Time," 109
"I've Got My Love to Keep Me Warm," 86
Imerman, Dr. Stanley, 161
In Old Chicago, 92–98, 99, 107–08, 111, 114, 123, 124, 132
In Search of a Sinner, 132
In-and-Out Hamburgers, 241
Indianapolis, Ind., 59
Irene, 221
Ironwood Country Club, 206
It's a Wonderful Life, 177

J. Walter Thompson Agency, 33, 40
Jack Benny Show, 4, 146, 150–51, 153, 154, 155, 161, 187, 193, 199, 200, 203, 218, 231
"Ja-Da," 121
Jacksonville, Fla., 37, 38, 54
James, Harry, 168, 219
Jazz Singer, The, 124
Jell-O, 150, 153
Jessell, George, 198
Johnson, Van, 225
Jolson, Al, 42, 120–21, 124–25
Jones, Jennifer, 163
Joplin, Scott, 220
Jordan, Marian, 194
Joseph of Hollywood, 145

"Journey to a Star, A," 166, 167
Joyce, Brenda, 127
Jungle Book, The, 218

Kalmus, Natalie, 126
Keaton, Buster, 125
Keavy, Hubbard, 91
Keeler, Ruby, 221, 235
Kelly, Gene, 198
Kelly, Judge Henry C., 99
Kelly, Nancy, 116
Kelly, Patsy, 87
Kemp, Hal, 4, 90, 106
Kemp, Tex., 216
Kent, Sidney, 51, 63, 65, 162
Kentucky, 133
Kiner, Ralph, 211
King, Betty. *See* Scharf, Betty
King, Florence, 246–47
King, Henry, 94, 96–97, 98, 100, 108,
    111, 112, 114, 127, 130, 167, 169,
    171, 179, 213, 237
King of Burlesque, 75–76, 85, 162
Kinskey, Leonid, 139
Kitten on the Keys, 185
Kleiner, Dick, 8, 10, 232, 243, 246
Kraft Hour, 84
Kramer, Regina, 244

L. A. Weekly, 243
La Costa, Calif., 241
Laden, Lester and Faye, 42
"Lady in the Tutti Frutti Hat, The," 167
"Lady Is a Tramp, The," 91
LaFollette Press, 5
Lang, Neil, 146
Lang, Otto, 62, 111
Lang, Walter, 157, 167, 214, 215
Langfeldt, Evelyn, 83
Langford, Frances, 64
Las Vegas, Nev., 168
LaShelle, Joseph, 175
Laura, 175, 176, 178
Lawford, Peter, 222

Lee, Gypsy Rose, 105
Leiter, Kelly, 5, 6
LeMaire, Rufus, 170
Leppert, Charley (father), 11, 12, 14, 15–
    17, 20, 24, 71–73, 107, 108, 170
Leppert, Philip (uncle), 14, 72
Lever Brothers, 201
Levy, David, 143
Lewis, Elliott, 194–95
Liberty Magazine, 220–21
Lightnin', 96
Lillian Russell, 131–32, 135
Lillie, Bea, 40
Linton, Ind., 148, 149, 239, 240, 241,
    242–43, 244
Little Old New York, 127, 129
Livingstone, Mary, 191, 203
Lloyds of London, 94
Loew's Circuit, 63
Loew's, Inc., 63
Lofner, Carol, 149
Lombard, Carole, 155
London, England, 190–91, 236
Long Island, N.Y., 25
Looks Familiar, 226
Lorre, Peter, 189
Los Angeles, Calif., 36, 49, 50, 59, 70, 79,
    83, 118, 155, 160, 176, 204, 219, 224,
    235, 238
Los Angeles Examiner, 51
Los Angeles Times, 51, 59, 184, 224
Love Boat, 226
Love Thy Neighbor, 87
Loy, Myrna, 126, 143
Lum & Abner, 154
Lurlene (ship), 113
Lux Radio Theatre, 4, 133, 160
Lux soap, 133

MacCarthy, Charlie, 87
McClelland, Doug, 142
McCrea, Joel, 80
MacDonald, Jeanette, 4, 42, 92, 94, 163
Maceo, Sam, 148, 189

McGuire, Dorothy, 177
McHarg, Judy, 184, 188–89, 205, 206, 224, 237
McHugh, Jimmy, 64
MacMurray, Fred, 127, 235
Madison Square Garden, 129
Magic of Lassie, The, 226
Malibu, Calif., 237
Mandarin Chinese, 81–82
Mandela, Nelson, 236
Mannix, Eddie, 95
March of Dimes, 197
Marshall Fields, 211
Martin, Dean, 212, 218
Martin, Mary, 226, 235
Martin, Tony, 8, 9, 44, 79–80, 82, 83–84, 89, 91–92, 99–101, 102, 104–08, 112–14, 118–20, 128–30, 134, 152, 155, 159, 168
Marx, Groucho, 209
Maxwell House Coffee's Good News, 123, 144
Maxwell, Marilyn, 191, 219
Mayer, Louis B., 65, 89, 94, 126
Mayo, Virginia, 177
MCA, 200–01
Melody Cruise, 149
Merman, Ethel, 28, 31–32, 34, 42, 109, 112, 133, 223, 224
Metzler, Dr. Gottred, 43
M-G-M, 3, 35, 42, 58, 63, 64, 65, 81, 92, 94, 95, 126, 131, 163, 210, 222
Miami, Fla., 129
Miami Herald, 199
Middleton, Phyllis Harris (daughter), 9, 168, 169–70, 172, 186–87, 188, 197, 204, 205, 206, 217, 225, 233, 235, 237–38, 239, 240, 241–42, 246
Mikulan, Steven, 243
Milland, Ray, 133
Miller, Marilyn, 21
Milwaukee Journal, 59
"Mimi," 34
"Miracle on 34th Street," 222

Miranda, Carmen, 133, 139, 144, 145, 157, 158, 167, 209
Mirror Chocolate Company, 17
Modern Screen, 55, 172
Moffitt, Grandmother, 13, 17, 18, 21
Mogel, Leonard, 220
Monroe, Marilyn, 6, 215, 247
Mordden, Ethan, 7, 105
Morgan, Helen, 45–46, 48
Morris, John, 205
Mother Wore Tights, 185
Motion Picture Academy, 80, 114, 116, 126, 149, 164, 236
Motion Picture Exhibitors, 129
Movietone, 63
Mr. Smith Goes to Washington, 126
Murphy, George, 102, 103, 235–36
Music from Hollywood, 4, 90, 91, 101, 106
Music Is Magic, 64–65, 68
My Gal Sal, 159
"My Mammy," 121
"My Man," 120, 121
"My Walking Stick," 109

Naish, J. Carrol, 139
Nashville, Tenn., 149
National Broadcasting Corporation (NBC), 35, 39, 123, 193, 199, 200, 202
National Hotel Chain, 150
Nelson, Gene, 225
"Never Say No to a Man," 214
New Orleans, La., 162, 213, 216, 229, 239, 242
New York Daily Mirror, 45, 71, 108, 116
New York Enquirer, 59
New York Evening Post, 72
New York Herald Tribune, 87
New York Journal, 43, 59, 72
New York News, 202
New York, N.Y., 10, 11, 13, 15, 21, 24, 25, 35, 36, 37, 43, 45, 59, 61, 65, 70, 72, 88, 91, 107, 109, 120, 122, 129, 130, 135, 146, 147, 160, 176, 197, 202, 222, 224

New York State Compensation Bureau, 59
New York Times, 23, 31, 35, 53, 58, 64, 68, 99, 105, 116, 122, 127, 134, 167, 221
New York World Telegram, 116, 199
New York World's Fair, 134
Newman, Lionel, 163
Newman, Paul, 227
"Nice Work If You Can Get It," 91
"Night and Day," 91
Night of 100 Stars, The, 227
Ninotchka, 126
"No Love, No Nothin'," 167
No, No, Nanette, 220, 221
"No Tabuleiro de Bahaiana," 134
Norfolk, Va., 43
North, Robert, 193
Northridge, Calif., 203
Norton, Inez, 56
Now I'll Tell, 56, 57, 58, 77, 123
"Now It Can Be Told," 109, 114, 133
Nugent, Frank, 105, 127
Nye, Bessie, 81

Oakie, Jack, 143, 147, 163, 164
Oakland, Calif., 91, 106, 107
O'Brian, Margaret, 198
"Oh, You Nasty Man," 5, 50, 51, 58
O'Kent, Ben, 118
"On Moonlight Bay," 246
On the Avenue, 84, 85, 86–87, 108
"One Never Knows," 81
Orient Express, 192
Over Easy, 226
Owensville, Ohio, 118, 120
Ozzie and Harriet, 193

Packard, 150
Palais d'Or (nightclub), 37
Paley, Bill, 170, 200
Palladium (London), 190–91
Palm Desert, Calif., 246
Palm Springs, Calif., 203, 204, 206, 209, 210, 225, 236, 238, 241

Palomar Ballroom (Los Angeles), 150
Panama Canal, 122
Paramount Studios, 52, 87, 134, 138
Paramount Theater (Los Angeles), 148
Pardo, Jaime, 152
Paris, France, 192
Parker, Helen, 226
Parsons, Louella, 42, 82, 128, 129, 146, 159, 160, 161–62, 168, 171, 172–73, 184–85, 192
Pasadena Playhouse, 52
Payne, John, 157, 162, 163, 164, 222, 223, 225, 236, 237
Pearl Harbor, Hawaii, 160
Peck, Gregory, 138
Pennsylvania Roof (nightclub), 45, 147
Peoria, Ill., 120
Perry Como Show, 212, 220
Pfizer Pharmaceuticals, 227–34
Phil Harris–Alice Faye Show, 4, 193–97, 198–203
Philadelphia, Pa., 36
Photoplay, 116, 130, 172
Picture Play, 58
Picturegoer, 88
Pigskin Parade, 80
Piperi, James A., 158
Pittsburgh, Pa., 36, 59
Pittsburgh Sun, 59
Playboy, 6
Please Don't Shoot My Dog, 232
"Polka Dot Polka," 166
Poor Little Rich Girl, 5, 76–77, 79
Porter, Cole, 6, 52, 136
Powell, Dick, 86
Powell, Eleanor, 4, 64
Powell, Jane, 198
Powell, Mousie, 210
Power, Tyrone, 79, 80, 89, 93, 94–96, 97, 98, 99, 100, 107, 108, 109, 111, 114, 120, 121, 122, 143, 144, 146, 162, 208, 230
Preminger, Otto, 3, 175, 176, 178
Preston, Robert, 133

"Pretty Baby," 121
Princess Theater (Honolulu), 149
Production Code, 58
Prohibition, 14, 25
Providence Sun Journal, 106
Public Enemy, 66
Publisher's Weekly, 232

Queen Elizabeth II, 190
Quinn, Anthony, 236

Radio, 4, 33–34, 39–41, 42, 52, 88, 90,
    122–23, 190, 193–97, 198–203
Radio City Music Hall, 87
Radio Mirror, 91, 151
Raft, George, 64
Rainbow Room, 220–21
Ralston, Marcia "Mascotte," 149, 152,
    154, 158, 189
Rancho Mirage, Calif., 189
Rasking, David, 176
Rather, Dan, 236
Raye, Martha, 146
Razor's Edge, The, 219
Regan, Alice Harris (daughter), 9, 140,
    157–59, 161–62, 168, 172, 186, 189,
    191, 206, 213, 216, 221, 229, 233,
    235, 238, 239, 240, 241–42, 244, 246
Reed, Rex, 218, 221
Remley, Frank, 191, 194–95, 200, 219
Revel, Harry, 88
Revere, Anne, 175
Rexall Drugs, 200, 201, 202
Reynolds, Debbie, 220–21
Richmond, Va., 36
Rienhardt, Max, 178
Rigby, Harry, 220, 221, 222, 223, 225,
    237
Rin Tin Tin, 65
Rio de Jainero, Brazil, 144
Ritz Brothers, 80, 86, 99
Ritz, Paul, 229, 231, 233, 242
RKO Studios, 52, 86, 87, 138, 154
Road to Hong Kong, 214

"Rock-a-bye Your Baby with a Dixie
    Melody," 121
Roe, Gale, 78
Rogers, Ginger, 4, 86, 87, 102, 115, 141,
    236
Rogers, Richard, 214
Rogers, Will, 62, 66–67, 96, 213
Romero, Cesar, 5, 74, 85, 139, 141, 157,
    162, 219, 236
Rooney, Mickey, 143, 226
Roose, Jeanine, 193, 194, 200, 208
Rose, Helen, 163, 164
Rose of Washington Square, 120–21, 124,
    151
Rosenfield, John, 58, 88, 104, 217
Rothstein, Arnold, 56
Rotterdam World Cruises, 226
Roxy Theater, 88
Roy, John, 98
Royal Palms Hotel, 129
Royal Scandal, A, 179
Rubin, Martin, 166
Russell, Jane, 227
Russell, Lillian, 131, 132
Ryan, Sheila, 166

Sally, Irene, and Mary, 104–06, 112
San Fernando Valley, 128, 147, 187,
    203
San Francisco, 92, 94, 163
San Francisco, Calif., 10, 113, 149, 218,
    226
San Francisco Chronicle, 220
San Francisco World's Fair, 138
San Mateo, Calif., 241
Sanders, George, 208
Santa Anita (race track), 103
Santa Fe Chief, 190
Santa Monica, Calif., 49, 170
Saturday Evening Post, 192
"Say It with Music," 133
Schaefer, George, 175
Scharf, Betty, 9, 23, 48–49, 50, 60–61,
    70, 71, 99, 130, 170, 188

Scharf, Walter, 32, 37, 39, 46–47, 48–49, 50, 57, 70, 71, 90, 100, 109, 120, 124, 134, 135, 138, 195, 198

Schenck, Joe, 65, 103, 107, 152, 170, 178

Schwab, Laurence, 222

Scotch Tape, 197

Screen Actors Guild, 61, 226

See America First, 80

Seiler, Lew, 104

Seven Year Itch, The, 215

Shaffer, Rosalind, 168

Shaw, Artie, 198–99

She Learned about Sailors, 59, 61, 62

Sheehan, Winfield, 57, 62, 63, 64, 68

"Sheik of Araby, The," 142, 143

Shelton, Jack, 241

Sheridan, Anne, 160

Shientag, Judge Bernard L., 72

Showman's Trade Review, 143

Silvers, Phil, 189

"Silvery Moon," 163

Sinatra, Frank, 189, 217–18, 240

Sing, Baby, Sing, 77, 79–80, 94

"Sing, Baby, Sing," 150

Singer, Ray, 194, 200

Skelton, Red, 41, 201

Skouras, Spyros, 65, 162, 196, 210

"Slowly," 176, 180

"Slumming on Park Avenue," 86

"So Help Me," 123

So This Is Harris, 149

Solomon and Sheba, 208

"Somebody Loves Me," 28

Song of Bernadette, 163

Sparks, Ned, 87

Spitalny, Phil, 198

Spokesman Review, 136

SS *America*, 146

St. Francis Hotel, 149

St. James Theatre, 224

St. Johns, Adela Rogers, 54

St. John's Hospital, 170

Stage Door, 115, 116

Stagecoach, 126

Stanwyck, Barbara, 80

"Star-Spangled Banner, The," 198

State Fair (1933), 213

State Fair (1945), 178, 213–14

State Fair (1962), 3, 213–17, 221

Staten Island Ferry, 167

Steward, Don, 239, 240

Stewart, Jimmy, 226

Sting, The, 220

Stonehouse, Ruth, 149

Stowaway, 5, 81–82, 84

Strauss, Theodore, 167

Streisand, Barbra, 70

Streets of Paris (Shubert review), 133

Studio system, 51, 52, 53, 58, 61–62, 69, 73–75, 79, 88–89, 101–02, 104, 121–22, 123, 132, 135–36, 179, 180, 183–84, 208–10, 215

Styne, Jule, 90, 99

Sugie's Tropics, 80, 99

Sullivan, Ed, 107–08

Sun Valley, Idaho, 201

Swanson, Clark and Florence, 206, 210–11

"Sweet Cider Time," 163

Sydney, Australia, 149

Tail Spin, 115–16, 118

Talbot, Lyle, 69

Tampa, Fla., 38

Technicolor, 123, 126, 132, 157, 158, 166–67, 173

Television, 122, 202–03, 212

Temple, Shirley, 5, 58, 62, 66, 67, 76, 77, 81–82, 94, 143, 144

Tetley, Walter, 193

Texas City disaster (Texas), 189–90

That Night in Rio, 144, 145, 146, 147

"There's a Lull in My Life," 88

This Is My Affair, 78

This Is Your Life (BBC), 235–36

"This Year's Kisses," 87

365 Nights in Hollywood, 61, 62

Thunderbird Country Club, 203, 206, 208, 210, 212, 217, 240–41
Tierney, Gene, 168, 210
Tiffin, Pamela, 215, 216
Time, 217
Tin Pan Alley, 6, 140–43, 145, 148, 157, 171, 214, 226, 246
"Toot Toot Tootsie Goodbye," 121
Top Hat, 86
Town Tattler, 147
Tracy, Spencer, 56, 57, 62, 92, 107, 126, 143
Tree Grows in Brooklyn, A, 170, 177
Trocadero (nightclub), 79, 99
Truex, Ernest, 132
Truman, Harry, 197–98
Twelvetrees, Helen, 56, 57
Twentieth Century, 61, 65, 66
Twentieth Century-Fox Studios, 3, 52, 65, 66–67, 70, 72, 73, 74, 75, 78, 80, 82, 85, 90, 92, 96, 98, 101–03, 107, 108, 112, 118, 120, 122, 126, 135–36, 138, 144, 146, 153, 158, 162, 164, 165, 167, 168, 169, 173, 175, 179, 180, 182, 186, 192, 195–96, 209–10, 213, 226, 247
Two-Faced Woman, 3

United Artists, 65
Universal Studios, 87, 100–03
University of Arizona, 213

Vagabond Dreams Come True, 34
Vagabond Lover, 49
Vallée, Rudy, 4, 8, 29, 31, 32–34, 35, 37–39, 40–45, 46, 48–49, 50, 51, 53–55, 56, 57, 58, 59, 68, 69, 72, 73, 83, 147, 186, 195, 225, 236, 237
"Vamp, The," 121
Van Horn, Harriet, 199
Variety, 64, 77, 88, 90, 93, 103, 164
Victoria, British Columbia, 169
Virginia Beach, Va., 43

Wabash Avenue, 204
Wake Up and Live, 87–88, 105, 231–32
Wakeling, Gwen, 112, 158
Waldorf-Astoria Hotel, 150
Wanger, Walter, 64
Waring, Seabury, 42
Warner Brothers Studio, 65, 77, 86, 120
Warner, Jack, 65
Warren, Doug, 134
Warren, Harry, 163, 164
Washington Review, 224
Wayne, John, 115, 204
We Still Are, 231–32
Wead, Frank "Spig," 115
WEAF (New York), 39
Webb, Fay, 35, 44, 49, 51, 53–55, 73, 83
Webb, Robert, 114
Weber & Fields, 132
Week-End in Havana, 153, 157–58, 214, 226
Welles, Orson, 41
"What a Wonderful World," 243
Wheeler, Lyle, 175
"When Did You Leave Heaven," 80
Whitaker, Nancy Chaffe, 205, 211, 217
White, George, 28, 30, 34, 36, 50, 53, 108; *Scandals* (on Broadway), 5, 28–29, 30–32, 34, 35, 36–37, 42, 49, 108
Whiteman, Paul, 26, 28
Whitfield, Anne, 193
Whiting, Richard, 80
Whoopee!, 167
Who's Who, 5
"Why Do They Always Pick on Me?," 164
Wickersham, Bill, 161
Wilkens, Cecile, 216
William, Warren, 132
Wilson, Don, 152
Winchell, Walter, 87–88, 105
Wings of Eagles, The, 115
Withers, Jane, 61, 84, 236, 246
Wizard of Oz, 94, 126
WJZ (New York), 39

Won Ton Ton, the Dog Who Saved Hollywood, 226

Woodlawn Cemetery, 72

World Series of 1919, 56

World War I, 65

World War II, 5, 122, 160, 161, 162, 163, 165, 166, 173–74, 185, 186

Wrather, Bonita Granville, 226

Wright, Dollie (Phil's mother), 148

Wrightman, Charles, 144

Wurtzel, Sam, 175

Wurtzel, Sol, 62, 80

Wuthering Heights, 126

Wyman, Jane, 116, 246

Yale University, 32

You Can't Cheat an Honest Man, 87

You Can't Have Everything, 89, 90, 91, 105

"You Make Me Feel So Young," 195

"You'll Never Know," 5, 164–65, 191, 236

Young, Loretta, 143, 246

Young, Robert, 81

"Younger than Spring," 243

Your Career in Motion Pictures, 52

Your Hit Parade, 80, 87

You're a Sweetheart, 100, 101–04, 211

Yuma, Ariz., 99, 100, 101, 113

Zamboni, Virginia, 238, 242, 243, 245

Zanuck, Darryl F., 3, 8, 65–67, 76, 77, 78, 79, 80–82, 85, 87, 89, 90, 91, 92–98, 100, 103, 104, 105, 108–11, 115, 116, 119, 120, 121, 122, 123, 124, 126–27, 131–32, 133, 135–37, 138–42, 152, 153, 157, 160, 162, 163, 165, 170, 171–73, 178, 179–82, 185, 189, 192, 196, 209, 210, 219

Zanuck, Virginia, 189

Ziegfeld, Florenz, 30, 120

Ziegfeld, 131